Clothes conscious. Manipulative. Affectionate. Bossy. Talkative. Even in an age of revolutionary change in the status of women, old myths about gender die hard. Ardent feminists throw up their hands in bewildered resignation when their toddler daughters reject trains, blocks, and overalls in favor of dolls, makeup, and frilly dresses. "How can you fight the culture and the media?" they demand defensively. More traditional parents point to behaviors that predated language—timidity, cuddliness, passivity—as proof that "femininity" is innate, biologically programmed, and fixed for all time. Whether nature or nurture is responsible, whether we approve or disapprove, our girls will be girls—right?

Not so fast. Appearances have a way of being deceiving, particularly in an area as complicated and ambiguous as gender roles. Most little girls today have working mothers: 25 percent of them are growing up in single-parent families. Ask a little girl decked out in beads and high heels what she's doing and she's likely to reply, "Going to work," not "Going to a party," as she might have said a generation ago. Economic fact, far more than feminist theory, has altered the old roles.

—from THE LITTLE GIRL BOOK

By David Laskin:

GETTING INTO ADVERTISING*
PARENTS™ BOOK FOR NEW FATHERS*
PARENTS™ BOOK OF CHILD SAFETY*
EASTERN ISLANDS
AN ANGEL A WEEK*

*Published by Ballantine Books

THE LITTLE GIRL BOOK

Everything You Need to Know to Raise a Daughter Today

David Laskin and Kathleen O'Neill

BALLANTINE BOOKS • NEW YORK

http://www.randomhouse.com

Library of Congress Catalog Card Number: 95-95086

ISBN: 0-345-38678-7

Manufactured in the United States of America

First Trade Edition: April 1992
First Mass Market Edition: April 1996

10 9 8 7 6 5 4 3 2

For our own little girls:
Emily, Sarah, and Alice.

Simone de Beauvoir's theory is that women, by some chargeable mischance of human affairs, live in immanence, men in transcendence. I can only say, some do and some don't, either way.

—KATHERINE ANNE PORTER, "Ole Woman River"

Contents

Contents

Acknowledgments

Our first thanks go to the parents who shared with us their thoughts and feelings about raising daughters—and, of course, to the little girls themselves who talked with us or simply let us watch them go about their lives.

We are grateful to Barbara Raber, principal of Lakeville School in Great Neck, New York, for inviting us into her school and for generously sharing her time, her knowledge, and her resources, and for giving us access to teachers and staff members, including Rochelle Stern, Dr. Ana Dybner, Terri Elias, and Betty Meron. Julie Olson, principal of the Diamond Path Elementary School in Apple Valley, Wisconsin, was also very helpful.

At The Spence School, Dr. Edes Gilbert and Doris Cottham were helpful to us.

We would also like to thank the following professionals in the fields of psychology, education, mathematics, and computer science for their guidance, their patience in fielding questions, and their openness in sharing their expertise: Jo Sanders with the Women's Action Alliance, Dr. Katherine Canada at Goucher College, Dr. Samuel Osheron at the Harvard University Health Service, Dr. Rhoda K. Unger at Montclair State College, Dr. Brad Sachs at the Father Center in Columbia, Maryland, Dr. Gail Melson at Purdue University, Dr. Elizabeth Fennema at the University of Wisconsin, Dr. Robert Gundling.

Thanks also go to Lolly Keys of the American Youth Soccer Organization, June Million of the National Association of Elementary School Principals, Tom Synder of the National Center for Education Statistics, Ellen Wahl of Girls Inc., Mary-Ellen Rood of the National Council on Child Abuse and Family Violence, Mary Allman of the National Resource Center on Child Sexual Abuse, and Amy Meyers of the American Anorexia and Bulimia Association.

We appreciate the help of Mary Dergin Bichanich, Daniel Laskin and Jane Cowles, William Englund, Sherry Wallach, Sandy McGrew, Cindy Olansky, Terry and Polly Blank, and Dan Polin for helping put us in touch with parents of daughters all over the country.

We'd like to thank Joëlle Delbourgo at Ballantine Books for coming up with the idea for *The Little Girl Book*, for signing us up to write it, and for her friendship. Thanks go to Virginia Faber, our editor, for her lightness of touch and her eye for detail. We're grateful to our literary agent, Diane Cleaver, for her grace in disposing of the business matters and her helpful comments on the manuscript.

Last, but by no means least, is our gratitude to *our* three little girls, Emily, Sarah, and Alice, whose very being is our major qualification for writing this book.

Preface

This is a book for parents of daughters, specifically daughters from birth to age eight. As parents of three young daughters of our own, we have tried to address the issues and questions that we encounter every day. We have learned that even seemingly ordinary dilemmas—whether or not to buy a four-year-old a Barbie doll, whether to sign up a six-year-old for the soccer team—have both a "philosophical" and a practical side. For example, you might object to Barbie's unattainable model of femininity, but your daughter will roast you alive until she has one. Thus we provide background in psychology and socialization to help illuminate the philosophical side and offer practical tips and applications to assist you in the day-to-day, moment-to-moment business of raising a daughter.

Chapter 1 discusses sex differences in general, taking on the ongoing debate about whether nature or nurture is more responsible for the differences between males and females. Chapters 2 to 6 follow a little girl's development from infancy through third grade. In each stage we consider how a little girl differs both physically and psychologically from a little boy, look at a girl's relationship with her mother and father, and describe how she is likely to interact with siblings and friends.

Chapter 2 covers infancy, Chapter 3 covers the preschool years, when little girls really begin to discover stereotypically "feminine" behaviors. The "Parenting Tips" sections at the end of these chapters contain practical advice on how fathers can become more involved with their daughters, on clothing and appearance, on a little girl's place within the family, and on her relationship with siblings.

Once your little girl reaches elementary school, academic and social issues become important, so Chapter 4 takes a look at girls in the classroom and on the playground, with special attention to girls' involvement in math, science, and computers.

Chapter 5 covers the social life of the schoolgirl, including her friendships, her relationships with boys (or lack of them), and her participation in sports. Chapter 6 deals with the behavior of five- to eight-year-old girls at home—their relationships with parents and siblings, as well as their attitudes toward new responsibilities.

Chapter 7 is devoted to the difficult subject of sexual abuse of girls, a topic that has received increasing attention in recent years. In Chapter 8 we discuss the special problems girls face in single-parent families and divorced families, and in Chapter 9 we look at the impact of maternal employment on daughters. Finally, we end with a look ahead at the special problems that girls encounter in adolescence.

We have tried as much as possible to avoid taking a particular political stance and to reflect many different points of view. We love our daughters' femininity and we want them to grow up feeling proud of themselves as girls and as women. We are also aware that we live in a sexist society, in which girls and women are still denied some of the privilege, power, and respect held by boys and men. We have tried to alert parents to sexist behaviors and attitudes that might hamper their daughters' development or relegate them to second-class status.

Girls and boys are undeniably different, but we believe

that our society tends to overemphasize these sex differences, usually to the detriment of the "second sex." Our research and interviews have confirmed our belief that the really major differences are between *individuals*, not between the sexes. As women and men become more and more equal partners in the family and in the workplace, our culture may begin to recognize this and incorporate it into its fundamental assumptions and attitudes. If and when this happens, our daughters can only be the gainers.

1

Myths and Facts About Little Girls

"Look at her—she's gabbing on the phone already," Aunt Meg says, half fondly, half critically of her niece, as the two-year-old prattles into her toy telephone. "A typical little lady."

"When boys play pretend, it's guns. When girls play pretend, it's cooking and cleaning," comments a father of a five-year-old girl and a two-year-old boy. "It's kind of funny. They certainly don't get it from *us*. I don't go off to work and spend weekends mowing the lawn while their mother stays home and cooks. We both work, we share household chores—and yet here's our daughter serving make-believe tea and our son going 'Pow! pow! pow!' "

"The instant she could crawl, she went for the dolls, but her brother never showed much interest in them," notes another mother.

"Can you *believe* how manipulative she is?" asks Linda, watching her friend's eighteen-month-old alternately wheedle and flirt with her older male cousins, then pout or throw a tantrum. "It starts *so* early."

"Nothing makes her happier than to dress up for a party," says Eric of his five-year-old. "Even before she could talk, she favored pink and purple. When she was three, she woke us up one morning dressed in this outlandish combination of colors. 'I'm ready for school,' she announced. 'Do I look beautiful?' Can you imagine a boy doing that?"

"So *soft*. So *delicate*. So *pretty*," were the adjectives parents used to described their newborn baby girls in a classic psychological experiment. Newborn boys of the same height and weight were described as strong, sturdy, and big.[1]

"Of course she loves clothes," says Jill, dressed in jeans and flannel shirt, of her toddler daughter Bonnie, turned out in lace-trimmed red velvet. "Bloomingdale's has always been her favorite store."

"She's always been affectionate, right from the start," says Jim of his three-year-old daughter. "And her five-year-old brother has always been a bruiser. His first reaction to any toy is to throw it across the room, while she tends to find a lap and crawl into it. His first word was *truck*, hers was *baby*."

"Boys are aggressive, but girls are bossy. They try to run the show," is Pamela's assessment of the interaction between her three-year-old daughter and her son.

Clothes conscious. Manipulative. Affectionate. Bossy. Talkative. Even in an age of revolutionary change in the status of women, old myths about gender die hard. Ardent feminists throw up their hands in bewildered resignation when their toddler daughters reject trains, blocks, and overalls in favor of dolls, makeup, and frilly dresses. "How can you fight the culture and the media?" they demand defensively. More traditional parents point to behaviors that predated language—timidity, cuddliness, passivity—as proof that "femininity" is innate, biologically programmed, and fixed for all time. Whether nature or nurture is responsible, whether we approve or disapprove, our girls will be girls—right?

Not so fast. Appearances have a way of being deceiving, particularly in an area as complicated and ambiguous as gender roles. Most little girls today have working mothers: 25 percent of them are growing up in single-parent families.

Ask a little girl decked out in beads and high heels what she's doing and she's likely to reply, "Going to work" not "Going to a party," as she might have said a generation ago. Economic fact, far more than feminist theory, has altered the old roles.

And yet, the myths persist. How far have we, as a culture, progressed beyond the assumptions that inform this summary of woman's nature written by the pioneering psychologist G. Stanley Hall in 1904?

> She works by intuition and feeling; fear, anger, pity, love, and most emotions have a wider range and greater intensity. . . . Women go in flocks, and in social matters are less prone to stand out with salient individuality. They are more emotional, altruistic, intuitive, less judicial, and less able to make disinterested and impersonal judgment. . . . [Women] excel in mental reproduction rather than in production; are superior in arts of conversation, more conservative and less radical; . . . [they] have most sympathy, pity, charity, generosity, and superstitions. . . . [A woman] is more credulous and less skeptical, more prone to fear and timidity, and has greater fidelity, dependence, reverence and devotion. . . . Man is best adapted to the present; woman is more rooted in the past and the future, closer to the race and a more generic past. . . . Woman is far nearer childhood than man, and therefore in mind and body more prophetic of the future as well as reminiscent of the past.[2]

Hall stood near the end of a long line of male thinkers, starting with Aristotle and continuing through St. Thomas Aquinas, Darwin, and Freud, who argued for the essential moral and intellectual inferiority of woman, due to inadequacy in her anatomy, brain, evolutionary role, or what have you. Well into the enlightened late twentieth century, respected volumes on female psychology reported that "femininity is largely defined by success in establishing and maintaining love relationships and by maternity."[3] It's no wonder that so many women take a defensive stance when balancing work and family and that so much of feminist social science appears to be a monotonous attempt to prove that the sexes are identical in ability and potential.

There is no getting around the fact that women have always been the "second sex," as Simone de Beauvoir argues so eloquently and exhaustively in her landmark book of that title; and any consideration of women, academic or popular, must take into account the long, dark shadow cast by the "first sex." Beauvoir was among the first to draw our attention to this shadow, and to begin pulling womankind out from under it. Her declaration that "one is not born, but rather becomes, a woman" is the point of departure for much of feminist social science. "No biological, psychological, or economic fate determines the figure that the human female presents in society," she writes; "it is civilization as a whole that produces this creature, intermediate between male and eunuch, which is described as feminine. . . . If, well before puberty and sometimes even from early infancy, [woman] seems to us to be already sexually determined, this is not because mysterious instincts directly doom her to passivity, coquetry, maternity; it is because the influence of others upon the child is a factor almost from the start, and thus she is indoctrinated with her vocation from her earliest years."[4]

Beauvoir and the feminist writers and social scientists who followed her may have consigned the idea of innate female inferiority—indeed, of innate femininity—to the scrap heap of intellectual history. But parents have a different take. Listen to what Mary, a Milwaukee mother of five, has to say: "Nine years ago, before my children were born, I thought, you treat them the same, they turn out the same. It wasn't until my first daughter was born that I realized there are true, innate differences between the sexes. It's what my heart told me. We give all five children the same love, respect, and sense that each is special—but the girls just do things differently from the boys. Sarah sat down with dolls, while Jordan always pushed them away.

She reads books without squirming. She seems to gravitate naturally toward 'girl things'—but she also tries to do everything the boys do, including sports."

Many other parents we interviewed agreed that each gender behaved differently *from birth*. As Cindy, the mother of a nine-year-old boy and a seven-year-old girl, put it, "When I was teaching school before I had children, I believed that boys and girls would act in the same way if given the same opportunities. This is what I learned in graduate school. But when I became a mother, I saw that the first thing my son picked up was a truck and then a ball. When I tried to give these toys to my daughter, she had absolutely no interest in them. She was always into dolls, and once she could walk, she loved dancing. I really tried to raise them in a nonsexist way. But there's a lot to be said for hormones."

Julie, a Minnesota high school principal with two sons and a five-year-old daughter, tells a similar story: "I came of age in the 1960s, and I still have some of those values. I never wore a dress when I taught, and I still don't wear makeup. But my daughter has *always* loved to dress up and she loves makeup. How can I possibly have a kid like this? Even though we try to broaden them, ultimately we just have to let them be who they want to be."

Rachel, a preschool teacher and the mother of two daughters, comments, "I would like to say I have not seen any stereotypical sex differences, but it wouldn't be true to my experience. In preschool, the boys grab trucks and try to make blocks into guns. The girls gravitate toward Play-Doh, housekeeping, and art. Every child does not do these things all the time, but by two and a half the behaviors are pretty well established."

Rachel's qualification that these stereotypical behaviors are common but not universal is one that we will return to again and again in the course of *The Little Girl Book*. Most parents we talked to said their little girls showed typically feminine behaviors and preferences, but a sizable minority described their daughters as rough, loud, active, aggressive, and boisterous—traits generally associated with boys.

Nonetheless, whether their daughters were ultra-fems or dyed-in-the-wool tomboys or something in between, the parents concluded overwhelmingly, though often reluctantly, that gender traits are preprogrammed in the womb. "I never cease to be amazed by how feminine she is," we heard over and over from mothers. "She certainly doesn't get it from watching *me*!" In the great nature versus nurture debate, nature is the hands-down winner among parents.

Science, however, refuses to take their word for it. To social scientists the question of how and why the sexes develop their differences in behavior, ability, and psychology is, if anything, more problematic than ever. To venture into the voluminous professional literature is to enter treacherous terrain in which sociopolitical snipers lurk behind every bush. Even a claim that baby girls smile more and earlier than boys has been riddled with feminist bullets:[5] from smiling in the cradle there is just one short step to flirting in the typing pool and a lifetime of degrading female wiles. Without much digging, you can find an "expert" and a "study" to support just about any position you wish to take, and a theory to go with it. At the male chauvinist extreme there are sociobiologists such as E. O. Wilson and Robert Trivers who posit a world of biological determinism, in which male and female social behavior has evolved along radically distinct lines because it benefits the survival of the species for males to be aggressive, sexually promiscuous hunter/warriors and females to be passive, protected, sexually discriminating childbearers and nurturers.[6] Representing the other camp is writer Anne Fausto-Sterling, who in *Myths of Gender* examines each of the major assertions of sex differences, from male aggressiveness to female inferiority in math, and tears them all to shreds.[7] As Ashton Barfield points out in an essay about the nature/nurture debate over explaining sex differences, "Since the evidence is essentially inconclusive, the generalizations are largely a matter of personal interpretation."[8]

Some years back a study was conducted comparing the political views of researchers of sex differences and their findings. It was discovered that those social scientists who preferred maintaining the status quo tended to find many more differences between the sexes than did their colleagues who favored political change.[9] "Objective" scientific research, it appears, is a relative term.

On this embattled ground, a few areas of truce have been declared. Jerome Kagan, a developmental psychologist at Harvard, notes that "in every known society males and females differ, not only in genes, physiology, and growth patterns but also in profile of behaviors and organization of beliefs." Yet, he asserts, researchers have found no good reason why these anatomical and physiological differences between males and females should hamper their pursuit of "the total variety of vocational and social roles available in our society."[10] Other researchers note that the overlap between the sexes is far more significant than the differences. Or, as psychologist Rhoda K. Unger puts it in *Female and Male: Psychological Perspectives*, "Individual potential is still a far better predictor of behavior than membership in any particular racial, ethnic, or sexual group."[11]

Both common sense and observation bear this out. Nadine, at age four, enters into (and wins) many more fights than her eight-year-old brother ever started, but she also likes pretty clothes and makeup. Kate, whom her father described as a "tomboy from birth," is far more passionate about sports than is her younger brother, but also far more sensitive about her appearance. Megan, now nine, climbed out of her crib before turning one and devoted herself to pulling everything off her changing table; she loves softball and soccer. Her sister Willa, on the other hand, has always stayed as far away from "boy's things" as possible, and would happily wear pink ruffles every day. Little girls, like little boys, come in a tremendous range of styles, interests, and capabilities.

Though you would be hard-pressed to find two researchers to agree on exactly how much the sexes differ, there is a general consensus among social scientists that nurture or nature alone cannot explain the differences between the sexes. The two work inextricably together to create gender.

Dismantling the Stereotype of Femininity

The definitive study of sex differences may never be written, but most theorists agree that the landmark book in the field is *The Psychology of Sex Differences*, published in 1974 by Stanford University psychologists Eleanor Emmons Maccoby and Carol Nagy Jacklin. Maccoby and Jacklin undertook to pin down which sex differences were "inevitable," that is, biologically determined, and which were "the product of arbitrary social stereotypes that could be changed if society itself changes."[12] Instead of extrapolating from their own research in one or two minutely defined topics, they conducted an exhaustive survey of the research of thousands of colleagues in every area of sex difference they could think of. In all, their book summarizes the results of some 1,400 studies conducted from 1966 to 1973. The categories that Maccoby and Jacklin chose to examine and the hypotheses they analyzed furnish an excellent register of the commonly accepted areas in which boys and girls differ.

The prevailing cultural myth that Maccoby and Jacklin set out to verify or debunk goes something like this: Compared to the little boy, the little girl is a sensitive, clinging, timid, rather needy child, cooperative and even submissive to authority, passive in her interaction with other children, quiet in her play, dependent on the approval and advice of her elders. In the area of sense perception, she is more sensitive to pain and tactile stimulation than boys; she listens more acutely and with more focused attention, but she lags behind them in visual perception. In the sphere of motor abilities, the little girl of the myth is dexterous with her hands and graceful in her movements, while the little boy is quicker, stronger, and more coordinated in his gross motor activities—jumping, climbing, running, for example.

The mythical little girl is a social creature practically from birth, more adept and responsive than boys in social situations, more keyed in to group interactions and more socially suggestible (that is, more likely to take cues from others and imitate their actions). Intellectually, she has an edge over little boys in verbal skills, talking earlier and better than boys, reading sooner and with greater comprehension, expressing herself more volubly and complexly. But boys have a clear advantage over girls in mathematical abilities, in the ability to visualize objects in space, in abstract reasoning and nonverbal creativity. Girls, according to this cultural myth, recall words and social situations better than boys, while boys remember objects and numbers. In general overall intelligence, our culture assumes that the little girl lags behind the little boy.

Traits such as passivity, sneakiness, vanity, subjectiveness, excitability, and tearfulness may be added to the myth.[13] The stereotypical little girl would be ideally suited to become a housewife or schoolteacher, secretary or nurse, hostess or waitress, while we could expect the stereotypical little boy to become an engineer or soldier, corporate executive or architect, mathematician or pilot. He would lead, she would follow; he would command, she obey. She might discuss and even write about his actions—in war, in business, in politics—but he would *act*.

So much for the "myth." Now what about the "reality"? What actual differences between boys and girls did Maccoby and Jacklin's exhaustive survey turn up? The researchers identified only three "well-established" differences between the sexes: that boys are more aggressive than girls; that girls have greater verbal ability, an advantage that surfaces in a meaningful way only at about the age of eleven; that boys have superior abilities in math and in spatial visualization, distinct but related advantages that show up only after adolescence. Their survey revealed no evidence that girls are more social or suggestible than boys, that they are more oriented to auditory stimulation, that they are less skilled in analytic reasoning or have lower overall intelligence. Similarly, no basis was found for the myth that girls learn more by rote while boys more easily master tasks involving "higher-level cognitive processing."

In a number of other areas, Maccoby and Jacklin lacked definitive evidence or they found ambiguous or inconsistent results. These areas include tactile sensitivity (most studies found no sex differences; in studies that did find differences, infant girls were more sensitive); fear, timidity, and anxiety (studies based on observation found no sex differences, but studies based on teacher ratings or reports by children themselves found that girls were more fearful and timid); activity level (infant girls are just as active as infant boys, but some studies found preschool boys to be more active than preschool girls); competitiveness and dominance (if the studies showed a difference, boys were the more competitive and dominant in group situations); compliance (girls tend to comply with adult demands more than do boys, but neither sex showed a greater willingness to comply with demands of their peers).

In the decade and a half since *The Psychology of Sex Differences* was published, psychologists and sociologists have chiseled away at Maccoby and Jacklin's findings, using new analytic techniques to suggest that the conclusions about male aggression may be overstated and questioning some of the conclusions on male superiority in spatial visualization.[14] A comparison of boys' and girls' scores on standardized college entrance aptitude tests reveals that "gender differences declined precipitously" from 1960 to 1983, with girls closing the gap in math and boys closing the gap in tests of verbal ability.[15]

Other psychologists claim, however, that Maccoby and Jacklin's "box score" approach to the data led them to understate the differences between boys and girls. Psychologist Jeanne H. Block of the University of California at Berkeley has been one of the more outspoken critics of Maccoby and Jacklin's findings. In a review of the professional literature published in 1983 she came up with these significant differences between the sexes: Boys are more aggressive in their play and verbal interaction; they attempt to dominate peers more than girls and prefer TV shows with more aggressive content. Boys are more active in their play than girls, more curious from ages three to six, and wander farther afield in their explorations. Boys suffer many more accidents requiring medical treatment from ages four to eighteen. Girls control their impulses better than boys, take fewer risks, and are better able to delay gratifying their desires. In addition, they are more socially compliant than boys, yield to group pressures more often, and show greater empathy with others. Females feel less confident of their abilities to solve problems and show a greater tendency toward "learned helplessness."[16] And so the debate goes on endlessly.

A Feminine Brain?

In recent years the "sexing of the brain"—that is, the idea that the brains of men and women show significant differences in structure and chemistry, and that these differences influence behavior—has sparked considerable interest. Proponents of the nature side of the debate have claimed evidence of brain differences as "hard" scientific proof that such fundamental sex differences as male aggression, female verbal superiority, and male superiority in math and spatial visualization are inescapable because they are biologically "programmed." "The constraint of our maleness and femaleness," as Jo Durden-Smith and Diane deSimone say in *Sex and the Brain*, is "wired before birth into the chemistry and circuitry of the male and female body and brain."[17] In other words, to oversimplify, your little girl behaves differently from your son not because she's imitating her mom or responding to parental/peer/media pressure, but because the predilection for such behavior is "wired in" to her cells. Biology as destiny rides again.

Two areas of brain research are particularly relevant: brain lateralization and the effect of sex hormones on behavior. The human brain is divided into two sectors, or hemispheres, which though more or less equal in size, have distinctly different functions. The left hemisphere, again to simplify, is the seat of language as well as of analytic and sequential thought. The right hemisphere specializes in processing visual information and figuring out spatial relations; it is also where we feel emotion and experience art and music. Now, though we all have this split inside our skulls, we don't recognize the division or lateralization of our brains because the two sides communicate via a thick bundle of fibers known as the corpus callosum. Researchers have found, however, that in girls, the left, or verbal, hemisphere develops more rapidly, while in boys, it is the right, or spatial, hemisphere that has a head start. The difference persists in the way the two hemispheres communicate as well. The average woman has a wider and larger corpus callosum than the average man, a difference manifested even in fetuses. The bigger bridge allows for more communication between the two hemispheres of the female brain; or, as scientists put it, women's brains are less completely lateralized (or more diffusely organized) than men's.[18]

This sounds like a possible advantage—after all, isn't it better if the right side knows what the left side is doing?—and may explain why girls often learn to read more easily than boys. (Reading involves communication between both hemispheres.) But, as it turns out, it may be a disadvantage for such visual-spatial tasks as map reading or rotating an object mentally or imagining how a two-dimensional drawing would translate into a three-dimensional object. According to some theorists, girls tend to use their left hemisphere, the verbal hemisphere, to work out visual-spatial problems, which are really the province of the right hemisphere. The greater lateralization of the male brain allows boys to tackle visual-spatial problems more single-mindedly, as it were, with more concentration and greater efficiency.

The two hemispheres also develop differently. In girls, the left, or verbal, hemisphere, develops earlier, in boys, the right, or visual-spatial, hemisphere. So, according to psychobiologists Jerre Levy of the University of Chicago and Marie-Christine de Lacoste, currently with Yale Medical School, girls have a built-in advantage in verbal abilities, as well as an inherent disadvantage in nonverbal, right-hemisphere tasks.

These findings have sparked enormous controversy. Critics point out that the alleged differences in the male and female corpus callosum are insufficiently substantiated.[19] Others argue that each brain is unique and that differences between individual brains are far greater than group differences between the "typical" male and the "typical" female brain. Roger Sperry, who won a Nobel Prize for his pioneering work on brain lateralization, suggests that individual brains may be even more distinctive in their physical structures than fingerprints.[20]

The other area of biological research has focused on hormones, particularly sex hormones. Researchers have found they can alter the behavior of female rhesus monkeys and rats by raising the level of testosterone, the male sex hormone, in utero. Female rhesus monkeys that have been "masculinized" in this way take on habits and actions typical of males, for example, roughhousing with other monkeys, mounting their peers, and actively initiating play with other young monkeys. From research on rats, scientists have concluded that not only do sex hormones influence behavior, they also have an impact on the very structure of the brain. East German researcher Gunter Dorner has extended the work to humans, going so far as to conclude that the level of testosterone to which a male fetus is exposed is critical in determining his sexual orientation. According to Dorner, a male fetus who, for some reason, was exposed to a low level of testosterone in utero has a far greater chance of growing up to be homosexual.[21]

June Reinisch, psychobiologist and director of the Kinsey Institute at Indiana University, points to a clear connection between male hormones and aggressive, rough-and-tumble play in children. Her research has shown that girls who were exposed to higher than normal androgen (male hormone) levels when their mothers took androgenizing drugs during pregnancy are more aggressive, independent, and tomboyish in behavior than their sisters who were not exposed to higher androgen levels. "The male and female brains are different structurally, and probably chemically," says Reinisch, "and that means that male and female behaviors are going to be different—overlapping, but different."[22] Reinisch also states that the "biological differences . . . are really quite small," but are amplified by the different socialization that boys and girls receive.[23]

Other researchers into the chemistry of the brain have discovered that females have a higher level of serotonin, a neurotransmitter that acts to inhibit aggression and control impulses.[24] Putting together the pieces of the puzzle and extrapolating from work with animals to humans, such strict constructionists conclude that our brains are sexed just as are other parts of our bodies, and that many behaviors considered typically masculine or feminine arise from fundamental differences between the male and female brain. In their view, attempts to raise our sons and daughters identically would be going against nature.

These theories about the sexing of the brain are intriguing, but they remain just that—*theories*. The notion that the feminine behavior we see in our daughters is somehow "wired in" to their brains and dictated by their hormones has by no means been proven, and some recent research has turned up contradictory results. Doreen Kimura of the University of Western Ontario has evidence that brain lateralization is not a simple black-and-white issue between the sexes, but that "depending on the particular intellectual function we're studying, women's brains may be more, less or equally diffusely organized compared with men's. No single rule holds for all aspects of thinking."[25] It seems clear that biology alone cannot account for the complexity and variety of human behavior and performance. As Jerome Kagan wisely notes, "We must never treat the biological and the experiential as separate, independent forces."[26] Attempts to isolate the two will of necessity distort the picture.

In any case, the differences between the sexes appear tiny when considered from the perspective of the range of differences between individuals. Carol Tavris, Ph.D., the coauthor of *The Longest War: Sex Differences in Perspective* and a columnist for *Vogue* on health concerns, feels that both the scientific community and the media may have a bias toward finding fundamental differences between men and women and ignoring similarities. "The main studies that fail to find sex differences are underrepresented in the scientific literature," she feels. "The question is: Why do researchers persist in looking for biological explanations for male-female differences rather than looking at differences in men's and women's social, economic, and cultural experiences?"[27] When it comes to living with and raising little girls, it may well be that biology has less relevance than our attitudes and expectations, the toys we buy, the behaviors we encourage, and the ways we interact. But of course such an assertion simply plunges us back once more into the thick of the great debate.

Now What About *Your* Little Girl?

Even this brief outline of the current state of the great nature versus nurture debate may leave you, the parent of a real little girl, wondering, "Who cares?" You may feel that the academic wars over sex differences are, well, academic. What does a 634-page study that comes up with only three definite differences between the sexes have to do with the sweet, warm body on your lap? Five-year-old Diana, who wouldn't dream of setting foot outdoors unless her outfit is perfectly color coordinated. Three-year-old Lauren, who spent an entire evening applying dusty rose polish in the vicinity of her finger- and toenails. Two-year-old Annie, who, when her dad tried to play baseball with her, placed the ball in her shopping cart and covered it with a blanket. Five-year-old Maddy, who flew upstairs to change into her frilliest dress when she overheard the word *party*. Four-year-old Andrea, who lives in a blush-pink fantasy world of Sleeping Beauty, Cinderella, and Barbie.

Few of us with daughters would deny that they are distinctly different from little boys. Their play is different, their obsessions are different, their fantasies are different; they notice different things in the world around them and respond differently; they watch different shows on television, choose different books, interact with peers differently, and use different equipment on the playground. An abyss seems to yawn between *our* little girls—the daughters we live with in our normal, day-to-day world—and *their* little girls, the female children whose behavior has led social scientists to dismantle, or at least challenge, the mythology of sex differences.

On a closer look, however, the abyss proves to be at least partly illusory. True, Diana is far more concerned with clothing than is her brother Steve, but that doesn't keep her from being quick with numbers, more assertive, and less hung up on her parents' approval. Lauren's older brother Jimmy polished his own nails too; they both had a wonderful time for an evening and were bored with the polish by the next day. Four-year-old Morgan fantasizes about being a ballerina, but on other days becoming a doctor or a farmer also appeals to her. When she tires of being a princess, Naomi joins her two older brothers at baseball or soccer and seems more coordinated than either of them. Betsy, age six, has finally stopped insisting on wearing dresses every day, realizing that she can have more fun on the playground in pants. Seven-year-old Connie talks incessantly about astronauts and space exploration. Maddy may be devoted to pink dresses, but that doesn't stop her from climbing trees or going to basketball games with her dad (she learned to count by watching the scoreboard). Annie never did catch on to baseball, but she can run like the wind and outclimb any child her age. Andrea's girlish fantasies seem to be a source of strength and confidence for her: the more passive she is in her fantasy life, the more assertive she has become in her interactions in nursery school.

Michael, who raised three sons before having two daughters with his second wife, takes a philosophical approach: "When Amira [who is now thirteen] was born, she was a delight—certainly quieter and gentler and less rambunctious than my three boys had been as babies. All the things people said about how different girls and boys are came true. We didn't foster it, but we certainly did enjoy it. But as she grew up, she developed a tough side, which she needs to survive in her school. She really knows how to take care of herself and she knows what's going on around her. She has the ability to use her femininity as a strength. We're proud of her, and she's proud of herself."

The little girls we know and the ones social scientists describe may not be so different after all. When we're observing our daughters or talking about them, many of us tend to play up their apparent femininity, whether out of pride or chagrin, but when we step back we may acknowledge it as just an aspect of their character, not its sole determining quality. There are ages and stages in a child's life when playing out an exaggerated gender role serves a purpose. A three-year-old girl's obsession with jewelry and makeup is a way of figuring out who she is, how she differs from her brother—and it may ultimately free her up to get in touch with other, less strictly gender-typed aspects of her personality. Like Amira, your daughter may be soft and gentle and yet tough enough to look out for herself. Typically feminine traits can coexist with typically masculine traits, and your daughter at different times in her life may draw on both as she needs them.

This is not to deny that at some fundamental level our little girls *are* different from little boys, and not just anatomically. Would you want them any other way? The notion of totally sex neutral child rearing that was batted about in the 1970s turned out to be an impossible ideal, and maybe for the better. What it often translated into on the practical level was that parents tried to get their girls to put aside dolls and frills in favor of trucks and overalls; boys, on the other hand, could continue being boys, so long as they eschewed the violent fringes of macho culture—the laser guns and death rays—and occasionally "nurtured" a doll or helped Mom bake cookies. "Defeminizing [girls]," as Stella Chess, M.D., and Jane Whitbread put it in their book *Daughters*, "treating them like boys, simply substitutes a new set of restrictions for the old ones."[28] Nonsexist child rearing, in other words, has its own sexist biases. Nowadays, we are coming to see that the hyperfemininity of certain periods of girlhood will not necessarily imperil our daughters' future prospects for self-fulfillment and we are questioning our unconscious assumption that feminine is in some way inferior to masculine. As Inge K. Broverman, program director in psychology at the Fielding Institute in Santa Barbara, California, notes, "The psychology of sex differences is changing so that we are no longer trying to make women into men, but are recognizing that women have traits we value."[29]

In *The Preschool Years*, Ellen Galinsky and Judy David of the Families and Work Institute of New York remark that "to the extent that traditional sex-typed roles restrict personal and professional fulfillment for males and females, we need to question them. At the same time, we side with parents who want their sons and daughters to grow up feeling good about being male or female. These goals—providing options and promoting a strong sense of gender—are not incompatible."[30] One of the biggest favors we, as parents, can do for our daughters is to let them be girls, even as we show them by example and precept that we think girls are as good as boys—not the same as boys, but their equals. Perhaps even better would be to let them be *children*—to encourage individual preferences without applying value-ridden gender labels.

Psychologist Samuel Osherson writes about his young son's craving for a toy sword. "How to do justice to the healthy masculine needs of our sons in this time of gender consciousness and changing sex roles?" Osherson wonders.[31] In the end, he comes to see that the sword is a perfectly normal outlet for some of his son's aggressive impulses. We may feel repelled at our daughters' choice of Zsa Zsa Gabor as a role model, just as Osherson dislikes his son's identification with Masters of the Universe. But in both cases, the best thing we can do for our children is to keep open minds about the messages they are conveying through fantasy play.

Our aim in *The Little Girl Book* is to help parents appreciate their daughters as children, as girls, and, most of all, as individuals, from birth to age eight. When we find gender differences, we'll try to explain their cause, their purpose, and how we as parents can help our daughters adjust to any special problems or issues that may arise out of these differences. We'll be looking at how the interaction of biology and culture, nature and nurture, produces some of the special qualities of little girls. What traits are inevitable? What traits are acquired? How have little girls changed as our culture has changed? We will compare "real" little girls— the daughters, friends, schoolmates, cousins, neighborhood children we see around us all the time—with the "ideal" little girls about whom social scientists draw their conclusions. And we will examine all the important relationships in a little girl's life—with mother, father, siblings, friends, caretakers, teachers—and how these change as she progresses through each of the phases of early childhood, from infancy, through toddlerhood, into the preschool and early school years.

Our daughters are growing up in a world far more complicated and stressful than the one we knew as children. The better we understand them, the more we'll be able to help them navigate the swift, dark waters ahead.

2

The Littlest Girls: Infancy and the Start of Socialization

How Little Girls Are Formed

Notwithstanding Simone de Beauvoir's magisterial pronouncement that "one is not born, but rather becomes, a woman," there is no question that one *is* born a girl. A girl's sex (as distinguished from her sex role) is fixed at the moment of conception—one of the many genetic messages that the sperm carries to the egg when it penetrates the outer membrane and initiates the awesome process of creating a new person. This new person has twenty-three pairs of chromosomes, half contributed by her father, half by her mother, one of which determines sex. The mother's egg cell always contributes an X chromosome to the pairing; but the father's sperm may carry either an X or a Y chromosome. When an X-bearing sperm fertilizes the egg, the new life is a girl—XX.

Initially, the male and female embryos both have a tiny, androgynous bump known as the ovotestes. It is not until seven or eight weeks after conception that the XY (male) embryo begins to transform the ovotestes into testes. The process of transforming the ovotestes into ovaries happens a couple of weeks later.[1] This is the only time that a girl lags behind a boy in any important development. Three months before her birth, your daughter's ovaries are structurally complete and stocked with a lifetime supply of eggs, about 400,000 on average.[2] When she reaches puberty, your daughter's ovaries will secrete sex hormones that trigger the release of one of these eggs each month, but no sex hormones are secreted prenatally. A male fetus, on the other hand, does produce androgens (male hormones) in utero: biologists believe that prenatal androgens account not only for the formation of the penis and internal male organs, but for basic differences in the structure and functioning of the brain (see page 11). The androgens coursing through the body of the male fetus leave a permanent impression on his hypothalamus, the section of the brain that controls the release of hormones. When the boy reaches puberty, his hypothalmus triggers a more or less continuous release of hormones; whereas in a girl, the hormone release is cyclical, hence the menstrual cycle.[3]

Interestingly, hormones, not genetics, cause male development to differ from female. If a fetus has the XY genetic makeup of a boy but, for some reason, is incapable of secreting or using androgens, it will develop along the same lines as a female. The female model, to put it crudely, is the basic life form, whereas becoming male requires that extra hormonal boost. "The effect of hormones on early development is really very much a matter of what you add to the basic female model," says John Bancroft, a behavioral endocrinologist at the Medical Resource Council's reproductive-biology unit in Edinburgh, Scotland. "Like anatomy, basic behavior is feminine. If you add androgen, it gets more masculine, and if you take it away, you get the opposite effect."[4] The Bible story of Eve created out of Adam's rib got it wrong: Eve was there first, and Adam sprung up only after God created testosterone.

Possessing the basic model gives your daughter certain advantages, even in the womb. The XX configuration makes the female fetus sturdier than the male, more likely to survive to full term and to be born whole and perfect.[5] She also matures more rapidly in utero. At birth, despite the fact that boys are on average a bit longer and heavier than girls, girls are skeletally more advanced by anywhere from four to six weeks, and behaviorally more mature. Her edge on maturity continues and in fact accelerates throughout childhood: a baby girl will sit, crawl, and walk earlier than a boy; she learns how to use the potty sooner; she gets her permanent teeth a few months sooner; she counts and prints letters earlier; and she enters adolescence on average two years earlier than a boy. On average, at any given point in childhood, a little girl will be about six months more advanced than a little boy of the same age.[6]

Scientists speculate that the Y chromosome not only slows male development (after the initial head start on genital development), but makes the male more vulnerable to congenital diseases such as hemophilia and to such anomalies as nearsightedness, autism, color blindness, allergies, dyslexia, and stuttering. It is possible that the double X configuration of females acts as a kind of genetic safeguard. A healthy X will cancel out the problem carried by a defective X, whereas in a male, with only one X, all defects will be expressed. For the same reason, some scientists believe that boys show greater mental and physical variation than girls: there are, according to this theory, more male geniuses but also more idiots, more extremely tall and extremely short males, and so on. (However, many psychologists, particularly feminists, convincingly reject the theory of greater male variability.[7])

Your newborn daughter may look tiny and extremely fragile. In fact, she is every bit as sturdy as a newborn baby boy—even more so in some respects.

Your Newborn Daughter: Everything Nice?

"We wanted a girl first," said Dan, a New York City father of a daughter and son, "because we thought a girl would be easier to raise. More is expected of boys. They are more aggressive. Girls are quieter on the outside, but they turn things inward." Dan didn't quite get around to reciting the old nursery rhyme about how girls are made of sugar and spice and everything nice while boys are made of snips and snails and puppy dogs' tails, but his comments were certainly headed in that direction. We expect our newborn daughters to be sweeter, more cuddly, quieter, and above all *easier* than our sons. "Girls squirm less," as one mother put it. "They will actually sit quietly on your lap and look around without wiggling all over the place." "He was fussier and needed to eat more," recalled another mother. "The girls were calmer." "I could never put him down," said a third. "My daughter seemed more self-sufficient right from the start."

What are the facts? Are girl babies really easier than boys? (Stella Chess defines *easiness* as getting hungry at regular intervals, eating with pleasure and without dallying, falling asleep promptly, sleeping for predictable stretches of time, enjoying hugs, and not being overly suspicious of strangers.[8]) The answer, though far from definitive, seems to be that yes, girls are on average somewhat easier to handle as infants—but not because of some innate docility. Rather, it's because of that developmental head start. Girls are not only four to six weeks ahead of boys skeletally, but more advanced behaviorally as well. Infant girls tend to sleep more than boys (about an hour more out of an eight-hour period), and they are generally less irritable and easier to soothe when they do get cranky. In addition, newborn girls tend to have longer periods when they are alert but inactive, whereas when newborn boys are alert, they tend to do more squirming, thrashing, grimacing, and eventually fussing.[9] Keep in mind, however, that, as with all sex differences, there is a tremendous overlap between the sexes and large variation among individuals of the same sex. One father of twins, for example, reports that from birth his daughter has always been more active, wakeful, and aggressive than her twin brother. Another family's first daughter was a model baby and the third outdid any boy in screaming, thrashing, and rebelling. These children are all perfectly normal.

A girl's head start may carry over into the sphere of

social awareness as well. Developmental psychologist Jerome Kagan asserts that "the infant female is a little more prone than the male to the state normally called fear," based on laboratory observations in which infant girls showed distress to a novel situation or separation from their mothers at an earlier age than boys. Kagan found that starting at around three to four months, girls would "freeze" when something frightened them and then start to cry, whereas boys were more apt to react by initiating some action. Kagan speculates that the infant girl's greater fearfulness may result from her "biological precocity": because she is more advanced than a boy, she is more fully aware of the strangeness and potential danger of a new situation. But Kagan also throws out the possibility that fearfulness may be an innate sex-linked trait, since it emerges at an age when "differential treatment by parents" cannot yet have taken effect.[10] Other studies of infants find no sex differences in fear response; and in studies of older children based on self-reports, girls may score higher in fearfulness because in our culture it is more acceptable for a girl to admit being afraid than it is for a boy.[11] And some studies show that infant girls cope better with psychological stress than boys, crying less when separated from their mothers.[12]

Body and Senses: Sex Differences Revisited

For those who like to keep score, here is a rundown of the major differences between infant boys and girls in physical strength and sense perception.

Boys, as we have seen, are born on average slightly longer and heavier than girls, and they also have more muscle and less fat. But because of their relative maturity and possibly because of their XX chromosomal configuration, girls are better able to withstand physiological stress and are less likely to die of an infectious disease, birth defect, or sudden infant death syndrome in the first year of life. Some, but not all, researchers have found that when placed on their stomachs, newborn boys are able to lift their heads up higher than newborn girls. And in some popular baby books, infant boys are portrayed as more "wiry" than girls. Again, studies conflict, and the notion of male infants as stronger, bouncier, and generally more athletic may simply be a reflection of cultural assumptions.

Similarly, the notion that girls hear better than boys at birth but that boys are more visually oriented can be taken as myth or fact, depending on which study you consult.[13] Maccoby and Jacklin assert that "it has not been demonstrated that either sex is more 'visual' or more 'auditory' than the other,"[14] and until a more exhaustive survey comes along, we'll stick with them.

Even more controversy surrounds the question of whether infant girls are more sensitive to touch. A number of studies have found that infant girls react more than boys when their heels are tickled or their tummies blown on.[15] The notion fits cultural stereotypes and has in fact been used to explain certain aspects of feminine behavior. In *The Psychology of Women*, J. M. Bardwick posits that the female's "greater reactivity to physical stimuli . . . [is] a necessary precondition for empathy and imagination."[16] Thus, from an infant girl's soft, delicate baby skin springs womanly sympathy and kindness. But, once again, Maccoby and Jacklin, in reviewing nine major studies, find "only hints" that baby girls are more sensitive to touch than baby boys, and conclude that "a conservative reading of the evidence is that no such difference has been demonstrated."[17]

Babies obviously do differ tremendously in their physical and sensory abilities, just as they differ tremendously in temperament and behavior. But, again, the really significant differences are those between individuals. "If we are unaware of a baby's sex," write psychologists Edward Tronick and Lauren Adamson in *Babies as People*, "we cannot tell by observing the infant's behavior if he or she is a boy or a girl."[18] From a practical point of view, it would be far better to try to figure out what your own baby is interested in and what she responds to than to assume that as a girl she *must* like music and soft pats but won't care about mobiles, pictures, or roughhousing. In a well-known study of 133 children from infancy through preadolescence, Alexander Thomas, Stella Chess, and Herbert G. Birch of the New York University Medical Center found that temperament remains remarkably constant through childhood and into adulthood, and that such traits as activity level, adaptability, intensity, and distractibility may be inborn to a greater degree than previously believed. In their initial study, the researchers found that 40 percent of the children could be described as temperamentally "easy," while about 10 percent were "difficult"—that is, intense in behavior, unfriendly, negative, and unpredictable in their eating and sleeping patterns.[19] Parents of daughters can take some comfort from the fact that although an equal number of boys and girls were found to be difficult in infancy, by age two many more boys than girls remained so.[20]

Another and perhaps equally important factor Thomas and Chess point to is "goodness of fit" between a parent's and a child's temperament.[21] "Goodness of fit" is obviously partly a matter of chance—being lucky enough to have a child whose moods, preferences, and habits accord well with your own—and partly a matter of parent and child adapting to each other. Gender-related factors may enter in as well. Susan, the mother of two school-age sons and a toddler daughter, said that when she was growing up she was a "stereotypical girl—shy, quiet, and totally into dolls." Hoping to find these qualities in her own daughter as well, instead she ended up with a little girl who is boisterous and far more aggressive than her brothers were as babies. Susan admits she has trouble relating to a girl so alien to her own personality. On the other hand, Alice, a world-class athlete who conforms to few feminine stereotypes, says she sometimes feels "unnerved" by her daughter's frilly femininity, in her opinion an inborn trait.

Although both Susan and Alice feel somewhat disappointed by their "fit" with their daughters, both acknowledge the importance of respecting their little girls' individuality and letting them develop their own styles. If you feel you and your daughter don't have a good fit, you might try to improve it by getting to know her temperament well enough to anticipate her needs and interests. Experiment, and keep your eyes open to her responses. Try not to expect her to be easy, sweet, and cuddly, simply because girls are "supposed to" be that way. In the first months of life, a child's temperament, far more than her sex, will help you understand what makes her tick.

Socialization Begins at Birth

Steve's daughter Vanessa is now four, but he can still recollect his thoughts when the doctor announced to him and his wife that they'd just had a baby girl: "I remember thinking of her as being this sweet, nice, gentle, soft-skinned, flowery kind of thing. I thought she would be into dolls, dress-up, makeup—you know, girl-type things. In fact, all of this has come true. She loves dolls and stuffed animals, lipstick, and nail polish. She demanded to have her ears pierced at four even though she knew it would hurt. It was worth it to her."

Not all new parents of daughters have as detailed a "script" of feminine behavior as Steve, but most of us step into the role of a little girl's mom or dad with at least a few preconceived ideas about what raising a daughter will be like. "I worried about having to look after her more and protect her more than if she were a boy," one mother from rural Iowa said. "Especially when she hit sixteen." "I figured I'd have to dress her up pretty and take her shopping," is how a Valparaiso, Florida, mother remembers her initial reaction. "It didn't bother me that she was so small," said a California mother. "It matters if a boy is short, but a girl can get by so long as she's pretty." "I thought I'd have to stand over her more," said a Georgia mother. "You don't want to think of a little girl falling down and getting a scar." Others of us joke in the delivery room about all the shoes she's going to go through, how much time she'll spend on the phone, how she'll have her daddy wrapped around her little finger—but even as we joke, we're setting the wheels of stereotype in motion.

As we reviewed in Chapter 1, baby girls and boys are more alike than they are different, but few of us treat them that way. As Edward Tronick and Lauren Adamson put it so eloquently in *Babies as People*, "While the studies on newborn sex-related behavioral differences are baffling and controversial, the research findings on how adults perceive these elusive 'differences' is not. We adults do not treat the sex of a baby as a trivial clue. To us, it is a central organizer, a potent description of who the newborn baby is."[22]

Think of the very first thing you tell your friends and relatives about the new baby: It's a girl! Think of how often you tell *her* that she's a girl. "Here's my little girl!" "What a gorgeous girl!" "Pretty baby girl!" we say. Not "Here's my darling little American" or "What a sweet little Episcopalian" or "Pretty baby Caucasian"—even though nationality, religion, and race are also crucial elements of her identity. Not as crucial as gender. Look at how you have furnished your daughter's room. Look at the toys that you and your friends and relatives buy her, even before she's old enough to hold them, let alone play with them. Look at the clothes you put her in and listen to what you say when you dress her up. Jerome Kagan points out that "each parent possesses an idea of one perfect set of traits for males and another for females. These ideals are, of course, influenced by the values of the culture. The parents' actions usually are attempts to mold the child in accord with the cultural standards."[23] And even if our ideals for girls and boys are quite similar, our children will eventually pick up the emphasis on gender differences from friends, relatives, teachers, television, books. It's in the very air we breathe.

Social scientists have detected some subtle but revealing differences in the way parents handle and speak to their sons and daughters, even in the first months of life. Howard Moss and his colleagues at the National Institute of Mental

Health spent a great deal of time in the late 1960s and early 1970s observing a representative group of first-time mothers with their boy and girl babies. Despite the wide range in behaviors displayed by the babies, Moss found that the boys were on average fussier and more wakeful than the girls. At three weeks, the boys received more handling than the girls: since they fussed more often, their mothers picked them up, and spent more time rocking them and attending to their needs. By three months, however, the mothers were handling their fussy boys less whereas the handling for the more even-tempered girls stayed the same. Moss speculated that the new mothers felt rewarded by their success at soothing their daughters and therefore had an incentive to keep it up; but since their efforts to calm their sons were ineffective, it seemed pointless to continue trying.[24] Moss also found that when the babies reached four months, the mothers tended to reinforce their daughters' social interactions more than their sons'. They responded more readily to the girls when the babies smiled and babbled, and used such social tools as speech and eye contact to soothe them. In contrast, the mothers soothed fussy boys by providing auditory or visual stimulus. Mothers were also found generally to put far more effort into arousing and stimulating their baby boys than their baby girls. Other researchers believe that at six months mothers often "wean" their sons from physical contact, giving them a firm push toward independence, whereas they socialize their daughters to be dependent by encouraging them to remain physically close.[25]

Even before speech, conversation seems to be central to the mother-daughter relationship, certainly more so than to the mother-son bond. Studies have shown that mothers talk more to their daughters at three months, and that three-month-old daughters "talk" (babble, coo, gurgle) more in response.[26] Moss's inescapable conclusion is that mothers "seemed to show greater investment in the social behavior of their daughters than that of their sons."[27]

The influence of fathers is rather different. To begin with, most men in our culture want a son much more than a daughter, and want a son more than their wives do.[28] Although we may shudder at the notion of female infanticide (a routine practice in some societies), men in our culture still commonly offer their sympathies to a dad on the birth of a daughter—or, God forbid!, a second, third, or fourth daughter. "I get a lot of teasing from my friends," said one father of four daughters. "They're always saying things like, 'Poor guy,' or 'Tough break.' I have this brother-in-law who says my life is ruined since I don't have a son. I think he's an idiot." On the other hand, a number of dads feel greatly relieved to have daughters because it frees them from the burden of masculine competition and sports. Men who have poor relationships with their own fathers talk about how refreshing it is to "start from scratch" with a little girl, with none of the father-son conflicts to contend with.

Nonetheless, son-preference remains common, and it can exert a powerful influence. According to Ross Parke, a noted psychologist at the University of Illinois, fathers handle, touch, and talk to their sons more than their daughters, even in early infancy, and they feed and diaper sons more often too.[29] Patti, the mother of a daughter and son who are eighteen months apart, notes that although her husband was not terribly involved in the care of either child, he was far more enthusiastic about his son. "He loved our daughter, but then when Brad was born his attitude was, 'Now I finally have my boy!' " In this father's mind, having a son excused him from paying much further attention to his daughter.

Despite all the media attention to the "new, involved father," most dads fall well short of their partners on the chores and daily routines of baby care.[30] Fathers get far higher marks, however, as playmates for their babies. "My husband gets the fun and games, and I get the real work," Donna, a full-time mother of three, complains, only half-joking. On a typical evening after work, Mal is likely to wrestle for an hour with Matthew, while Bonnie joins in intermittently. After the roughhousing subsides, Mal will scoop up Bonnie and sit quietly with her on the sofa. Studies have found this pattern even in the early months of life. Dads commonly toss their sons in the air, roll around on the floor with them, and hold them upside down. Once sons can crawl or walk, fathers are likely to encourage them to get up and start exploring. It's not that fathers *don't* play with their daughters; rather, as with Mal and Bonnie, they play less often and less roughly. When their daughters can walk, fathers prefer to keep them close by, discouraging wandering and independence. And, like mothers, fathers reward their little girls for talking.[31]

Perhaps even more significant is the role fathers play in gender typing. In an oft-cited study called "The Eye of the Beholder: Parents' Views on Sex of Newborns," mothers and fathers were asked to describe a group of newborn boys and girls who were nearly identical in size, weight, and robustness.[32] Although both parents described the girls as softer, smaller, and more delicate, fathers were even more prone than mothers to make such gender-based distinctions. Throughout infancy and childhood, and more than moms, dads pressure their boys to act like boys and their girls to act like girls. It's especially important to dads that their sons *not* play with dolls and tea sets.[33] Tomboys are more acceptable than sissies to just about everyone.

Rhoda Unger, a professor of psychology at Montclair State College in Montclair, New Jersey, feels that it's not only fathers but the culture as a whole that puts more pressure of this sort on boys. Girls, perhaps because they have less status in our society, are free to deviate from such stereotypes.[34] Most of us feel far more comfortable watching a little girl play baseball than watching a little boy play with Barbie. But this freedom is short-lived. According to Unger and other psychologists, at adolescence girls run up against the same sort of pressure that boys feel from birth. Adolescence is also the time when girls start to lag behind boys in academic achievement.[35] Carol Gilligan, a professor at the Harvard Graduate School of Education, finds that girls undergo a kind of emotional and moral crisis at adolescence in which they frequently lose the confidence and resilience of childhood. As they wake up to the place of women in our culture and its demands, they become confused, silent, and less forceful about their own needs.[36] (See Chapter 10 for a more detailed discussion.)

As your daughter dumps her pablum on the floor or struggles to grab this book with sticky hands, these concerns may seem rather remote. But it's worthwhile keeping the big picture in the back of your mind, even at the start.

Parenting Tips: Sexist Attitudes, Dads and Baby Daughters, Clothing, Family Life

Sexist Attitudes

While social scientists endlessly wrestle with the great nature/nurture debate, our time might be better spent on the question of how to raise our daughters more fairly and more creatively. As we've seen, physical and behavioral differences between the sexes are minimal, especially when compared with the differences in our attitudes and assumptions. "I always thought I wanted boys," said one mother whose daughters are now seven and ten, "because boys are always outside running around. I thought girls would be prim and proper and ladylike. But I'm not that way, and after a while I realized that it didn't have to be this way with my daughters. I think I've lucked out with my girls, and my husband feels the same way."

Lots of us share this mother's assumption (or fear) that our daughters will be prim and proper, and many of us reinforce these behaviors, consciously or unconsciously. Researchers have conducted a number of studies in which they "trick" parents by cross-dressing infants or randomly assigning pink or blue outfits. In one study, mothers who insisted that they treated their sons and daughters alike were asked to play with a six-month-old baby, and were provided with three toys: a doll, a train, and a fish. The mothers who were given the blue-dressed baby proffered the train; the pink-dressed baby was offered the doll.[37] In another experiment conducted in England, six-month-olds were cross-dressed. The women (not the mothers of the babies, obviously) who were given the girls disguised as boys encouraged them to crawl, stand, and pursue other vigorous motor activities far more than the other half of the group.[38] And in still another study, researchers John Condry and Sandra Condry showed adults videotaped sequences of a baby crying in a frustrating situation. When told that the baby was a boy, subjects speculated that he was crying from anger; when told that the same baby in the same videotape was a girl, they said she was probably crying out of fear.[39]

The point is not that we fail our children if we behave in a more sexist fashion than we intend to or believe is right. Rather, we should try to become aware of our often unconscious attitudes and beliefs about sex roles.

Tips for Fathers of Newborn Daughters

"I come from a family with three boys," says Barry, the father of six-year-old Maddy, "and when my daughter was born I remember thinking, 'Oh, no! What do I do now?' I knew about ball playing and roughhousing, but I didn't know what to do with girls."

Not all new fathers snap out of the initial "shock" of having a daughter as quickly as Barry did.

Barry found an excellent way out of this dilemma: he rolled up his sleeves and got into the dirty day-to-day business of infant care. In the early months, the "business" and pleasures of bringing up baby are very often linked: you play peekaboo while changing her diaper; feeding and burping are occasions for cuddling and kissing; bathtime is an opportunity to introduce new sensations and toys. Fathers who remain aloof from their daughters until they can *really* play may find that it's impossible to catch up when that day finally arrives, if it ever does.

Stereotypes may also stand in the way of a good father-daughter bond in the early months. Several fathers mentioned the pleasure they took in their baby girl's prettiness: even more than their wives, they loved to see their daughter dressed up in frilly clothes and looking adorable. As the studies cited earlier indicate, the dad who roughhouses with his baby son is more likely to restrict his interaction with a daughter to low-key social activities such as talking or singing. This may suit some little girls perfectly, but others would respond joyfully to the wild antics if only Dad would give them a chance. Similarly, fathers tend to be more protective toward their daughters: when carried too far, this can be oppressive and even retard independence and confidence.

Some men may, from the very start, feel excluded from what they perceive as the "woman's world" their wives and daughters inhabit. Brad Sachs, Ph.D., director of the Father Center in Columbia, Maryland, notes that men's general tendency to defer to women as the "experts" in child care is even more pronounced when the baby is a girl. But Sachs points out that a father need not be alienated. "Men can see it as an opportunity to access their feminine side more deeply," he says. "This doesn't mean becoming like a woman, but rather enhancing their masculinity by gaining a broader sense of manhood."[40] Sachs also believes that some men may feel uncomfortable diapering or bathing their baby daughters because of the intense awareness of child sexual abuse these days; they worry that they might touch their daughters in the wrong way, and they may use these worries to avoid getting involved in child care. *Day-by-Day Baby Care* by Miriam Stoppard, M.D. (Ballantine Books, 1983) is one recommended title (among many) with clear pictures and text on "cleaning a girl." The basic rule is to clean the outside of her genitals *only*, never to pull back the labia or try to wipe inside her vagina.

If a father wants a playmate to roughhouse with, he can

encourage his daughter's motor activities—and maybe start by combining his games with basic caretaking routines. "My husband is very athletic and I was disappointed for him when our first child was a girl," said one mother. "But he became super-involved right from the start. He took her everyplace, cared for her as much or more than I do, and later on played all sorts of ball games with her. Now she's really the athlete in the family."

Mothers can help by surrendering some of the child care responsibility and by easing up on the ultra-feminine accoutrements. A father who finds his baby girl dressed like a Victorian china doll is more likely to treat her like one.

Clothing and Appearance

There is no denying that dressing up baby girl is more fun than dressing up baby boy, and that clothing is likely to loom larger in her adult life. Department stores, boutiques, and catalogs brim with irresistible little outfits with which we can indulge our fondest fantasy of fledgling femininity. And even if we deliberately restrict our purchases to sex-neutral overalls and stretchies, chances are that friends and relatives will shower us with tiny ruffled dresses, beribboned sunbonnets, mini barrettes, even pocketbooks and jewelry.

If you enjoy bedecking your infant daughter, fine. But keep these pointers in mind:

- Clothing can restrict your daughter's ability to move freely. Binding elastic and tight-fitting skirts can make it hard to kick and stretch. When your daughter starts to crawl, she'll have far less trouble getting around in pants, shorts, or overalls than in a dress or skirt.
- Dress your daughter appropriately for the situation. A desire to show off a new outfit or use it before she outgrows it is understandable; but you will only saddle yourself with conflict if you put on her best velvet for a trip to the park or an outdoor gathering. You also risk

falling into the habit of discouraging her from active play so that she won't soil or tear her outfit. Remember that baby girls need to move around as much as little boys. Don't sacrifice her physical development to her wardrobe.

- Keep the future in mind. Parents who make a huge fuss about their infant daughter's clothing are teaching her that appearance is important, that what she wears is an essential part of who she is. This can come back to haunt you in a year or two, when *she* starts making a huge fuss over her clothing. Many parents find themselves pulling out their hair at eight in the morning when their two-year-old refuses to wear anything but her white satin party dress and patent leather shoes. They forget that they were the ones who applauded every ruffle during infancy.
- Ultra-feminine clothing may alienate a girl's father, as discussed above. It may also contribute to the stereotypical notion of girls as more fragile and delicate than boys. One way out of this bind is for the mother to let the father dress the baby occasionally (and not to criticize the results).

A Daughter's Place in the Family

A little girl's position in the family, the sex of her siblings, and the way her parents divide up family work all help establish her sex role and her view of herself. As we have seen, both mothers and fathers may prefer to have a son, especially for a first child, and parents who have only daughters may value each succeeding little girl less. On the other hand, there is evidence that many parents consider the ideal family to be both a son and a daughter.[41] "Everybody wants to have vanilla *and* chocolate," joked one psychologist. A little girl who arrives after a little boy may find herself in the best of all possible worlds.

We've heard a lot of parents use the "you can't fight nature" argument, pointing out that their son has been domineering and boisterous from birth, and their daughter always more passive and timid. It's possible that in some cases these parents are actually creating or reinforcing the behavior they believe is innate. Remember also that although temperament may remain fairly constant through life, preferences in toys, companions, and activities change frequently and rapidly. Your little girl may move from dolls to blocks, and on to puppets or dress-up clothes at various times. Try to let her take the lead in expressing her interests, rather than imposing sexual stereotypes on her or "freezing" her in one phase.

Although family patterns are changing, mothers by and large continue to be the primary caretakers and fathers the primary breadwinners, and your daughter may well grow up taking this division of labor for granted. Babies generally associate Mommy with comfort, food, and the daily routines of care, while they associate Daddy with spontaneous play, unpredictable behavior, and a higher level of motor activity.[42] As one mother of two put it, "My husband works long hours and it's hard for him to be very involved with caring for the kids. When he gets home, he tends to throw the kids up in the air and then throw them back at me." Willy-nilly, in her first year your daughter learns how mothers and fathers (and, by extension, women and men) differ in their family roles and in their behavior toward her. She sees who changes her diaper, who does the dishes or takes out the garbage; she feels the different ways her mother and father pick her up, she sees her parents buy different toys for her brother and make different demands on him. But, as Letty Cottin Pogrebin points out in *Growing Up Free*, even as parents continue to assume different roles within the family, they can consciously strive to share the tasks of family work and the joys of family play along nonsexist lines. "Nothing is wrong with division of labor," writes Pogrebin, "so long as the role split is based on individual specialties, not on sex."[43] Ellen Galinsky of the Families and Work Institute in New York notes that a quarter-century of research has revealed that children develop broader ideas about sex roles when their mothers are employed (see Chapter 9) and when their fathers are highly involved in child care.[44] Not surprisingly, girls stand to gain more in the way of self-esteem and status in this regard than boys.

Even when parents succeed in presenting nonsexist models, the children very often persist in sexist behaviors and expectations. A little girl (or boy) is more likely to call out to Mommy for help, for reassurance, or a gentle hug, even if Dad is equally gentle, comforting, and available; and when a child first learns to talk, the word *mommy* often means both mother and "Come here," "I need you," or "Pick me up."[45] As we will see in the chapters ahead, as a little girl grows, and particularly as she enters the preschool period, she may define quite rigidly the appropriate behaviors and activities for each sex. A child makes sense of the world in black and white and in bold, simple patterns (mommies take care of babies; daddies work and play ball) before she can begin to add shading, nuance, and varied textures.

3

The Dawn of Femininity: The Preschool Years

From Baby to Girl: Gender Identity and Gender Roles

Ask your one-year-old daughter whether she's a boy or a girl, and the likely answer (if you get any answer at all) is "baby." Point to a picture of a couple and ask which is the mommy and which is the daddy, and she's likely to reply with a bemused smile or by tearing the picture out of your hand and sticking it in her mouth.

Repeat the experiment a year or a year and a half later. Your two-and-a-half-year-old is likely to tell you proudly that she's a "little girl" (or a "big girl," depending on her mood). Without stopping to ponder the picture, she knows that the daddy is the one playing ball and the mommy the one cooking dinner, and she can sort out objects by gender category: purse for women, shaving cream for men, and so on.[1] (Interestingly, and maddeningly for feminists, toddlers very often adhere to far stricter gender categories than their parents do: a thirty-month-old girl is likely to sort the hammer with the "daddy things" even if her mother does most of the household repairs and the pots and pans with the "mommy things" even if her father does most of the cooking.)

By age three, your daughter is firmly established in her sense of herself as a girl (her gender identity) and she is likely to emphatically prefer stereotypically feminine activities and toys.[2] "She's into dolls, ballet, skirts, and dresses," one mother summed up. "She won't have anything to do with a toy or activity if it can possibly be construed as masculine." Though the house was full of her brother's trucks, trains, planes, and balls, Cara at age three rejected them all in favor of dolls and kitchen equipment. On vacation three-year-old Liza pined for her patent leather party shoes.

Most girls this age also prefer female playmates and react more positively when introduced to a new little girl or group of girls than to an unfamiliar boy or group of boys.[3] Researchers have found, however, that although a toddler knows and boasts that she is a girl, she doesn't yet really grasp that gender describes a class of people and not just her alone. As Eleanor Maccoby points out, a three-year-old girl will get furious if you call her a boy—but she's likely to react just as furiously if you call her by the wrong name.[4]

During the preschool years, ages two to five, your little girl gradually figures out a good many of the implications of girlhood. As she comes to realize that her gender is something she shares with other girls, and with her mother and grandmother, she also acquires a more detailed and comprehensive sense of how girls are "supposed to" behave and how this behavior differs from that of little boys. When she was two or three, Zeva, a little girl from a small town in Ohio, tended to imitate the activities of her two older brothers, ages eleven and eight. Her play was loud and boisterous, she tried to urinate standing up, she rejected dresses, ribbons, and dolls, and even went so far as to insist she was a boy. But once she went to preschool at age four and started to make friends with other little girls, Zeva began to identify more with her friends' feminine preferences and behaviors. "She thinks she *ought to* like to wear feminine things, so she tries to," says her mother. "I think that, because her best friend is very feminine, she's decided that being a girl is okay. She accepts the fact that she's a girl, but she still doesn't want to make a big deal about it."

A psychologist would say that Zeva is acquiring a sex role or gender role. Gender role should not be confused with gender identity (a girl's ability to label herself as female). Zeva eventually understood that she really was a girl, even though she doesn't always enjoy acting and dressing like one. Gender identity comes into focus first, and gender role follows, though in widely varying degrees. For Cara, feminine gender role means wearing frilly dresses every day, twirling around like a ballerina, and refusing to play baseball. For Becky, it means copying her mother, from helping care for a baby brother to adoring arts and crafts to organizing her "work" papers (her parents run their own advertising agency). For Maddy, climbing trees is fine as long as she's wearing a pink dress. Again, to quote Maccoby, a girl can have a firmly established sense of her gender identity but still reject certain (or most) aspects of the feminine gender role: "A girl can know that she is a girl, expect to grow up as a woman, never seriously want to be a boy, and nevertheless be a tomboy—enjoying boys' games and toys and preferring to play with boys. She has a firm, fully accepted female *identity*, but she does not adopt all the *sex-typed* behaviors that her culture labels feminine, nor avoid those labeled masculine."[5]

Our preschool daughters constantly surprise us with their funny mix of innocence and sophistication, factual knowledge and pure fantasy. When asked the difference between men and women, four-year-old Wendy explained that women wore jewelry and men didn't, then amended the explanation that men sometimes wore one earring while women usually wore two. To Wendy, clothing, hairstyle, and jewelry were the crucial cues to a person's sex—not their genitals, even though she knew the correct words for the male and female sex organs. She knew she would always be a girl "because I was born a girl," as she put it; but she hadn't yet extended this same knowledge to include everyone else. A man who put on two earrings, grew his hair, and wore a skirt would not only *look* like a woman, but *be* a woman. The idea of "gender permanence" does not usually emerge until ages five to seven.[6] There is some evidence that at that point, children's fanatical devotion to gender stereotypes wanes. At five, Amy wrapped herself in a frilly cocoon and shuddered at the thought of short hair because "girls don't do that." Now, at thirteen, Amy hates to wear dresses, stands up to the tough kids at school, and loves to go fishing with her dad, while her little sister Ellie, age five, keeps the ultra-feminine fires burning. Her parents, now accustomed to the vicissitudes of socialization, are confident that Ellie will grow up to be a rounded, strong, and independent person, just as her sister did.

Learning to Be a Girl: Theories of Gender Acquisition

You don't have to teach, coax, correct, or pressure your baby into becoming a little girl. In fact, you probably won't be able to stop her even if you try. "We really worked against the sex stereotypes," said Judy, a Midwestern free-lance editor and mother of Hanna, age four. "We dressed her in unisex clothes as a baby, gave her blocks as well as stuffed animals and dolls. But as soon as she had a say in the matter, she asked for pink and purple. It shocked us, but we're not putting up a big fuss. For now, we're going with the Barbie business."

How does it happen? And why? Social scientists have advanced a number of theories and, of course, debated them at great length. Without getting too tangled up in the debate, here are the three major theories.

1. Identification. The essence of the various theories that fall under this heading is that during the preschool years children come to identify with the same-sex parent. According to Freud, the originator of identification theory, both sexes initially identify with the mother because she is the source of nourishment, care, and love and they fear her withdrawal. However, when a little girl realizes that little boys have penises and she doesn't, she blames her mother and turns to her father. Since she can't have a penis, she desires to have a baby instead, and so must seduce her father. Hence a preschool girl, according to Freud, imitates her mother's behavior in order to take her place.

"Penis envy," the cornerstone of Freud's theory of female psychology, has come under attack, particularly by feminists, who point out that there is little evidence in studies of actual girls that it exists or that it is the prime motivating force of their psychology.[7] Other critics note that the Oedipal myth that is central to Freud's theory—the story of the prince in ancient Greece who was abandoned as an infant and returned to slay his father and wed his mother—pertains only to males, and consider the notion of "penis envy" a lame attempt to "fit women into [Freud's] masculine conception."[8]

2. Social learning. In this theory, advanced by Albert Bandura and Walter Mischel, among others, reinforcement is one of the prime agents of socializing children in all aspects of social behavior, not just sex roles. Along with relatives, child care providers, and teachers, parents approve of girls for feminine behavior and discourage or fail to reward them for acting like boys. Children, in turn, closely observe the people around them to pick up cues about sex roles and imitate what they perceive as appropriate behavior.

3. Cognitive development. Lawrence Kohlberg, the leading proponent of this theory, departs from the theories above by emphasizing the internal developmental abilities of the child rather than external forces. Kohlberg follows French epistemologist Jean Piaget's belief that there are set and predetermined steps of mental development through which all children progress. For Kohlberg, the young child's gender identity—her notion of herself as a girl, which emerges shortly after age two—is the crucial fact around which she organizes experience and perception. The notion that "I am a little girl" colors not only her sense of self but her perception of the world around her. The three-year-old sees everything in black and white: objects and activities become rigidly "for girls" or "for boys." A girl thus comes to value feminine behaviors and activities because they are like herself—they fit with her own sense of self. Instead of acting like a girl because her parents reward her for doing so, a little girl acts like a girl because she knows she is a girl and therefore finds it rewarding.[9]

A body of research supports these basic assumptions. Experiments have shown that as soon as little girls and boys learn the words *girl* and *boy*, they begin to so label themselves, very seldom making mistakes. Furthermore, children as young as three showed clear preferences for gender-appropriate objects in a study in which certain objects were labeled "for girls" and others "for boys."[10]

Gail Melson, professor of child development and family studies at Purdue University, notes that psychologists in the area of gender acquisition are currently moving toward a synthesis of the social learning and cognitive development theories.[11] Melson points to a recent study that found that toddlers who learned to label themselves by gender early on tended to be children of parents who reacted strongly and positively to their sex-typed play. Thus, within a cognitive development framework, these two-year-olds had reached the stage where gender was a key way of organizing their experience; in a social learning context, they were receiving clear reinforcement from their parents for gender-appropriate behavior.

There is also the possibility that children are born with a certain genetic predisposition to conform with or reject certain aspects of their gender role. Social scientists who lean toward this more biological view of gender acquisition have posited the "constraints on learning" model, which suggests that an individual's biological sex makes it easier for him or her to learn the appropriate gender behavior: acting like a girl somehow comes more naturally to girls.[12] When coupled with the factor of inborn temperament, a case can be made for the view that some little girls "take" to femininity simply because it suits them, and similarly other girls react against it right from the start. Certainly, this theory would make sense to those parents who describe with amazement how they could never wrestle one daughter into a dress, while her sister was practically born clutching a Barbie doll to her breast. For example, Sandy, a Maryland mother of four girls (ages nine, six, four, and eighteen months), says that Megan, her oldest, has always been rough and tumble and extremely curious—attributes typically associated with boys—while Lindsay, age six, seemed much more stereo- typically feminine from birth. "You can't say 'girls act this way,' " Sandy concludes. "It depends on the individual child."

One factor that does *not* seem to play much of a role in a girl's acquisition of gender role is the degree and aspect of her mother's femininity.[13] In fact, feminine daughters are more likely to spring from masculine fathers who are both warm and assertive in their attitudes toward their children and who value and encourage their daughters' femininity.[14] The fact that highly feminine mothers do not produce highly feminine daughters (and that masculine fathers don't necessarily produce masculine sons) is an important rebuttal of the strict social learning theory. Eleanor Maccoby notes that to the extent that children adopt the personalities and behaviors of their parents, they tend to follow the dominant parent, regardless of sex. She concludes that "parental so- cial pressure to behave in sex-appropriate ways will not necessarily lead to adoption by the child of the same-sex parent's own sex-typing style."[15]

Dressing, Playing, and Acting Like a Girl

While social scientists debate the how and why of gender acquisition, parents and their daughters are in no doubt at all about the what: we see it and feel it and live with it every day. Lauren's first word was *baby*, and she cradled her dolls as soon as she could sit up. Betsy wore a dress every single day between her second and fourth birthdays. Ashley, age four, insisted that only boys could play with blocks and GI Joe dolls, while ponies with long pink and purple manes were for girls. Jennifer, age three, will not leave the house without a pocketbook. Her cousin Rachel is obsessed with Cinderella. Shannon, not yet three, crosses her legs "like a lady" and keeps one hand limp at the wrist when she speaks. Our two-year-old twins love nothing better than to rifle through their grandmother's purse in search of lipstick, eye shadow, and necklaces. "Where the heck do they get it from?" wonders Karen. "My husband cooks half the time, but when the kids play, it's always the girls who do the cooking. My son likes to play baseball, but both my daughters avoid team sports. I could see my six-year-old wanting to be a cheerleader. This drives me crazy." The story of the physician mother overhearing her preschool daughter announce that only boys can be doctors (girls, of course, have to be *nurses*) has been told so often that it's entered the realm of myth.

The sex differences in behavior that looked so negligible in infancy emerge with a vengeance in toddlerhood and the preschool years. Clothing, toy preferences, book preferences, fantasies: chances are that your daughter will demonstrate a strong feminine bent in all of these during her third year, or even earlier. Psychologists studying toddlers as young as fourteen months have found that girls tend to choose dolls and soft toys even when they have a whole array of toys, including trucks and cars, at their disposal.[16] By the time they get to preschool, most girls will gravitate to the doll corner, the kitchen, the crayons and paints, while boys spend most of their time with cars, trucks, blocks, and airplanes. However, books, puzzles, and Play-Doh seem to appeal equally to both sexes.[17]

More subtle, but farther reaching in their implications, are the differences in group play. Our cultural attitudes (see Chapter 1) would lead us to expect a big difference between girls and boys in energy level, but this, like many other sex stereotypes, has little foundation in fact. Preschool girls zoom around the playground, swing on the monkey bars, and jump on trampolines as wildly as any Tarzan.[18] Sandy's oldest daughter Megan has never had trouble keeping up with boys in sports or rough play. Fran says that her three-year-old daughter is more of a natural athlete than her big brother. Cindy points out that her daughter Cara, despite being ultra-feminine in her interests, is physically robust and that she would be good at sports if she wanted to be.

The key sex difference, it seems, is not in the amount of energy girls and boys burn up in play, but in their styles of play and social interaction. In a fascinating study conducted by a Stanford University psychologist, same-sex preschool girls and boys were turned loose in groups of three in a mobile home equipped with soft carpeting, a trampoline, and a beach ball. Although the girls were nearly as active as the boys in the amount of jumping and running they did, they organized their playtime very differently. Before having at the trampoline, the girls negotiated a set of rules governing taking turns and sharing. When one of the girls broke the rules, the others would argue with her, but seldom did they grab her and try to haul her off. The boys, on the other hand, abandoned themselves to all-out, free-form roughhousing. They wrestled and pounced on each other, they bopped each other with the beach ball, they yanked and shoved each other and played tug of war, shouting with joy all the while.[19]

This distinction seems to be deeply rooted in human nature across a range of cultures; even male nonhuman primates engage in more rough-and-tumble play, while their female counterparts tend to find ways of cooperating.[20] Another trait that goes back into our evolutionary past is the tendency for children to segregate themselves in same-sex groups. Walk into any preschool or day care center anywhere in the world and you are likely to find the same basic pattern: girls playing with girls (with a couple of boys hanging around the fringes of small groups), and boys playing with boys (with a few girls mixing in). "They might as well have separate entrances for the boys and girls at the nursery school for all the mixing they do," said one mother, laughing. As one social scientist writes, "Sex is a more powerful determinant of 'who plays with whom' than age, race, social class, intelligence, or any other demographic factor, with the possible exception of propinquity."[21]

Evelyn Goodenough Pitcher and Lynn Hickey Schultz studied the social interactions of 255 preschool children (ages two to five) in the Boston area during the late 1970s.[22] They found that the preference for same-sex playmates varies for boys and girls according to age. At age two, neither girls nor boys showed very much social behavior: children of both sexes tended to play by themselves or alongside another child ("parallel play"). For the most part, interaction took the form of watching another child or trying to grab her toy. However, by age three, girls have begun banding together, with a consequent rise in prosocial behaviors (sharing, talking, instigating play or fantasy) and tapering off of antisocial behaviors. For boys, the process is slightly different. At age three, boys display more negative behavior, and to the extent that they seek out prosocial contact with other children, they turn to girls slightly more often than to other boys. Pitcher and Schultz speculate that the reasons for this marked difference between these three-year-olds are that girls mature earlier and that they have a stronger sense of gender identity and "ego control." Caretakers, whether at home or at preschool, are likely to be women, an advantage for girls in defining themselves and in "figuring out" what girls should or should not do. Since boys tend to have limited contact with adult men at home or preschool, they take longer to consolidate their sense of gender identity. When starting preschool boys also tend to have more trouble with separation anxiety than girls.

When boys do get around to grouping together, at around age four, they spend a lot of time "vying for power," fighting for dominance. "When I see preschool boys playing, I'm so glad I have girls!" one mother of three daughters remarked after enduring a birthday party at which the girls played quietly while the boys trashed the house. "It's almost as if the boys feel *compelled* to be violent—they don't consider it really fun unless they're fighting and knocking things over." Interestingly, Pitcher and Schultz point out that the boys' squabbling and jockeying for position may actually enrich their friendships: "the greater amount of conflict present among the boys resolves into same-sex relations that are more highly developed than those of girls."[23]

By age five, to some extent the tables have turned: the boys are pretty much ignoring the girls, but the girls are now trying to get in on the wild games of the boys (often without much success). It may be that girls have already perceived the higher status and greater freedom of being male. Or perhaps they figure that since the boys are making more noise, they must be having more fun (see page 51). Nevertheless, same-sex groups pretty much prevail throughout childhood. However, for girls, they tend to shrink, and by middle childhood, most girls have one best girlfriend or a couple of very close playmates, while boys are more likely to play in gangs.[24]

Several parents found that their daughters seem light-years ahead of their sons in social awareness and in the ability to express feelings. "In a group of girls," says one father, "they all seem to have an instinctive sense of the social 'vibe.' They talk about their feelings all the time, and they all seem to know who's 'in' and who's 'out.' Boys seem either not to have all these feelings or to be unaware." Mary agrees. "Zeva is more socially tuned in at age four than her brothers are at eight and eleven," Mary says. "She will come out with statements like 'You hurt my feelings' or 'That really makes me mad.' Although the boys have always been highly verbal, I've never heard them say things like that. When her best friend throws her out of her room, Zeva will say, 'Oh, she just has to be by herself for a while.' She seems to have an understanding of another person's point of view that the boys totally lack."

Many of these differences reflect the power and pervasiveness of socialization. Girls and boys as young as three are behaving exactly as our cultural stereotypes indicate they *should* behave. Preschool girls spend a good deal of their time in playhouses, enacting elaborate mother-daughter-baby games. Pitcher and Schultz found that when girls make believe they are mothers, they tend to be "guardians of propriety, order and superior know-how," rebuking other girls and boys for making messes or breaking rules.[25] They are also terrifically busy around the house with cooking, cleaning, hauling sick babies back and forth to the doctor, and chasing disruptive boys away. To the extent that five-year-old boys enter the playhouses, they tend to disrupt domestic order. When one five-year-old boy in the Pitcher and Schultz study pretended to bake bread, he announced that the bread was filled with fire and it killed the whole family.[26] One preschool teacher told us that she tried to involve the boys in the kitchen corner by putting out play money for them to use to buy groceries. Instead, one boy decided he was a robber, stole all the money, and went streaking through the classroom with it, while the girls scolded him for spoiling the game.

Unlike boys, girls show a keen interest in their own appearance and that of their peers, and compliment others. One father noted that his daughter has almost always loved flowery dresses and will cry if she gets a spot on one; her brother, on the other hand, would happily sport the same grubby T-shirt for days. Girls hug, pat, and address each other fondly, whereas boys, as they get older, restrict physical contact to playful wrestling and shoving matches and tend to tease each other with bathroom epithets. Girls are frequently "bossy": as young as three, they play the role of the know-it-all in domestic matters, and at five, they insult boys for their disruptions and "yukky" behavior and dispense "Miss Priss" warnings and advice. Boys, on the other hand, hit, tease, grab, and wreck other children's work. When a five-year-old girl gets pummeled by a male peer, she is more likely to insult him or appeal to an adult than to hit him back.

Of course, anyone who has endured an unsuccessful preschool "play date" knows that little girls can shove, grab, tear, and hoard as energetically as little boys. Cathy outdoes most boys in her class in daredevil feats on trikes and scooters. Shannon, not yet four, is far tougher than her older brother and has been known to use her fists to defend her "turf" at the day care center. And even timid Annie occasionally forsakes her Little Ponies for superhero fantasies. "Given the choice between Ninja Turtles and Sleeping Beauty," says the father of four-and-a-half-year-old Kate, "she'll take both."

As children respond to shifts in our society, we may be seeing more little girls like Kate, who cannot be stereotyped as "typically feminine." Already a number of nursery school teachers have noted the impact of the prevalence of working mothers and the huge increase in single-parent families. A mother facing the daily stresses of a full-time job may very well encourage her daughter to be assertive, because the quality will benefit her in the future.

Is It True Boys Have More Fun?

Preschool girls and boys may be growing more alike in their behavior—the research has yet to catch up with social changes—but there is pretty close to universal consensus that boys remain, on balance, more aggressive. Boys hit more, threaten more, swagger more, and bully more than girls.[27] Impulse control is another widely reported sex difference: girls can delay gratification more successfully than boys, they take fewer risks, and they deal more evenly with frustration. Girls tend to stick closer to home or closer to a parent when outdoors. They are generally more compliant; they are better listeners to each other and to authority figures; and they tend to submit to the wishes of the group more readily.[28] Boys have more temper tantrums and far more accidents requiring medical treatment. "Boys are into destruction for the sake of destruction," said one mother. "If they see a shelf of books and toys, they can't rest until they've knocked all of them down. If they don't have guns, they make them out of sticks. Girls don't."

By all these measures, girls are easier to manage and less trouble to raise. But is it also possible that our "good" little girls are having less fun than all those "bad" little boys? Fun is a tricky concept to gauge objectively, but a few telling signs have emerged in recent studies. As young as age four, girls laugh twice as much when they are paired with a boy than they do when paired with another girl, and humor continues to be a predominantly male trait right into adulthood.[29] "You don't see those big belly laughs and falling-down-on-the-floor laughing fits as often with girls," one mother of three said. Think of how many more men than women are clowns, stand-up comics, and comedy writers. In the study in the unfurnished trailer, the boys' pushing and tackling and belly flopping on top of each other also seemed to release more sheer joy. In another study, researchers found that in sex-segregated groups boys tend to gain dominance by shoving each other aside, and girls were more likely to dominate by verbal persuasion. Nonetheless, despite the physical aggression, the boys seemed to be having a better time than the girls. They argued and whined less, and were more enthusiastic.[30]

Several preschool teachers have remarked that the boys can't wait to get outside and hit the playground, while the girls seem more content to play quiet indoor games. One mother of two daughters and a son said with exasperation that the girls seem resigned to stand on the sidelines while her son jumps in and *plays*. "This drives me crazy. I'd rather she played on the team." Another mother noted that her daughter whines and complains far more than her son, and sometimes declines to play because she doesn't want to mess up her hair. "My son is breezy, but that's his personality," she concludes. Other parents remark that the old stereotype about girls being bossy has some truth to it. While the boys are hurling themselves into competitive games, the girls are more likely to be reeling off instructions to each other, hassling each other for disobeying rules, and complaining to adults when their bossing leads to trouble.

It may be, of course, that we are projecting our own image of childhood fun. Two girls engaged in a gentle fantasy of being horses, trotting around the yard, and chatting about who is the mommy horse and who is the baby horse *seem* to be having less of a rip-roaring good time than two boys whooping it up as Batman and Superman with much shooting, shouting, and explosive laughter. It could be that girl fun is simply quieter and less exuberant. "Lindsay is my shiest daughter," says Sandy, mother of four girls, "and when I see her next to boys I sometimes wonder whether she's having as much fun. I've concluded that she just has fun *differently*." Another mother wonders, "Is running around with sticks more fun than playing house? The difference I've seen between preschool boys and girls is concrete versus imaginative play. You can't assign a value to it."

Parenting Tips: Learning from Mom, Discovering Dad, Sexuality, Encouraging Independence, Clothing, Siblings, Friends, Tomboys

Learning from Mom

I definitely believe that there is a special bond between a mother and a daughter. Maybe it's because they are alike in so many ways. When one of my daughters gets hurt or feels scared, they always want Mommy. . . . Of course, we also have more conflict. In many ways, I find I get angriest at my oldest daughter—maybe because I have higher expectations of her.

—SANDY, MOTHER OF FOUR DAUGHTERS

The special closeness between mother and daughter? I'm still waiting for it. Right now I feel much more resentment than love from her. She's always been closer to my husband, and I've always been closer to my son, maybe because I nursed him when he was a baby, which I didn't do with her.

—ELLEN, MOTHER OF A DAUGHTER AND A SON

I knew from the moment of conception that I was having a girl. I was dying for a girl because I wanted someone to dress frilly, someone I could relate to and someone who would do the things I did as a child, someone to dress like me and take to places I liked. . . . She's three now and she has not turned out as I had hoped. She is rough and wild. When I dress her in frills, she'll be tearing them off. Her father is a really aggressive man, and I see a lot of him in her, especially when she runs up and down, screaming and hollering. I keep hoping she'll become more like me.

—YVONNE, MOTHER OF A DAUGHTER AND A SON

For a woman, it's nice to have a girl because there will always be that special relationship and companionship that she can't share with her sons, that feeling that she can't let her daughter go so easily. I really feel that I have that with my daughter. I understand Cara's feelings—for example, her need to appear perfectly feminine all the time—because I was like that myself. We think along the same lines, and I can easily put myself back at her age and think, 'That's what I would have done.' My mother had trouble coming to grips with what I was—I never measured up to her. I've finally decided I am who I am, maybe only since I've been a mother. I don't think Cara and I will have that problem. Our femininity is something we share and accept.

—CINDY, MOTHER OF A DAUGHTER AND A SON

I hated my mother and went into therapy to deal with it. I very much want my relationship with my daughter [age five] to be happy. We have worked toward that goal, and I think we have succeeded. . . . In many ways she is a clone of me. She shares my interests, she says the things that I say. Far from being threatened by this, I found it comfortable and gratifying. It feeds my ego.
—SHERI, MOTHER OF A DAUGHTER AND A SON

I feel that my daughter [age four] and I are real, real different people, and I wish we were more alike. I wish there were more areas where our personalities meshed.
—DALE, MOTHER OF A DAUGHTER

As different as their attitudes and experiences with their preschool daughters are, all these women share one assumption: that a mother and daughter should have a special bond. The fact of shared gender—so elementary on the surface—is the basis for the complicated, demanding, richly rewarding, and maddeningly intense relationship between mother and daughter. When the assumption of a special mother-daughter bond is fulfilled, as between Cindy and Cara, it can be one of the deepest sources of satisfaction in a woman's life. But Cara may come to feel stifled by a mother who views her as an extension of herself, and she may devote more and more energy to establishing and accepting her separateness from her mother, as Cindy did with her own mother. At the opposite pole is Yvonne, who may end up having a healthy and happy relationship with her daughter if she can accept their differences. But first she must overcome her regret over the reality. Identification and alienation, an instinctive connection, and a desperate push for freedom—these are some of the contrasting themes considered in this section about the mother-daughter relationship in the preschool years.

Nancy Chodorow is perhaps the most prominent of the social psychologists who have found enormous significance for a girl's psychological development in the basic fact of shared gender. In her influential book *The Reproduction of*

Mothering, Chodorow writes: "Because of their mothering by women, girls come to experience themselves as less separate than boys, as having more permeable ego boundaries. Girls come to define themselves more in relation to others.... A girl does not simply identify with her mother or want to be like her mother. Rather, mother and daughter maintain elements of their primary relationship which means they will feel alike in fundamental ways."[31]

Carol Gilligan has interpreted and extended Chodorow's argument into the area of gender identity. In her influential book *In a Different Voice*, Gilligan writes that

> For boys and men, separation and individuation are critically tied to gender identity since separation from the mother is essential for the development of masculinity. For girls and women, issues of femininity or feminine identity do not depend on the achievement of separation from the mother or on the progress of individuation. Since masculinity is defined through separation while femininity is defined through attachment, male gender identity is threatened by intimacy while female gender identity is threatened by separation. Thus males tend to have difficulty with relationships, while females tend to have problems with individuation.[32]

The women we spoke with all take for granted that this intense connection between mother and daughter is natural and fitting. When it exists, the mothers are proud and pleased; when it doesn't, they feel hurt and disappointed, or sometimes merely baffled. Sheri, the mother of a five-year-old daughter and a two-year-old son, was intrigued by the notion of "permeable ego boundaries" and felt that it aptly described an aspect of her relationship with her daughter: "I really don't see her as significantly different from myself. She really is a 'little me.' She copies me, and she does it in a cute way.... Of course, I also see her picking up on parts of me that I don't like."

Gilligan further argues that because of the basic difference between the mother-daughter bond and the mother-son bond, girls grow up with empathy "built in" and thus tend to live by a different moral code that involves sensitivity to the needs of others and feelings of responsibility. Women, in her view, "not only define themselves in a context of human relationships but also judge themselves in terms of their ability to care."[33] When Mary speaks of how her four-year-old daughter is so far ahead of her eight- and eleven-year-old brothers in expressing her feelings and acknowledging the emotional needs of her playmates, she is offering a real-life illustration of this. Other parents have noted how the little girls in a group of children will stop playing when another child cries or gets hurt, while the boys may glance over at the commotion and then go back to their play.

It's easy to see why Gilligan's theory has infuriated many feminists, for it seems to play right into the old male chauvinist view of the nurturing, "relational" woman minding the kids and warming casseroles while her spouse goes off to slay dragons at the office. In fact, psychologist Gail Melson points out that little boys show "nurturing" behavior too, especially in experiments in which they are observed with pets (a socially acceptable object of affection for both sexes) rather than dolls. And Dr. Kyle Pruett, a psychiatrist with the Yale University Child Study Center, in his study of "nurturing fathers" finds that girls raised primarily by men behave pretty much like their mother-raised friends emotionally, socially, and intellectually.[34] One difference that Pruett noted in the preschool period was that father-raised girls, although just as feminine as their mother-raised peers, did not restrict themselves to stereotypical feminine activities: in preschools, they played with dolls *and* blocks.[35]

Nonetheless, putting the debate over the implications of mother-daughter attachment to one side, a kernel of truth in Gilligan's and Chodorow's ideas shows up in the relationships of many of the mothers and daughters we have seen. The idea of "a boy for you and a girl for me" still holds sway in our culture, as does the notion that a daughter should remain close to her mother not only throughout childhood, but all her life. Cindy speaks for many mothers when she describes how attuned she and her daughter are and how much she cherishes the closeness. Whether this bond with her mother will make Cara more empathetic and "relational" than her brother remains to be seen. It's reasonable to assume, at the very least, that a girl who identifies so closely with her mother will want to re-create this bond, particularly with her own daughter.

On the other hand, mothers who fail to develop this sense of identity with their daughters may regret it keenly, and may come to blame either themselves or their daughters for its absence. Kate noted how disappointed she feels that she and her daughter are not the "same type." She'd have preferred a more athletic daughter with more spunk, just as Yvonne yearns for the opposite. Alice, a world-class athlete, has come to accept the fact that her four-year-old prefers Barbie dolls but still marvels at the difference between them. Judy, a '70s feminist, also voices bafflement at her four-year-old's hyperfemininity, and hopes it won't get in the way of developing a close relationship with her daughter. Heather feels let down that her two daughters are so whiny and dependent. "I certainly wasn't that way as a child," she muses. "I don't know where they get it from."

Sonia, a sensitive and reserved musician, feels exasperated at times by the wild antics of her five-year-old daughter, Cathy, who seems to be happy imitating her rambunctious seven-year-old brother. An extremely gregarious person, Deb found it hard to accept the fact that her daughter Jessica, now in high school, had few friends throughout her early childhood and would often spend an entire day alone in her room. Deb feels she has "adjusted" to Jessica's personality, but she has never felt as close to her daughter as she'd hoped.

Although key to the mother-daughter bond (or its absence), shared gender is far from the only dynamic at work. As one mother of three daughters pointed out, just because they share the same sex, it's absurd to conclude they would "feel alike in fundamental ways." "I have a very different relationship with each of my daughters. Each of them is like me in some ways, but separate from me in many more ways. I think personality is far more important than gender in shaping your relationship with a child."

That makes a great deal of sense. It's also important to note that Gilligan is writing about internal "voices"—voices that may have more to do with women's feelings and motives than with their actual behavior. The notion that mothers and daughters "feel alike in fundamental ways" should be taken as one strand, out of many, in the complex and evolving mother-daughter bond, and given more symbolic than literal weight.

Conflict also arises when a daughter turns from her mother to her father (or plays one off against the other) and later, in adolescence, when a girl asserts her separateness from her mother, sometimes violently.[36] In a short story called "Cold Heart," Jamaica Kincaid eloquently describes a nineteen-year-old so overwhelmed by her identity with her mother that she is compelled to cut all ties, not even opening her mother's letters. "I had spent so much time saying I did not want to be like my mother that I missed the whole story," she says bitterly. "I was not like my mother—I was my mother. . . . I could not trust myself to go too near [her letters]. I knew that if I read only one, I would die from longing for her."[37]

Even a toddler's need to declare her independence, to stake out the borders of her self, can raise prickly issues. In *My Mother/My Self* Nancy Friday writes of a child's need for "refueling" by touching base with her mom before she is ready to go off and face the world again. "The good mother understands the frightened return, but does not use it as a warning not to leave again; in fact, once she sees the child is refueled, she encourages it to go off again." Mothers who cannot let their daughters "go off again" may, in Friday's view, end up burdening them with their own fears and with the compulsive need "to feel *connected* at all times, at any cost." Friday also notes that a mother who interrupts a daughter's contented play before she needs to be "refueled" can nip her sense of adventure in the bud. In addition, a mother of a daughter may feel entitled to hold herself up as an expert on girls because she has passed through girlhood herself and thus, in her own eyes, "knows all about it." A daughter's attempt to break free is seen as a rejection not only of "appropriate feminine behavior" but of the all-knowing, all-protecting mother.[38]

"Separation is not loss, it is not cutting yourself off from someone you love," Friday writes, summing up the thesis of her book. "It is giving freedom to the other person to be herself before she becomes resentful, stunted, and suffocated by being tied too close. Separation is not the end of love. It creates love."[39]

In contemplating these psychological theories, you may feel forced to walk an impossibly fine line between empathizing with and overwhelming your daughter, between mothering and smothering. There is no easy solution or quick fix. As parents, we have always found it most useful to digest the expert advice and then tackle each individual problem as it arises. Just as it helps to think of your daughter as a *child* first (rather than a *girl* first), so it makes sense to think of her as her *own* person first and as *your daughter* second.

Discovering Dad

During the preschool years Dad steps out of the wings and into the limelight. Now, after three or four years of preferring (or demanding) Mom for everything from getting dressed in the morning to getting tucked in at night, many little girls can't get enough of their dads, who become the parent of choice. Those who have been wondering where the phrase "Daddy's little girl" came from now find out with a vengeance. "There came a point when only Daddy would do for everything," as one mother put it. "It's nice for him to be adored."

However, the shift doesn't happen overnight, nor is it as uniform and all-consuming as it may appear. A preschool girl may feel intensely guilty about switching allegiances and anxious that her mom will punish her "betrayal" by rejecting her. Such anxiety is a sign that their intense bond persists. "Mommy has always been number one, and this really hasn't changed too much," one father said of his five-year-old, with a shrug. "I've just become more available and my wife less so, so my daughter and I spend more time together." As Nancy Chodorow points out, "Every step of the way ... a girl develops her relationship to her father while looking back at her mother—to see if her mother is envious, to make sure she is in fact separate, to see if she can in this way win her mother, to see if she is really independent. Her turn to her father is both an attack on her mother and an expression of love for her."[40]

Fathers continue to pressure their children to conform to gender roles during the preschool years. True, a father is more likely to tolerate his four-year-old daughter playing Batman than his four-year-old son playing Cinderella; yet he, even more than the mother, is often the one who encourages his little girl to grow her hair long, to dress neatly, and to appear "ladylike."[41] Ron said that even though he and his wife have tried to steer clear of sex stereotypes, he nonetheless enjoys seeing his five-year-old in ballet costumes and party dresses. "She's so delighted by it," he happily admits, "and I love the fact that she looks beautiful." Marcella notes that her husband actively encourages their three-year-old to like girly things. He wants her to know about cooking and dressing up. "With our son, he'll say, 'What are you crying for?' But with our daughter he'll say, 'It's not ladylike to sit with your legs wide open or up in the air.' " Barry was the one who bought Maddy her first bikini, even though his wife does most of the routine clothes shopping. Some psychologists believe that fathers actively feminize their daughters out of an urge, perhaps unconscious, to make them sexually attractive.[42] Predictably, studies have found that the most stereotypically feminine women have fathers who are both strong and warm, and who approve of femininity, both in their daughters and in adult women.[43] Interestingly, Kyle Pruett found that the primary caretaking fathers in his study had totally abandoned this paternal tendency to enforce sex stereotypes: they neither pushed footballs on their sons nor tutus on their daughters, but instead encouraged individual interests and talents.[44]

There is nothing wrong with fostering a little girl's budding femininity, so long as you are aware of the potential traps. In *Beyond Sugar & Spice*, authors Caryl Rivers, Rosalind Barnett, and Grace Baruch caution fathers against encouraging their daughters in the "Princess" fantasy. "There is a natural instinct among fathers to want to protect their little girls who seem so small, so vulnerable, so helpless," they note.[45] An overprotective father may, unwittingly, be teaching a daughter to be helpless, to depend on a man or on "feminine wiles" to get her through a difficult situation rather than draw on her own inner resources. We've noticed fathers in playgrounds or at children's birthday parties step in and "rescue" their daughters from potentially frustrating or upsetting situations—fitting in the puzzle piece for her, guarding her place in line at the slide, making sure she gets her "goody bag." Very often the same father will push his son in the same situation to "fend for himself" or "tough it out" with the other children. Steve, a father of a four-year-old daughter and a two-year-old son, noted with some chagrin that "my impulse with Vanessa is to think she needs help, whereas with Max I think, 'He's a tough kid, he can handle it by himself.' When she bursts into tears, I tend to want to rescue her, but with Max I'll tend to say, 'Come on, Max, get up.' I try to make a conscious effort not to do this with either one of them."

The best piece of advice one mother ever heard about dealing with the conflicts and frustrations of preschool children was to "sit on your hands." A father like Steve would do well to remember to "let them work it out." The authors of *Beyond Sugar & Spice* recommend that fathers praise their daughters for what they accomplish, not just for how pretty they look, and to try to involve them in tasks "where they can see a lasting result." A little girl will have a more enduring sense of accomplishment if she helps Dad (in however rudimentary a way) put up a new swing set, build a deck, or grow a garden than if she helps with chores such as straightening up the house or washing dishes that must be repeated daily.

Yes, your little girl has a long way to go before the subjects of womanliness and success arise, but their foundations are being laid now, and fathers are vital to the process. Just as mothers have the challenge of balancing attachment and separation, fathers must endorse their little girls as girls without undercutting their capacity for independence, self-assertion, decisiveness—and pure fun. An obstacle is the tendency, even in the preschool period, for many dads to remain more involved with their sons than with their daughters: dads may chat and relax with their little girls, but they demand excellence from their sons.

As discussed in Chapter 2, mothers sometimes "take over" and leave a father feeling shut out. This phenomenon can become even more intense now when the child is so wrapped up in discovering and asserting herself as a girl. "For Eva [now five], it was clear from the start that the parent of choice was her mother and this remains true," said Michael. "I do a lot of parenting and caretaking, but Eva has always preferred to be with her mother." Michael, however, has by no means given up; he has found a number of activities that the two of them can share, such as going for long walks, listening to music, cooking, and writing letters that she dictates. Steve admits that he can't relate to his daughter's obsession with nail polish, jewelry, and flowery dresses, but then, neither can his wife. Each of them has found other aspects of her personality to connect with: Vanessa and her mother share a love of animals; Steve takes her along to the health club or heads into the hills for long walks. Phil comments ruefully: "This weekend I killed an hour in various shoe stores while [his wife and daughter] waited to be served. I can see the future looming expensively ahead." But Phil takes his five-year-old into New York City, on Sunday morning bike rides, and out to lunches at Chinese restaurants.

Other fathers, however, have more trouble finding—or creating—common ground. A father who would happily play ball or wrestle with his son may feel uncomfortable or unwilling to help his preschool-age daughter try new outfits on her doll or choose the right shade of eye shadow. Psychologist Brad Sachs, director of the Father Center in Columbia, Maryland, concedes that it may be a challenge for some fathers to maintain a good bond with their daughters during this period. Sachs suggests a father "let her know that she's valued for many things, not just her appearance. It's *who* she is, not how she *looks* that is important."[46] Psychologist Sam Osherson notes that sometimes all it takes is for a father to devote a few moments to acknowledging his daughter's games or fantasies. "You don't have to spend hours on the floor playing with her dolls," he comments, "but just take the time to say, 'That's great!' when she holds the doll up to you."[47]

One of the benefits of the contemporary blurring of sex roles is that fathers are finding out that their daughters will happily join them in lots of traditionally male activities. Even though five-year-old Maddy loves nothing better than to don her frilliest pink party dress, she also enjoys attending baseball and high school football games with her dad, a physician who specializes in sports medicine. "She learned two-digit numbers from watching Mets games," says her father with a laugh. "And she was very upset when Mookie Wilson got traded." When Maddy's mother, an advertising creative director, travels on business, her dad makes it a special occasion by "becoming one of the kids. We do fun things like eating dinner in the living room, which my wife would never permit, or I take her to my office on weekends." Vanessa, age four, loves to go to swim class with her dad; afterwards they go out for a hot chocolate together. Five-year-old Stacy is not wild about baseball, but she looks forward to going to games so she can be with her dad and indulge in unlimited hot dogs and sodas. Her twelve-year-old sister, however, is a rabid Phillies fan. Ted, the father of five, encourages his sons and daughters alike to help wash the car. No matter how cold the water in the pool, Ron always gets in with his daughter, who has become an excellent swimmer.

Daughters often surprise their fathers by their willingness to try something new. Even the prissiest little miss may welcome the chance to shuck her dress—or ignore it—and tear around the park with Dad. Our local Saturday morning five-year-old soccer league has two or three avid girl players on each team. Joe is delighted that his girls now commonly play in Little League and T-ball leagues. Jennifer, the three-year-old, is the family athlete, and Joe thinks it's great.

Try not to be discouraged if you sometimes strike out. Phil blames himself for being "derelict in teaching five-year-old Caroline about kicking and throwing," but he admits that it bores her and that her toddler brother has always shown more interest in it. Stuart felt relieved when he had daughters because it freed him from the obligation to play sports, something he has always loathed. Neal gave up trying to fight "nature" in encouraging his daughter to get involved in sports; instead, he expresses his "silly side" with her by playing hide-and-seek, tag, and tickling. Paul was annoyed when Becky refused to join the soccer team, but then he realized that he'd never kicked the ball around at home with her; he's planning to get her accustomed to the game before taking her down to the playing field again. Our daughters' version of football bears only the vaguest resemblance to the actual game; but at least it gives them a chance to chase around the yard with their dad after dinner.

"The continuing attention and support and availability of the father is crucial to his daughter's development," notes Sam Osherson. Each father, if he takes the time and interest, can figure out the best way to make himself available to his daughter, to support her, and to pay attention to her special needs.

The Dawn of Sexuality

As a little girl moves closer to her father, she may also begin to exhibit signs of emerging sexuality. "She spends an awful lot of time in my lap, talking baby talk, stroking my arm," one father said of his four-year-old. "I was never modest around my daughter until she turned four," another father said. "Then she started coming out with statements like, 'Eli [her baby brother] has a little penis, but daddy has a big penis.' I figured it was time to cover up." Another father noticed that his daughter became "obsessed" with her baby brother's penis when she was about four. "She says penises are disgusting, but she loves to look at his, and giggles when he plays with himself."

If a preschool girl directs this new sexual energy toward her father, her mother may feel caught uncomfortably in the middle. Even the most self-assured, understanding mother may lose her composure when she sees a surly, sulky five-year-old turn into a fluttering coquette the moment Daddy walks in the door. Some women complain of being maneuvered into vying with their daughters for their husbands' attention and love. "When my husband hugs me, my daughter inserts herself between us," said Mary of four-year-old Zeva. "She wants to know that she's tops." Marv said his daughter is so wrapped up with him that he sometimes literally has to peel her off; he sometimes feels trapped between two jealous women. When Jill kept insisting that she was going to marry Daddy, her mother gently reminded her that Daddy was already married to Mommy. "That's all right," Jill replied. "I'll marry him, too." Husbands who haven't flirted with their wives in years may flirt outrageously with their daughters. And little girls know how to use feminine wiles. As Barry put it, "When she's done something rotten, she thinks that if she hugs and kisses me, she'll get away with it."

Both parents may be shocked, but it's natural for a preschool girl to become interested in sex (especially in the question of where babies come from) and curious about her parents' sexuality. Freudians would point out that a little girls' sexuality is not something that suddenly pops out during the preschool years, but is an aspect of her nature that has been present from the start. As soon as a baby girl gets control over the movement of her hands, she will reach between her legs and touch her vagina when her diaper is off. There is nothing wrong with this form of masturbation in infancy or childhood so long as it isn't obsessive. A three- or four-year-old who masturbates in public can be gently reminded that her private parts are private—for her to touch only when she's by herself. In *Dr. Balter's Child Sense*, Lawrence Balter suggests that parents curb public masturbation by giving a child something to do with her hands, such as holding on to a box or bag at a store or coloring or doing a puzzle.[48]

Parents should keep in mind that a preschooler's sexuality is really an extension of her joy in being physical—that it flows from the same energy source as jumping, skipping, and hugging. Although she may act the coquette and touch herself in a way you find shocking, remember she is innocently doing what makes her feel good. Experts in preschool development advise parents never to punish a child for her normal curiosity and natural enjoyment of pleasurable sensations.[49] Michael says he sometimes finds his five-year-old examining her vagina with a hand mirror. "She seems totally absorbed and totally innocent."

Although some psychologists, particularly feminists, contest the Freudian concept of "penis envy" (a little girl's grief and rage and feeling of betrayal by her mother for the lack of a penis), there is no question that most girls start to notice the difference between their anatomy and a boy's sometime during the second year. Herman Roiphe, M.D., and Anne Roiphe, in *Your Child's Mind*, pinpoint eighteen months as the age. She may try to compensate by placing sticks or dolls between her legs, or she may suddenly become very tense for seemingly no reason, particularly if toys break or if a doll loses its nose or eyes. Some girls, according to the Roiphes, wonder if they once had a penis that broke off or whether they will grow one,[50] though we've never heard any parents mention this. Several parents have, however, noticed that their two- and three-year-old girls show a sudden burst of interest in watching their fathers or brothers urinate and become annoyed at their mothers for pointing out that they both have vaginas. For example, Vanessa, at three and a half, said she wanted to have a penis when she saw her little brother urinate standing up. Ashley, four, and Caitlin, two, giggled in nervous glee when a neighboring boy urinated against a tree. Our two-year-old twins, Sarah and Alice, make loud comments on their cousin's "peenee" when he has his diaper changed.

The Roiphes advise parents of a little girl who seems overly upset by the genital difference to reassure her that she is made "just the right way" and that they are glad she is a girl. A father can help a daughter through this crisis by praising her for being a girl and by taking an interest in her feminine activities. One positive outcome of this flurry of phallic anxiety, claim the Roiphes, is that it forces girls to confront "real world" issues earlier than boys, and thus may give them an intellectual edge.

If your daughter is the flirtatious type, you may be troubled by a new sexual aspect to this behavior in the later preschool years. It is not uncommon for a girl between the ages of three and six to wrap her legs around her father and rub herself erotically against him. She may become extremely interested in her father's body and stare at him when he gets undressed or goes to the bathroom. In *The Preschool Years*, Ellen Galinsky and Judy David advise that "when parents feel young children are becoming too 'sexual' or too 'intimate,' they should set firm limits."[51] A father can gently steer his daughter away, explaining that he prefers to go to the bathroom in private or that she sit next to him instead of on his lap. He may want to cover up now, and he may also begin to discourage her from cuddling up with him in bed or bathing with him. Barry still enjoys giving his five-year-old daughter a bath, but now he tells her to wash her private parts herself. He and his wife keep sex from seeming "dirty" by using the real words for genitals and not giggling about it.

This does not mean that all physical affection between father and daughter has to come to an end or that an atmosphere of strict Victorian prudery should suddenly be imposed on the household. Bob and his wife had always walked around naked in front of their daughters; now that the girls are getting older, he simply turns his back when he undresses; he feels that he would be unduly emphasizing the issue if he suddenly insisted on total privacy. Michael noted that his older daughter Amira became a little less physically intimate with him when she was six or seven. It happened naturally and mutually and they didn't make a big deal about it. A girl in the grip of the oedipal drama needs her father's love and respect more than ever: she needs him to help her control her powerful feelings of arousal and jealousy and she needs to learn that Daddy can love both her and Mommy at the same time but in different ways. Nancy Friday in *My Mother/My Self* notes that when a four- or five-year-old girl asks questions about sex (where babies come from is much on the minds of girls now, especially if a sibling has recently appeared), she needs not only factual answers, but clear signs of physical affection between her parents. If a mother has "given up" on sex herself, says Friday, her daughter will pick up on this and may grow up fearing her own sexuality.[52]

Galinsky and David suggest that if a little girl says she wants to marry her daddy, he can tell her how much he loves her and reassure her that he'll always be her dad but also let her know that he's already married to Mommy.[53] An embarrassed father who turns a cold shoulder conveys a clear message that sex is naughty and that his daughter's sensuality makes her unlovable. "We may come on as if to steal him away from Mommy," writes Nancy Friday of the five-year-old girl, "but we'll happily settle for his smile, his fond kiss, his lighthearted acknowledgment that we're just about the prettiest little girl he's ever seen."[54] On the other hand, a father who encourages his daughter's girlish sexuality too warmly, who becomes aroused by her, or who flirts with her as a way of getting back at his wife is engaged in a dangerous game that can veer into emotional or sexual abuse (see Chapter 7).

Several parents have mentioned with surprise how little interest their daughters show in sex. "My wife and I have marveled at their lack of curiosity about sex," said Tim, the father of four daughters. "We walk around nude and they never pay any attention." "I kept waiting for an Electra complex with my daughters," said another father of two daughters, "but I never got it. I've never seen any evidence of a great Freudian change." Girls develop and mature at different rates, and they express themselves in very different ways. There is nothing wrong with a little girl who continues to prefer the company of her mother, just as there is nothing wrong with a girl who has to have Daddy constantly at her side. The "great Freudian changes" may take place in utter silence or so subtly that you do not recognize them. "Normal" embraces a wide range of behaviors, styles, and paces of development.

In discussing the facts of life with your little girl, follow her lead and try to be as factual as you can in your explanations. If you're expecting another baby, this might be the perfect opportunity to explain to your daughter how the baby got in there and how it will get out. A new litter of puppies or kittens in the neighborhood is another easy way to broach the topic. Usually, by the time a little girl is four or five, she's old enough to grasp the basics of reproduction. You can start off by asking her how she thinks babies are made to find out how much she knows. (When we asked our girls how they thought babies were made, Sarah, age three, replied, "First one arm, then the other arm, then the legs, then the head, then the face," and so on. We decided to hold off for a while with the standard scientific explanation.) Keep the discussion matter-of-fact and low key.

Again, it's a good idea to use the correct anatomical terms. Your goal is to convey the idea that sex is natural and something that your daughter can discuss openly with you whenever she wants or needs to.

Little girls who show no interest in the facts of life may be too shy to ask or may have somehow gotten the idea that sex is bad. If your daughter hasn't asked you about it by the time she's five, it's probably a good idea to bring up the subject yourself. Ask your librarian for an appropriate book to get the conversation started.

One father said candidly, "We men grow up learning how to seduce women, and there is a natural tendency for us to carry this over into our relationships with our daughters." Part of what he has learned as a parent—and as a man—is how to incorporate this "seduction mode" into his love for his daughters. "Father [is] . . . the first man a girl loves," writes Sam Osherson, "and there *is* a normal emotional seduction between father and daughter, a resonance that is different from that between father and son."[55] One of the challenges—and joys—for fathers of preschool girls is letting his "normal emotional seduction" flower without becoming too luxuriant or too stifling.

Encouraging Independence and Achievement

As discussed in Chapter 1, there is no hard evidence that little girls are innately more dependent than boys. In this, as in so many other social traits, individual differences outweigh sex differences. "It's personality, not gender," as one long-time kindergarten teacher said. "Some of the girls are leaders; they insist they know how to do things and want to have their own way. Others are more passive and look to the teacher to tell them what to do."

Nonetheless, many parents complain that their daughters are more clingy and less outer-directed than their sons. With no hard evidence that dependence is a trait determined by biology, we have to look elsewhere for its origin. A study of twenty-four families with toddlers conducted in the late 1970s revealed some of the ways parents inculcate dependence in their daughters, often unconsciously. Parents left their toddler sons to play on their own more, but when they were with their sons, they tended to join them actively in their games rather than just sit with them, talk to them, or do housework alongside them, as they did with girls. Girls asked for help more than twice as often as boys, and parents both praised and criticized their daughters more than their sons. One clear theme that emerges from this study is that sons are given more room to develop independence "to wonder and think more about life," while daughters are kept more firmly under the protective wing of parents.[56] It also seems likely that the little girls asked for help more because they knew they were likely to receive it: with boys, on the other hand, parents were more apt to say, "Do it yourself."

If you object to your preschool daughter's clinginess, if you wish she would go off and play by herself more, fight her own battles, or cease to demand your help and attention so often, you might think about your own behavior in the light of this study. Are you likely to step in when she gets into a conflict with another child? Do you suppress her boisterous behavior? Do you give her less responsibility than her brother? Do you try to keep her close to you at home or when you're out in a playground or other child-friendly public place? You might also think about her toys and games. A well-known study of how parents furnish their children's rooms found that boys' rooms had far more sports equipment, cars, machines, and military toys, while girls' rooms had more dolls, domestic toys, and decorations of lace, fringe, and ruffles. The researchers concluded that "boys were provided objects that encourage activities directed away from home—toward sports, cars, animals, and the military—and the girls, objects that encourage activities directed toward the home—keeping house and caring for children."[57] Of course, some girls will ignore soccer balls and trucks, just as some girls have no time for dolls.

It's not a matter of replacing all the feminine objects with masculine ones, but rather of introducing a greater variety, and taking the time to help your daughter learn to use and enjoy them.

But try not to go overboard. Before despairing when a timid three-year-old refuses to stray more than six inches away in the park, we might step back and consider why we value independence so highly. Is it an absolute necessity for attaining maturity? Yes, if by independence we mean a healthy sense of individual identity; no, if we mean total autonomy or a strict weaning of a child from the attention and approval of her parents. Independence (in the second sense) is a relatively recent goal of child rearing. Arlie Hochschild perceptively points out in *The Second Shift* that the notion of what children need and how they should behave accommodates to cultural and economic conditions. In the nineteenth century, when middle-class women stayed home, children were thought to need their mothers at their beck and call throughout childhood. Now that the majority of mothers work, children, says Hochschild, are "increasingly imagined to need time with other children, to need 'independence-training,' not to need 'quantity time' with a parent but only a small amount of 'quality time.' "[58] These days, we praise our children for how little they need us—for playing by themselves or with other children, for going off obediently and cheerfully to a full day of day care, for cruising through a strange situation without a glance behind at Mom or Dad. We value independence in our children because we can't allow dependence.

Independent children are far more convenient for working parents. If our daughters don't fit this contemporary mold, we should try to understand *their* needs. If possible, we should let our dependent daughters cling a little longer if they need to—not necessarily more than our sons, but more than our rigorously work-oriented society condones.

Striking the right balance can be tricky. Perhaps one favor we can do for our daughters in this area is to take them on their own terms, to respect their individual needs to cling to or to separate, to let *their* requirements shape *our* expectations. Separating is an intense drama for all children during the preschool years; they vacillate wildly between the desire to break free of home and parents and the desire to remain firmly anchored in the familiar.

For many children the preschool years are a hill of fears, fears often inspired by brushes with the outside world—other children, preschools, group activities. A number of parents reported that their daughters became obsessed in the late preschool years with playacting the evil female character in fairy tales: the wicked witch in *The Wizard of Oz*, the evil stepmother in "Cinderella," the bad queen in "Snow White." Possibly the girls are acting out their ambivalence about independence: just as the wicked witch gloats over Dorothy's inability to return home, so a preschool girl's mother "wickedly" tries to shove her away, by sending her off to preschool, by returning to work, or by having another baby.[59] By playacting the role that makes them anxious, the girls are asserting some control over the situation as well as expressing their own anger. The wicked witch figures are also among the few models of strong, effective women our daughters are exposed to.

The drama of independence is cyclical, recurring each time a child has a cognitive or developmental breakthrough. As Ellen Galinsky and Judy David note, but "for each step away from their parents, children find a new way to reconnect with them."[60] Psychologist Mary Ainsworth and those who subscribe to her "attachment theory" believe that a baby who was permitted to be dependent in infancy, whose mother met her needs sensitively and lovingly, is likely to grow into a "securely attached" child. This doesn't mean a child who continues to cling helplessly to the mother, but just the opposite: a child with the self-confidence to become more and more independent and adventurous when she reaches the preschool period. But even the most securely attached preschooler needs to touch base and "refuel" with Mom and Dad, sometimes even regressing to behavior that looks infantile.

The issue of independence is intimately bound up with the issue of achievement, especially, perhaps, for our daughters. It may seem premature in relation to a preschool child, yet toddlers and preschoolers who are expected to be helpless and needy are likely to become passive and mediocre in a school setting. "Learned helplessness"—the acquisition of a defeatist attitude toward new tasks and challenges—is a problem that afflicts girls far more often than boys. One father had unconsciously been teaching his daughter to be helpless by rushing to her side when she met with frustration, while urging her younger brother to fend for himself in the same situations. "My goal is to let both my son and daughter learn to take responsibility for their own well-being, within reason, of course," he declares. "I just have to make more of an effort with her."

Adopting a positive "you can do it" attitude in the preschool years will give your daughter a real boost later on, when she'll have to rely on her own resources. Try to find tasks for her that she can accomplish on her own, for example, making her own sandwiches, dressing herself, caring for a pet. Encourage her to devise her own solutions to problems and to carry them out. Asking a needy preschool girl "What can *you* do about it?" is (sometimes) an effective way of prodding her into taking action (though other times it merely provokes a temper tantrum). And when it works, the child is justifiably pleased with herself. Our five-year-old came up with the idea of hanging hooks at her level in her closet so she could get her jacket and backpack without asking for help. Three-year-old Amy whined when the other children in the pool took her boats away and whined more when her mother suggested that she ask for them back. So they made a deal: her mother would come with her if Amy did the talking herself. A year later, Amy didn't need her mother's assistance, nor did she need to hang on to all of her toys all the time.

For more about how to encourage girls to perform in school see Chapter 4.

Clothing and Appearance

Alice was as ornery about her clothing as a preschooler could get. She insisted on wearing woolly tights on blazing summer days and beach "jellies" for her December birthday party. The only constant in her own peculiar (and, to our way of thinking, atrocious) sense of style was a dress—the longer and floppier the better, unless, that is, she could find one that was two sizes too small. We followed the textbook advice: offer two choices. Alice howled. Left to her own devices, she froze in frustration, standing in the middle of her room in her underpants. As 9:00 A.M. and the nursery-school carpool approached, we would thrust her little, angry limbs into something, anything, and push her out the door, often in tears. Not a good way to start the day.

Given this history, we're not terribly well-qualified to give advice. But here goes, anyway. The standard advice is to back off. Unless your child's choice of clothing is likely to do her harm, i.e., cause her to freeze, roast, or trip in the playground, you should let her pick her own outfits, if that's what she wants to do. One nursery school director said, "We can tell who dresses their children and who lets them dress themselves." It does not reflect badly on you if your child goes to preschool or daycare with orange stripes, purple checks, and a bizarre hat. In the end, it's probably worth the slight embarrassment not to have a knockdown fight every morning.

Other standard advice is to stock your child's drawers only with items that you find tolerable. One mother, who had gotten sick of the orange-and-purple look, told us that she simply limited her clothing purchases to red, white, and blue so that everything would go with everything else. This advice sounds easier than it really is. We found, for example, that it is impossible to eliminate every seasonally inappropriate item. Some fall days are hot; some cold. You have to leave a few T-shirts around and a few sweatshirts, and if you have a child like Alice, you know which she'll pick on the first frosty morning.

The key thing to understand is that, while any given battle over party dress versus pants may seem silly to you, this whole issue is very important to your child and, for that reason, it's not easy. For many children, perhaps especially girls, their attire is a form of self-expression, one of the few they may have.

Few mothers we talked to insisted on dolling up their litte girls. If anything, most mothers these days wear jeans as often as they can and are sometimes shocked to find their little girls pursuing anything that has ruffles. You don't have to worry that your little girl's choice of style at this stage will determine whether she grows up like Betty Friedan or Nancy Reagan. Remember that, in the preschool years, children work on defining their gender identity in ways that often strike adults as exaggerated or even comical.

The real issue is about control. Who is going to make the rules? At ages two and three, our little girls are playing out versions of the same battle that most of us remember waging with our parents as adolescents. The bottom line is that you and your daughter are most likely to emerge from this phase happily if you try to respect her right to choose. We emphasize *try*. As veterans of a prolonged clothing war, we know it isn't easy. She may refuse to choose or may choose such inappropriate clothes that you are forced to intervene. And intervene you should, because at those times your child is probably less interested in expressing herself than in testing your limits. But, short of that, let the orange stripes and purple checks multiply.

And Alice? Well, she turned four while we were writing this book. Sometimes now, she will nod sagaciously and say "It's a frosty morning. I think I'll wear my flower pants, today!" We nod, as if nothing could be more obvious.

A Daughter's Place in the Family: Dealing with Siblings

A preschool girl must come to terms with independence not only *from* the family but *within* the family. The arrival of a new sibling frequently triggers regression. All of a sudden, being the "big girl" seems distinctly unappealing when compared to such obvious advantages of infancy as constant attention, coddling, and heaps of presents. We may be particularly surprised by the regression of our daughters because they often seem so much more grown up than our sons: more articulate, more socially aware, more demure and controlled in their behavior. It's important to remember, however, that even the most advanced five-year-old girl still has a strong streak of baby in her, and she may abandon all her poise and social skills for thumb sucking, whining, pants wetting, and temper tantrums when she finds herself thrust into the role of big sister.

Regressive behavior, competition, and jealousy sparked by the arrival of a new baby are common among both girls and boys. However, the transition to being an older sibling may be particularly rough for a girl because the parents expect her to help care for the new baby and feel angry or disappointed when she refuses. Research into the question of whether girls are innately more "maternal" than boys is, like so much of the research into sex differences, inconclusive.[61] There is some limited evidence that firstborn preschool girls play more with infants than firstborn preschool boys, but this has not appeared in all studies. There is also some evidence that a younger sibling in need of comfort, help, or a morale boost is more likely to turn to an older sister than to an older brother.[62]

Families report mixed findings. Michael and Kathy's daughter was dying to have a baby to take care of, and specifically requested a sister; she got her wish and she has always loved helping care for her little sister (except when she's jealous). Karen felt lucky that her four-year-old daughter showed so much interest in "mothering" her little sister, and her six-year-old son also got involved in his own way. "My four-year-old will be a good baby-sitter," she remarks. "She wants to do adult things, and she helped even when her sister was an infant. My son will sit and show the baby a book or bring me her bottle, but my daughter wipes her face." Barry reported that although he and his wife bought their daughter miniature toy versions of every conceivable baby care item when their son was born, she showed far more interest in bathing her dolls than her brother; she never got into the "Little Miss Mother" routine, and instead ignored him until he could walk and talk. Diane found no sex differences in her children's interest in babies: her older daughter loved to help care for her brother when he was a baby, and he in turn was a big help when his little sister arrived. Steve was delighted—and surprised—that his daughter showed such a "motherly instinct" in feeding, rocking, and hugging her baby brother. "We didn't expect her to help at all, so we were pleasantly shocked at her nurturing instinct." He noted, however, that this "instinct" has been waning now that Max, age two, is very much his own person, and fights back.

Psychologist Gail Melson, who has studied sex differences in empathy and nurturing behavior in preschool children, feels that children as young as age three have acquired the concept that care for babies is a female activity, because in most households, and in most books and TV shows, they see mothers taking the primary responsibility. Since, as we have seen, preschool-age children tend to see gender roles in stark, black-and-white terms, they will label baby care "something for Mommy" no matter how much time their fathers spend feeding, diapering, and holding the baby. However, as noted earlier, when we leave the highly gender-typed area of baby care and move into a gender-neutral area such as pet care, the sex differences in nurturing disappear. "Little boys are as warm and cuddly with their pets as little girls," Melson concludes.[63]

Even if our daughters don't have more built-in nurturing capacity than our sons, we expect it. "Run along and play while I change the baby," we say to our four-year-old son when his newborn brother wakes up. "Come and help me with the baby," we say encouragingly to a four-year-old daughter. Again, what's important is respecting each individual child's interests and temperament. Each of Sandy's four daughters tended to go through a "little mommy" phase when a new sister arrived but quickly lost interest. She tries to encourage them to be close without pressuring the older girls into helping with the baby care against their wills.

Judy Dunn, who has studied sibling interactions extensively at Cambridge University, finds that family structure, that is, the sex of siblings and the age differences between them, cannot be used in any clear or simple way to predict how the children relate to each other.[64] Dunn's work does not bear out the common assumption that siblings of the same sex are fated to be close. Sibling conflict is high in all sorts of family configurations—one study cited by Dunn revealed that 29 percent of behavior between siblings was hostile.[65] A prime factor in determining how siblings get along with each other is temperament: the same "goodness of fit" that can make or break a relationship between parent and child—and friends too, for that matter. It's wonderful when our daughters fulfill our fantasy of the loving sisters, with a charming, helpful older sister eagerly entertaining a new baby and taking her under her wing as she grows up. But this fantasy, like most, has a way of coming true only in part and on occasion. How well did you get along with your siblings, especially when you were four or five? One mother had great hopes that her daughters would be close in part because she and her brother are so distant. Another, who never had a sister, thus feels especially disappointed that her two daughters are not close. Expecting our children to be lambs, especially when we as children were lions, is unfair and unrealistic. Remember, also, that the preschool years are marked by strong and rapid mood swings. Contented play erupts into conflict in the wink of an eye; angry teasing subsides just as quickly. "I hate having sisters!" our older daughter screams, punctuating her ferocity with a slam of her bedroom door. Five minutes later she's out playing delightedly with them on the teeter-totter.

Among Judy Dunn's few significant findings was that a girl with an older sister is more likely to have feminine interests than a girl without one. To take another example from our own family: "Alice has a list of girl things in her head," five-year-old Emily commented about one of her two-year-old twin sisters. "What's on the list?" we wondered. "Things like Barbie, Sleeping Beauty, party dresses, nail polish." We didn't have to search for the source of Alice's list: it corresponded perfectly with Emily's own interests. Alice, in fact, has dedicated herself to emulating Emily since birth. Cathy and Zeva, both of whom have older brothers, have much less detailed "girl's lists" in their heads than Alice and devote much more of their energy to emulating boys.

A far better predictor of sibling interaction than family structure is family process—how parents behave when their children are together, how they deal with fights, how they introduce a new baby into the family. Dunn reports that a child is far more likely to be friendly with a new baby, regardless of either child's sex, when a parent takes the time to sit down with the older sibling and discuss the new baby as a person, "with wants, needs, and feelings, for whom they could both take responsibility."[66]

Here are some tips for dealing with other issues that commonly crop up between siblings:

Assigned roles. Parents very often assign roles to their children based on a few pronounced character traits. A shy, withdrawn daughter is "the sensitive one"; a boisterous, athletic one is "the tomboy"; a highly feminine, coquettish girl is "the princess" or "the flirt"; a stubborn, headstrong daughter is "the bear" or "the stinker." "The problem with roles is that they are self-limiting," note Galinsky and David in *The Preschool Years*.[67] A child may become trapped in a role that fit her at age three but no longer applies at age five. Or parents may have trouble acknowledging or encouraging behavior that does not fit the role: the princess may never get a crack at soccer or fishing; the sensitive one may be shielded from situations that would bring her out of her shell and help her grow. Beware of the power of roles and alert to how your daughter feels about being "type-cast."

Staying out of fights. "Parents take fighting between siblings far more seriously than the children do," said one grandmother, a veteran of two generations of internecine warfare. Fighting between siblings is not only inevitable, it's normal and sometimes even beneficial. Sibling warfare may teach young children how to stick up for themselves, how to take responsibility for their own actions, and, eventually, how to settle disputes themselves. To the extent possible, stay out of the fights between your kids.

Avoid comparisons and an obsession with equality. In one family the three children, all quite close in age, always receive three identical inflatable rings for trips to the beach, three identical backpacks for carrying books, three identical stuffed dogs, and so on. The rationale is eliminating pretexts for fighting—but we've never seen three children bicker more viciously or senselessly. Each of our children is different, as is our relationship with each, and there is no reason to treat them all alike. Being fair does not mean enforcing strict equality, but treating each child as an individual. On the other hand, in acknowledging the differences between children, we should avoid overt comparisons as much as possible. Statements such as "Why can't you be neat like your sister?" or "Your sister never had tantrums when she was your age" will only provoke conflict and resentment.

Constructive responsibility. One mother reports that her five-year-old and her three-year-old fought bitterly and constantly. The more she tried to cajole, threaten, or punish them into getting along, the more they fought with each other or whined at her. Finally, she hit on the idea of giving

Annie, the five-year-old, some limited responsibility for her sister Betsy. When Annie and Betsy wrangled over the swings, their mother asked Annie if she could help Betsy climb up and push her. Annie also agreed, occasionally, to "read" her books to Betsy or help wash her hair. The responsibility made Annie feel more important and grown up than her sister, and Betsy reveled in the extra attention. Of course, they still fight, but now at least they have a few avenues for positive interaction. It is, however, important not to force a child into taking responsibility for a younger sibling, since this breeds resentment.

Making Friends

Children usually make their first friends in the toddler years, but these are for the most part short-lived, rather primitive relationships. Toddler friendships typically involve a good deal of imitation, parallel play, sharing, and inevitably, a certain amount of tussling over toys. Toddlers sometimes seem to conduct their friendships unconsciously or in ways that we don't perceive as friendship. Your daughter may tell you all about a new friend at the park or in her play group, and then at their next meeting the two will scarcely acknowledge each other. On the other hand, some toddler friendships endure and deepen into important, long-lasting relationships. The fact that our five-year-old daughter has known her best friend "since we were babies" (actually, since age two) is an important bond between them. If you watch your three- or four-year-old daughter in social situations, you'll probably see her gravitate toward other children who share her interests and temperament. Marcella says that her loud, aggressive three-year-old seeks out the roughest kids in a group for playmates. Sheri's active, verbal four-year-old found another nimble little girl with whom to clamber all over the jungle gym, chatting all the while.

By the preschool years, self-imposed sex segregation is usually well established (see pages 47–48). In a preschool or nursery school, your daughter is likely to play with two or three other girls, and she may inform you with utter conviction that boys are "yucky" or rough or dumb. "My daughter wouldn't let me come to her fourth birthday party," complained one father. "No boys allowed." On the other hand, a preschool-age girl may go through a phase of preferring the company of boys or she may include a boy or two in her "circle." Five-year-old Lena, angry that she had been excluded from a boy's birthday party, tried to break into the boys' groups at her preschool and traded her dresses and braids for jeans and a bob. Jill's best friend at four was a boy, and she even tried riding a dirt bike because that was his passion (she secretly hated it). However, when they started school, he rejected her "because he realized it wasn't cool to be friends with a girl," as Jill's mother put it. "He stopped seeing her so he wouldn't get teased. That is crazy." Five-year-old Emily has both girl and boy friends, and though she often quarrels with the boys and can't always find a game that both of them enjoy, she insists that they are really her friends and she wants to keep on seeing them. She explains that there are two types of boys—the rough and wild kind, whom she secretly admires for their aura of glamorous danger, and the "girl-type" boys, who are quiet and gentle and unthreatening. She complains, however, that even the quiet boys have recently joined the "boy's club" at nursery school; now her quiet boy friends will only play with her after school, when the wild boys are not around to tease them. This male embarrassment at being seen with the opposite sex usually intensifies during the early school years.

Most parents feel that trying to counteract sex segregation in the preschool and early school years is a losing battle. Even if our daughters are eager to play with little boys, like Emily, they often run up against a "boy's club" with a far more exclusive policy than any bastion of adult male solidarity. Feminist writer Letty Cottin Pogrebin believes that the greater pressure on boys to conform to their gender roles leads them to abandon girls as playmates far more avidly than girls abandon boys. She sees girls' separatism as a defensive reaction, and notes that girls tend to orient themselves *"toward* boys long before they are *with* boys." "Childhood sex segregation," Pogrebin concludes, is "a stepping stone to male supremacy."[68] To remedy the situation, Pogrebin suggests that we let children see cross-sex friendships among adults; that we cease identifying all children and dividing all activities by gender; that we encourage our little girls to play in all sorts of games, with all sorts of toys, and in all sorts of situations. Our daughters may avoid, or at least be less bound by, the claustrophobic all-girl cliques that tend to emerge in grade school if we help them become accustomed to playing team sports, to play in changing groups of children, and if we try to offer them a good balance of group activity, parent-child interaction, and solitary quiet time.

Whatever Happened to Tomboys?

Despite the prevalent sex segregation, some preschool girls, determinedly swimming against the current, seek out boys for playmates and show far more interest in typical boyish activities than in typical girlish ones. We used to label a girl who dressed in jeans and played baseball with the boys a tomboy, but that term seems to be falling out of use. As one mother of such a daughter put it, "You don't hear the word *tomboy* anymore; now it's, 'there's a girl who's into active things.' I like the fact that my daughter is assertive and physically active, but I do wish she'd wear a dress now and then." Another mother, who has a twelve-year-old and a three-year-old daughter, noted that "we live in a changing world, where both boys and girls get involved in football and volleyball now, and girls play on Little League teams all the time." Psychologist Gail Melson feels that "a lot of tomboyism is simply unladylike behavior. If Grandma came for Sunday dinner and found her granddaughter tossing a football around with her brother, she used to say, 'Oh, she's such a tomboy.' But the concept is no longer applicable today."[69]

The fading out of "tomboys" into "active girls" marks a real step forward in the breakdown of rigid definitions of gender. (Unfortunately, the advance is one-sided: "active girl" persists in being more acceptable than the male equivalent, the "sissy" boy. And even without the pejorative label, the passive, quiet boy who shuns sports, rough play, and male company is likely to make his parents anxious and encounter social pressure.) Rare is the girl who abandons the female camp altogether and plays with boys exclusively. If this does happen with your daughter, try to figure out why she has put such a low value on femininity, and help lead her to a more balanced view of the world.

If your daughter does go through a tomboy phase, or if she has always had a rough and aggressive style of play, try to be sparing with labels, especially in her presence. You may boast about how athletic your tomboy is, or how readily she gets herself dirty or sticks up for her rights, but your daughter might hear it as a criticism or as pressure to be more feminine. Maybe a sex-neutral term such as *athlete* or *fearless flyer* or *free spirit* would be a better way of describing a very active, daring, unruly girl. Also, if we've branded one daughter a tomboy or "jock," no matter how approvingly, we may fail to recognize or cultivate some of her more traditionally feminine traits, or pass on the subtle message that we only approve of her to the extent that she rejects her femininity. Too often our culture predisposes us to make mutually exclusive, either/or distinctions—either passive or aggressive, dependent or independent, masculine or feminine. Our complex, multifaceted daughters may well elude this crude categorizing: they may be tomboyish *and* frilly feminine; they may want girl *and* boy friends; they may enjoy dress-up *and* football. The less we try to fit them into rigid, limiting categories, the happier and freer we will all be.

Girls in Preschool

Attendance at some kind of preschool program is considered de rigeur in many parts of the country today, and attendance at preschool rose sharply through the 1980s, jumping 25 percent for three- to five-year-olds from 1981 to 1986.[70] (Preschool here is broadly defined to include private nursery schools, play groups, day-care centers, and programs for preschool-age children run through the public schools.) Although the increase in the number of working mothers and single-parent families is responsible in part, it is by no means the sole factor. Parents representing the entire social and economic spectrum feel that their daughters have benefited from preschool.[71] The little girls have gained social skills, have enjoyed new toys and playground equipment, and have picked up all sorts of new games, expressions, and information from the other children. It stands to reason that they will adjust more readily to elementary school, and studies back this up.[72]

All of this does not mean, however, that a preschool is an absolute necessity for your daughter's well-being. If both you and your daughter prefer having her at home until elementary school begins, if she has opportunities to play with other children in the neighborhood or at local parks, if the preschool programs available strike you as inadequate or inferior, then your best course may well be to forgo preschool altogether or limit her attendance to a few mornings each week. As Barbara Brenner, author of *The Preschool Handbook*, notes, "Statistics proving that preschool makes all kids better or smarter or more sociable just don't exist."[73] Mary, a Milwaukee mother of five (two boys and three girls), said her older three children attended preschool, but she is strongly considering keeping the two younger daughters (ages three and fifteen months) out. "As much as Sarah, my five-year-old, liked preschool, I think it was ultimately an average experience for her. I think a parent can do even better with a preschool child if he or she has the time to be there. Preschool isn't necessary for a child. I only work part time, the kids are my first priority, and so I can provide the little ones outings, special crafts projects, and activities that wouldn't be available to them in preschool."

If you do opt for some type of preschool program for your daughter, the overwhelming odds are that her teachers or care providers will be women. It stands to reason that women bring some stereotypically female values to the classrooms and playgrounds—for example, a preference for quiet, peaceful play; a greater interest in art, music, and crafts than in sports and roughhousing; a desire that the children enter into mutually supportive relationships rather than competitive hierarchies based on domination. As one female teacher candidly wrote, "When the children separate by sex, I, the teacher, am more often on the girls' side. We move at the same pace and reach for the same activities, while the boys barricade themselves in the blocks, periodically making forays into female territory. . . . I seem to admire boys most when they are not playing as young boys play."[74] Interestingly, according to one study of men in early childhood education programs and day-care centers, the male teachers scored just as high in feminine traits as their female counterparts: like the women, the men teachers emphasized such activities as dressing up, doll and kitchen play, painting and artwork, and were less likely to encourage climbing, hammering, building with blocks, or playing with cars.[75]

All of these factors may be to your daughter's advantage when she enters a preschool program, assuming she is stereotypically feminine in her behavior. On the other hand, a very rough and aggressive girl may get into just as much trouble (with both teachers and children) as a rough and aggressive boy. The care givers at a large day-care center complained to Marcella that her daughter Shannon, age three, was a bully because she was hitting other children. Marcella, however, felt that she was simply protecting herself from the kids who had beat up on her. Despite the flak, Marcella was proud that her daughter was developing a tough skin and "street smarts." She jokes that someday Shannon will be protecting her brother, a gentle and retiring eight-year-old. Psychologists observing girls in preschool believe that Shannon's behavior may be typical of daughters of working mothers (Marcella works full time as a secretary). "Girls are now taking on more of the superhero roles," comments one child development specialist. "Girls demonstrate more power than they would have in play situations ten years ago—and frankly, it's very nice to see."[76]

Because girls are on average a few months ahead of boys developmentally, and often more adept verbally, they may have an easier time meeting the challenge of preschool. As we have seen previously, some studies find that preschool girls have less separation anxiety than boys, that they cry less often in school, and that they go through less turmoil in the preschool period. Some speculate that boys have a tougher time making the transition to preschool because it coincides with the stressful process of establishing their gender role. They move from the feminine world of home to the feminine world of school, often with only scant exposure to their fathers. The same forces that make boys rebuff their mothers at home lead to disruptive behavior at preschool. For girls, on the other hand, the preschool teacher may become a surrogate mother—another strong female figure with whom she can identify, to whom she can turn for approval and support, and on whom she can model her own behavior.

Julie expected that her four-year-old daughter Morgan would shrink into a corner at nursery school because she tends to be shy, and, living on a farm, she had little contact with other children. However, her daughter joined in right from the first day. Pamela, who runs a toddler play group out of her Florida home, notes that her three-year-old daughter Alexis does not let herself be pushed around by the boys; she thinks Alexis learned to stand up for herself from her older brother. Karen, on the other hand, found different behavior at the small nursery school at a local church. "Even at age three, the boys were intimidating the girls and taking over the toy box," she noted. "The girls were passive and in awe of the boys." Steve said that when he picks up his four-year-old daughter from nursery school, the children are usually out on the playground and he sees no real difference in the way the two sexes play or the equipment they use. All the kids have equal access to the monkey bars and swings.

Parents can encourage preschools to counter gender stereotypes by recommending display materials with pictures of women in a variety of roles, such as doctors, farmers, fire fighters, as well as homemakers. Other suggestions include turning the dress-up corner into a "Me" center where children can role-play without necessarily adopting sex stereotypes. Substituting bathrobes for dresses and stocking the "Me" center with briefcases, purses, play medical equipment, and so on, might help children expand their repertoire of roles. Introducing rubber or wooden animals and dolls or play figures into the block center might attract more girls to this activity. Preschools can also break down sex stereotypes by placing toy woodworking tables and tools in the "house" and adding a toy typewriter or calculator to the available household objects.[77]

Parents can also encourage preschool teachers to work closely with very shy girls on learning how to stand up for themselves and make their needs known. One teacher told an anecdote about how two girls could not get the boys to give them a turn on the swings. The girls suggested that the teacher come and chase the boys away, but she pointed out that this would only help for now—the next time the boys were on the swings they'd have the same problem. Instead, she told them to get a few friends and stand up to the boys together. The girls gathered together a group of girl and boy friends and solved the problem themselves, learning in the bargain a good lesson in independence.[78]

Parents can also help counter sex stereotypes by coming into school to do special projects. For example, a mother who works as a pediatrician or dentist might talk to the children about her job and show the children what happens at an examination. One four-year-old daughter, who attended a nursery school in a church, especially enjoyed visits from the female minister. It really impressed the little girl that a woman could hold a position that commanded so much respect in the community. All of us have noted that dads are more on the scene at preschools than they used to be—they drive in car pools, attend meetings, and, occasionally, come in as parent helpers—which is inherently helpful in correcting gender stereotypes. You can learn more about combating sexism and other sorts of bias in preschool from a brochure entitled "Teaching Young Children to Resist Bias: What Parents Can Do," available from the National Association for the Education of Young Children (NAEYC), 1834 Connecticut Ave. N.W., Washington, D.C. 20009-5786.

Your daughter's temperament is a far more important factor than her sex in determining how she will react to a preschool. If at all possible, take it into account when selecting a program. Annie, a very timid four-year-old, got lost in the shuffle in the large nursery school class at a local synagogue; in retrospect, her parents felt she might have done better in a program that had more structure. Nell, age three, who is task-oriented, musical, and adept at defending her own turf, is thriving at a Montessori school, where there are a variety of activities and materials available for the children to use as they see fit, with minimal direction or pressure from the teachers. Rebecca, who was somewhat traumatized by a tough little boy in her play group at age two, learned by age four to avoid confrontation with the self-described "pirate" boys in her private nursery school; she had a great year in a program that emphasized crafts, dance, and cooking. Sensitive and shy Emily was intimidated at age four by a nursery program that emphasized perfection in art projects and a spotless classroom; at five, she blossomed at a looser program that offered a wider range of activities. It also helped her enormously to attend the same preschool as her best friend.

You may not have a choice of different preschools, or

your decision may be bound by such factors as convenience, cost, hours, and accreditation. But if you do have a choice by all means make time to visit the various programs with your daughter, meet the care givers, watch them in action, and chat with the director. You may want to ask some searching questions about how girls tend to adjust to the program, whether the care givers emphasize sex typing of the children, and typical activities. Beware of programs that stress early learning. Tufts University educator David Elkind cautions parents against preschool programs in which the children spend long hours at desks, in which workbooks are used extensively, and in which memorizing the alphabet is considered more important than playing, exploring the environment, and making friends.[79] NAEYC maintains in a position statement on good teaching practices for four- and five-year-olds that children learn by doing, not by rote drills.[80] NAEYC and the National Association of Elementary School Principals note that four- and five-year-olds can be made to memorize all sorts of facts and statistics so that they seem to be getting a jump-start on kindergarten, but in fact such children may "burn out" by the time they reach elementary school. Girls may be at particular risk because they tend to be more compliant than boys.

NAEYC recommends providing preschool children with a variety of activities such as dramatic play, blocks, games, puzzles, books, art, and music that the children can choose themselves; emphasizing small, informal groups rather than large, teacher-directed instruction sessions; having teachers help children develop social skills by talking with them about sharing, helping, and cooperating; preparing children to learn to read by having them listen to stories, dictate stories of their own, participate in class plays, and experiment with writing and copying letters.[81]

When screening preschool programs, if possible bring your daughter along. Does she seem to take to the setting, or does it make her uneasy? Are there many objects she wants to examine and play with? Is there any equipment on which she could hurt herself? Most important of all, does she seem to like the teacher/care giver? First impressions are extremely important to children. All three of our daughters surprised us with how much they remembered of their first visit to a preschool and how consistent they were in their reactions to teachers. During the five months that clapsed between their spring screening visit to "Ms. Judy's Playgroup" and their fall enrollment, our two-year-old twins spoke often of their teacher and the toy eggs and play money that she had let them handle. This smoothed their adjustment in September.

After your daughter has been in preschool for some time, you may notice that she is becoming more and more feminine in her interests and play. She may insist on wearing a dress every day; she may focus more attention on playing with dolls or ponies or begin to use more feminine mannerisms. This, as we have seen, is the age in which children of both sexes take on exaggerated gender roles, a process which may be hastened by exposure to other little girls. Furthermore, your daughter's preschool classmates may be exerting far more pressure on her to "act like a girl" than do you and her teacher.[82] Olivia began to show an interest in feminine things for the first time once she became friends with other girls in her nursery school class. Ariel sparked a craze among her preschool girl friends for fancy dress-up (complete with eye shadow and lipstick).

On the other hand, a preschool may be your daughter's first daily exposure to boys, and you may find that she brings home as many boyish activities as girlish ones. Annie seemed to get a huge vicarious thrill from the naughty antics of her male classmates. Her parents began to hear the names of the current crop of superheroes for the first time, and when she brought home one of the wild boys for a play date, she merrily joined him in trashing her room and soaking her little sister with the garden hose, pranks she had never indulged in on her own.

Finally, don't be overly alarmed if your daughter does not warm up to her preschool program right away. Children adapt to new situations at different rates and express their reactions to change in different ways. The little girl who comes zooming out of preschool hollering about how terrific it is may actually be having a tougher time making the transition than the girl who sidles out evasively and offers no comment. Some children seem to enjoy "punishing" their parents by complaining about every little mishap at school, when in fact teachers report that they have lots of friends and participate well in the activities. Other children tell their parents what they think they want to hear—school is wonderful, the teachers fun, the other kids super—as a way of disguising guilt at having "failed" at school. If your daughter seems miserable in a preschool program, try to find out what has gone wrong and how the two of you can fix it. One delicate three-year-old who was being tormented by bigger, bullying boys needed a bit of assertiveness training: her dad taught her to hold up her index finger in the bully's face and shout, "You bud, don't bother me!" It worked. Another girl tended to hang back when the other children were playing; her teacher suggested that it might help if her parents arranged after-school play dates and she recommended a few other girls for her to play with. A little girl born late in the year might be better off spending an extra year in preschool and then entering kindergarten as the oldest girl in her class. (For more on school readiness, see Chapter 4.)

Remember that starting preschool is a big step, particularly for a sheltered, firstborn girl. It may be the first time that she faces the fact that she is not the only child in the world. Give her time to adjust, to find her niche, to settle in.

Lots of parents of daughters remark that five, the last year of the preschool period, is their favorite age. Most of the whining and negativism of the terrible twos is over, and the incessant testing of limits tapers off as a little girl becomes more confident of herself, her gender identity, her place in the family, and her ability to move back and forth securely from home to the world outside. "At five, they are real people, but they still have their childhood innocence," one mother summed up. Our five-year-olds may still parade around in outrageous parodies of femininity—bedecking themselves with frills, jewelry, and makeup at every opportunity—but they also show a much more rational and complicated understanding of the world around them. A five-year-old is starting to grasp that being female means a lot more than long hair, dresses, and babies. In their fantasy play, our five-year-old daughters are princesses and Ninja Turtles, evil stepmothers and wild ponies, schoolteachers and mommies. They keep house and hold down jobs; they gallop off into the sunset and croon for a prince to rescue them. They're picking up more and more information from television, friends, preschool teachers, books. When we see the "big girls" chatting together on the way to school, executing high leaps in ballet class, or scoring goals in soccer league, we think, "Hey, someday my daughter will be doing all of that." Early childhood is drawing to a close. Your five-year-old daughter is about to embark on the next leg of her journey to maturity: the school years.

4

Girls at School: Elementary Education from Kindergarten Through Third Grade

The conventional wisdom is that elementary school is designed for little girls. This image has little girls sitting quietly at their desks, listening carefully to the teacher, and learning their lessons with ease, while the boys practically have to be strapped to their seats. Many little girls may actually behave like this in school because they are happy and stimulated by the classroom activities, but others may in fact be sitting quietly because that's what they are *expected* to do. Their apparent good behavior may mask boredom, passivity, and fear.

In this chapter we get behind the conventional image so that parents can really assess how good an education their daughter is getting from kindergarten to grade three. We discuss the special strengths of girls as well as their special needs, which are often far less obvious. And we look at how schools can foster or hamper our daughters' acquisition of basic skills, love of learning, and self-confidence—and what a parent can do about it.

At the start of the chapter we discuss how to assess a little girl's readiness for kindergarten or first grade, and also some typical ways in which a girl may respond to school differently and be treated differently from a boy. We'll also show you some of the many techniques you as a parent can use to ensure that your little girl has a stimulating, pleasant academic experience in her first years of school, one that prepares her and motivates her for the challenges ahead. We'll focus particularly on what you can do to inspire your daughter with love of those traditionally "masculine" areas: math, science, and computers.

Starting School: Is Your Daughter Ready?

There was no question in my mind that Jamie was better prepared to start kindergarten than her brother Brian had been. She had been playing a fantasy school game for over a year. She could concentrate longer than he could, and sit still longer. She knew her numbers, and her letters, and she could color inside the lines. With Brian, we weren't sure what he knew because he was afraid to say the alphabet. But the main thing was she just *liked* being in school. Brian did not want to give up his playtime. He took much longer to adjust to the school routine.

—HEIDI, A MINNESOTA MOTHER OF TWO

When it comes to starting kindergarten, little girls are lucky. Like Jamie, five- and six-year-old girls are generally happier to march off into the kindergarten classroom than their male peers, and they are better able to adapt to school schedules and routines. "Sarah was five and two months when she started kindergarten, and we would have held her back if she had been a boy," noted Mary, a Milwaukee mother of five children, including six- and nine-year-old sons. Because Sarah's older brothers had found the transition to kindergarten rather tough even though each boy had actually been a few months older than Sarah when he started, Mary and her husband Tom seriously talked about keeping Sarah in preschool for another year. But ultimately, they decided Sarah could hold her own. Now, two months into kindergarten, they feel they made the right choice. "Socially and emotionally she was ready," says Mary. "She wants to learn. She gets along well with the other children. Her teacher thinks she's doing fine."

Studies bear out Jamie and Sarah's experiences. The Gesell Institute, a Connecticut-based organization devoted to studying child behavioral development, has found that, for children five to six years old, girls are approximately six months ahead of boys in almost every tested category. Because of this developmental edge, a five-year-old girl is more likely than a little boy the same age to be ready for the relatively structured group learning required in many kindergartens.[1] Dr. Ana Dybner, an elementary school psychologist, noted that the major difference she has seen between kindergarten girls and boys is in social ability: "In social skills, by and large girls seem to develop earlier. They are more verbal, they put their thoughts and feelings into words more than boys do, and they have more patience. However, in terms of academics, a child's background, previous experience with groups, and stimulus at home are more important factors than gender."

Numerous parents and teachers have echoed Heidi's comment about how her daughter Jamie could sit still better than her son Brian. As Rochelle Stern, an elementary school teacher with fifteen years' experience, puts it, "The girls are more school-oriented right from the start. They love to keep their desks neat, to have nice little piles of neat papers. With boys, you get the feeling that you are interfering with their lives, with their Ninja Turtle and Nintendo games. The boys just can't sit still. They love to be running around outside. I sometimes worry that we're doing a disservice to boys by keeping them cooped up in small classrooms. That issue generally does not arise with girls." "Girls really want to be in school, but boys are there because they have to be," is how one mother summed up the differences.

By five and a half, your daughter probably knows her alphabet and may even be able to write all the letters. She prints her name easily. She may recognize simple words and probably spends quite a bit of time pretending to read books she has memorized. She can count to twenty or more. She walks, runs, and climbs with new fluidity. She can spend twenty minutes or more carefully coloring within the lines in a coloring book. But even more important is her relative emotional and behavioral maturity compared to the average little boy of the same age. She is more likely to pay attention and follow a teacher's directions; she can probably concentrate on a single task longer; she will probably be somewhat more adept at playing with the other children, organizing games, waiting her turn, resolving conflicts without fisticuffs. In short, her teacher is likely to tell you that she is doing well and that she is a pleasure to have in the class. "My daughter's teacher praises her for going along with the planned activity," one mother reports. "She says Meredith is mature, friendly, and considerate of others. And she has a good sense of humor." Another mother was pleased to hear the teacher mention her daughter's leadership qualities, her helpfulness with the other kids, and her readiness to do things without being told. Still another mentioned that the teacher praised her daughters for being friendly, able to get along well with the other children, and able to speak up and express their needs.

"School readiness" is the term in vogue today to describe a child's emotional, social, and developmental ability to begin school. Because of girls' developmental edge, parents of boys are generally far more preoccupied with the question of school readiness. These days, the conventional wisdom is that if there is any doubt whatsoever about a boy's school readiness, the best course is to hold him back. A long-term study of children in the Chicago area links failure in first grade to adolescent problems for boys but not for girls. Researchers speculate that immature boys get stuck in a vicious cycle of failure, low self-esteem, and loss of confidence that permanently alienates them from school.[2] Girls, however, are not totally immune from such problems. Researchers at the Gesell Institute find that children of either sex who get discouraged about their ability to master new skills in school tend not to catch up, but instead slip further and further behind each year.[3] Although your daughter may be less at risk than your son, it's still wise to weigh her individual abilities, needs, and maturity level carefully before starting her in kindergarten.

Jane, a Massachusetts mother of three daughters ages eight, six, and three, said she kept both of her older daughters back in nursery school for an extra year, and in both cases it was the right move. Meredith, a September baby, would have been eligible to start kindergarten just around the time she turned five (most states require that a child entering kindergarten turn five by December or January), but she had absolutely no interest in going to the "big school." Jane notes that holding children back an extra year is a widely accepted practice in her community, so she had no problem at all with keeping Meredith in nursery school. A year later, Meredith was far more enthusiastic about school, and she is now thriving as an eight-year-old second grader. Although Meredith's sister Christina was born in May, and so would have been nearly five and a half when kindergarten began, Jane and her husband decided to hold her back as well. "Christina is a very quiet, rather passive child," says Jane, "and we didn't want her to be overwhelmed in school. An extra year in nursery school gave her more confidence."

It's important to understand that school readiness is not a measure of a child's intelligence or a predictor of her future academic success. Your daughter may be intellectually gifted, yet not ready to profit from group instruction or kindergarten activities. She may be a very quiet child like Christina who would get lost in the shuffle at a large public school. The fact that your child did beautifully in nursery school does not mean that she is necessarily ready for the very different environment and agenda of formal school. Maddy was one such nursery school "star" who suffered by being pushed too quickly into kindergarten. As her father tells it, "In nursery school she was the class leader, and the teachers couldn't believe she was the youngest in the class. She had an older friend who followed her around. She loved it. The next year, all the nursery school kids went off to kindergarten, but Maddy was technically too young to start. We didn't want her to be in nursery school another year—we felt she'd be bored—so we sent her to a private kindergarten at a local synagogue. She had a miserable adjustment. The day lasted from eight until four, and the bus schedule made it even longer. She acted like a depressed kid. After raving about nursery school, all of a sudden she would say she hated school. When we went away for winter vacation, she became her old self again. Clearly, school was the problem." The next year, Maddy entered kindergarten in the public school system, and she's doing beautifully. Being one of the oldest children and going back to a half-day schedule both work to Maddy's advantage, and her parents are vastly relieved to hear her looking forward to school once again.

There is no magic formula for determining whether or not your daughter is ready to start kindergarten, but these pointers will help.

• Kindergarten is quite different from nursery school. More of the day is spent in structured group activities. There is more of an official aspect and less emphasis on play. There is far less supervision—in fact, the ratio of students to teacher usually doubles from nursery school. The school building itself is likely to be far larger and more intimidating than the nursery school, with long institutional halls, crowded and noisy play areas, and scores of classrooms. Can your daughter really deal with this? Is she easily frightened and likely to "freeze up" in a new situation? Does she become overwhelmed in crowds? Think about how she acts at home, in group settings, what you have observed at nursery school, and what her teachers have said about her.
• How well does your daughter concentrate on quiet activities, such as coloring, reading, putting together puzzles? How advanced is her fine motor coordination? Indications that your child may not be ready for kindergarten are an

inability to concentrate on an activity for more than a few minutes, an unwillingness to follow simple directions, a lack of interest in writing her own name, or an inability to hold a pencil with three fingers as an adult would.

- How well does your daughter participate in group activities, for example, at nursery school, birthday parties, summer or church programs? Little girls who strongly resist taking direction from others, who refuse to join in with other children, who seem to be dreaming or hovering somewhere in a private universe while a teacher or group leader is talking may have a hard time coping with the group activities of kindergarten. Again, such traits reflect a lack of social maturity, *not* a lack of intelligence. Very often extremely bright and creative children are too independent-minded or wrapped up in fantasy to join other children in group play. Such children very often profit from an extra year of nursery school.

- Consider your daughter's age relative to her classmates. The Gesell Institute advises parents of children born in the fall to give special attention to the issue of school readiness. Keep in mind that since holding children back has become a common practice in many communities, your September- or October-born five-year-old may very likely be the youngest child in her class. We're not suggesting you hold your daughter back in nursery school because everyone else is doing it, but rather that you anticipate problems that could arise because she is the youngest, and possibly the smallest, child in her class.

- Keep in mind that children change quickly. Your daughter may have a developmental burst over the summer and rapidly acquire the skills and abilities she needs for kindergarten. The new opportunities of kindergarten itself may trigger such a burst. Try to assess how well your daughter rises to new challenges and whether you have seen her make other sudden leaps forward in the past. Were you surprised at how well she adapted to nursery school? Does she seem to be gathering new confidence in making friends and joining up with groups of children?

Your daughter may be on a roll developmentally, and kindergarten may become one more experience that she sails through with flying colors.

Even if your daughter is clearly ready for kindergarten, she may still take some time to make the adjustment to the newness and bigness of "real school." Barbara felt a little worried about how tired her daughters seemed after a day of kindergarten, far more tired than they were after nursery school. Abby said her daughter seemed to like school well enough, but she was terrified of the rowdy big kids on the school bus and cried each morning at the bus stop. Accustomed to the close supervision of nursery school, Emily had trouble taking responsibility for her own belongings: she was forever forgetting her backpack or leaving her lunch money in the classroom. Tracy was always scared she'd get lost in the long school corridors as her class shuttled from classroom to gym to auditorium. Freda felt bored during recess because the play was totally unsupervised: the gruff playground aides merely watched. Randi was lonely without her two best nursery school friends, who had gone to different schools.

The question of school readiness doesn't end with kindergarten; the step to first grade can be just as big. As every parent—and every child—knows, first grade is the beginning of real school, where a child's academic progress will be measured and judged. The first-grade teacher has a definite academic agenda. While your child's kindergarten teacher may not have been concerned if your child didn't learn to read, the first-grade teacher will expect her to learn. Classroom time will be more structured, with more time devoted to traditional instruction and less time to activities that feel like play. First grade may also be the first year in which your little girl goes to school all day and every day. If the kindergarten teacher expresses doubt that your child is ready for first grade, or if you feel your child may not be ready, you should seriously consider having her repeat kindergarten. Although many parents worry that being "left back" will stigmatize their child and that the child will miss her friends, children at this age are much less conscious of such issues than adults are. Although we think that you should be truthful with your child and explain that she is going to repeat kindergarten and why, you will probably find after summer vacation that your child will happily return to kindergarten without much concern for the children who were her former classmates. And it will be much easier for your five- or six-year-old to repeat kindergarten than it will be for her to suffer through a year of first grade before she's ready.

Whenever your little girl does begin kindergarten or first grade, the best advice for helping your daughter (and you!) make the transition is to *give it time*. If possible, cut back a bit on your work schedule for a while so you can be more available to her in the first days of school. Try to help her make new friends by inviting one or two children to your home to play for an hour or two after school. Try to avoid pressuring her or comparing her unfavorably with siblings or friends. And avoid overscheduling. Your daughter will probably need some extra rest and quiet time as she adjusts to all the new demands on her attention. If serious adjustment problems persist after a month or two, then by all means discuss the situation with your daughter's teacher.

Sexism in the Classroom

Our elementary schools have been called feminine strongholds, where female teachers enforce and reward traditional female values, such as compliance, neatness, and decorum, and punish boys for unruly pranks and irrepressible high spirits. Our schools have also been branded as bastions of sexism, where boys are encouraged to achieve in academics and star in athletics, while girls are subtly indoctrinated to accept second-class status.

Over the past two decades, feminist psychologists, social critics, and concerned parents and teachers have made us aware of the special needs and problems that little girls face in school. There is no question that our schools and teachers have made progress in correcting sexism and in addressing the academic and social issues unique to girls. Nor is there any doubt that young schoolgirls nevertheless face certain disadvantages. It remains disturbingly and perplexingly true that although in elementary school girls outperform boys in all academic subjects, by high school boys have narrowed the gap in most subjects and pulled ahead in math. Why does this happen? How can we change it?

As we have seen in previous chapters, there are no hard-and-fast answers. We've talked to, observed, and heard about eight-year-old soccer stars, six-year-old Barbie enthusiasts, a five-year-old who felt lost and lonely in kindergarten but was too shy to do anything about it, a seven-year-old who led the class in an exciting geology project. Teachers have told us about girls who love and loathe math, girls who outcompete boys on the playing fields, girls who band together in "cool crowd" cliques, and other girls who suffer from being excluded. As you might expect, our daughters become even more varied in their passions and their temperaments as they grow up. Good teachers, like good parents, take individual needs into account.

If a girl does confront sexism, it's likely to be much subtler than the kind her parents faced. Think back to your own elementary school experience: boys and girls forming separate lines to march into school; gym class in which the boys played ball games and learned gymnastics while the girls touched their toes and ran in place; readers in which girls in pretty clothes stood around admiring the rough-and-tumble games of little boys ("Run, Dick, run!"); "unenlightened" teachers who deliberately or unconsciously encouraged boys to lead and girls to follow, directing boys to sports, academic achievement, and toughness and girls to social skills, cooperation, and decorum.

Walk into your daughter's kindergarten or first-grade class today and you are likely to see a very different world indeed. Girls and boys are "mixed up together in one pot," as one teacher put it. They crowd into their classrooms together in a noisy, integrated jumble. They are likely to sit together in little coed groupings of four or five desks. They take gym and woodworking together; they learn to cook and sing together; they have equal access to the computer; their storybooks and math problems are designed to appeal equally to both sexes. It may be exaggerating to say that elementary school classrooms have undergone a revolution since the early 1970s, but there has certainly been a strong, clear evolution in the direction of providing equal opportunities for girls and boys.

One sign is the change in elementary reading materials. In the early '70s the National Organization for Women funded a study of basal readers. References to girls and women were few and far between; the few that did appear uniformly portrayed women in domestic roles.[4] The study documented that boys were cited much more often for active mastery themes, such as ingenuity and bravery, while girls were cited for dependence and incompetence.[5] Educational publishers responded with new editions that have removed the most blatant types of sexism and sex stereotypes. Girls and women now receive approximately equal attention, and women are not uniformly portrayed wearing aprons and serving soup. Girls are more likely to be seen playing active roles in the stories, and some effort has been made to portray women working outside the home, though the readers are still criticized for portraying an idealized, predominantly white, middle-class life, in which two-parent families live in the suburbs.

A federal law, known as Title IX, enacted in 1972, reflected congressional recognition of the problem of sexism in education. The law prohibits sex discrimination in any educational program or activity that receives federal funding. Since most school programs receive federal aid, directly or indirectly, this law probably applies to some or all of the programs in your child's school. This means, for instance, that if the school offers woodworking or sponsors an after-school computer club, both activities must be equally available to girls and boys. The law has received the most publicity, much of it critical, in its application to sports where critics have raised the specter of girls getting mauled in coed high school football games. In fact, Title IX has at least up until now probably had more symbolic than practical impact: the federal government has not sent investigators into schools to root out instances of subtle, or even blatant, sex discrimination.[6] But even if the law is not primarily responsible for all the increased opportunities our daughters now have in school, the effects of those changes have been overwhelmingly positive: particularly in athletics, little girls have responded with tremendous enthusiasm to the increased access to sports in school, and after-school team sports for girls have also proliferated nationwide.

Nearly all of the parents we spoke to praised their daughters' elementary schools and teachers for their fairness. "Sexism is an issue that has been raised for some time and people are very aware of it," says one Massachusetts mother of three daughters. "I really see no evidence that my daughters are being discriminated against. I look at their readers and I think they go out of their way to put girls in active roles. The only problem I've ever seen in this area is that occasionally you'll hear a teacher spoken of as 'a great teacher for boys' or as someone who likes boys better." Holly, the mother of two girls (in fifth and second grades), has observed that the older and more traditional kindergarten teachers are likely to prefer girls to boys because girls behave more quietly in the classroom, but she has seen no other evidence of sexism in the school. "My older daughter took woodworking, and you see girls playing kickball with the boys on the playground now. None of this was available when I was in grade school." "The schools have really come up-to-date," summed up another mother whose four daughters span eleven years. "There are more opportunities today for girls, and there is more acceptance for girls to be involved with activities that were once thought of as male, such as carpentry or karate." "When I was in school, the girls took home economics, the boys took shop. All this has changed," said a Minnesota mother of two, a daughter and a son. "Today there is an awareness that you will need all these skills no matter what sex you are." An elementary school principal in our school district said that in her school one week each year is set aside as "Women's Herstory Week," when students study the lives of women athletes, scientists, artists, and writers. "It's an exciting time," she comments. "Too bad it's only one week."

All of this is very encouraging, but it's also a little too good—and too simplistic—to be true. Yes, schools and teachers have come a long way; but no, sexism has not vanished altogether from early childhood education in America. It's more subtle, in many cases it's unintentional, but it still exists and it holds our daughters back. David and Myra Sadker, psychologists with the School of Education at American University in Washington, D.C., were involved in a study of 100 elementary school classrooms in the 1980s. They found clear evidence that sex bias continues, even when teachers are unaware of it or are deliberately trying to correct it. Myra Sadker says, "We've met teachers who call themselves feminists. They insist there is equity in their classrooms. Then I videotape them as they're teaching, and they're amazed."[7] Specifically, the Sadkers found that teachers call on boys far more often than girls; they ask boys more complicated, searching questions involving abstract reasoning, while girls are asked questions that require them simply to repeat memorized facts or are supplied with the answer if they hesitate; they make eye contact with boys more often; they interrupt girls' answers to questions more often; and in the later grades they foster boys' achievement in math and science more than girls'. In rankings of how likely children are to receive attention from their teacher, white males came in first, minority males second, white females third, and minority females ranked last. The Sadkers conclude, "Boys were the central figures in the classroom and girls were relegated to second-class participation." And they further argue that "the idea that sexism will disappear naturally, becoming extinct as time and environment change, does not reflect reality."[8]

In 1994, the Sadkers published *Failing at Fairness: How Our Schools Cheat Girls*, a comprehensive study of sexism in America's schools based on a decade of classroom observations from elementary school through high school. Their conclusions remain disturbing. Despite the fact that our society has become far more aware of sexism since the 1970s, girls are still "second-class education citizens" in schools throughout the nation—dominated by boys, ignored by teachers, invisible, unheard, silent, and frequently teased or harassed on account of their gender. "Despite proclamations that equity had been achieved," the Sadkers write, "the cover-up was transparent: Bias persisted from the elementary grades through medical and law school." Often the "bias" masquerades as sound educational policy: teachers insist that the boys need more attention and discipline, that girls are by nature quiet and retiring, that sexism *can't* be a problem because they're using gender-neutral materials or have attended conferences on gender issues. But again and again, the Sadkers demonstrate that these are excuses, rationalizations, and smoke screens for a stubborn problem. *Failing At Fairness* sounds a sharp, clear alarm for parents of daughters: "Each time a girl opens a book and reads a womanless history, she learns she is worth less. Each time the teacher passes over a girl to elicit the ideas and opinions of boys, that girl is conditioned to be silent and to defer. . . . When female students are offered the leftovers of teacher time and attention, morsels of amorphous feedback, they achieve less. . . . Like a thief in school, sexist lessons subvert education, twisting it into a system of socialization that robs potential."

Other findings indicate that teachers tend to compliment girls for neatness and boys for analysis, thus guiding children to conform with sex-role stereotypes (the tidy girl, the achieving boy). In addition, elementary school teachers have been observed calling on girls only when they sit in the first row, but calling on boys no matter where they sit in the classrooms. Girls thus are subtly taught to be dependent: if they stray too far from teacher, they are forgotten or ignored; boys, on the other hand, learn that they will be noticed and listened to no matter what. As Dr. Katherine Canada, an assistant professor of psychology at Goucher College in Towson, Maryland, sums up, "Many people assume that the problem of sexism in schools has been solved. You hear people say, 'Oh yes, we took care of all that in the late '70s.' But it's folly to believe the problems are over and that we have achieved the goal of a sex equitable classroom. The kinds of sexist behaviors are so subtle, they are so deeply ingrained, and they happen so rapidly, it takes more than lip service to correct them."[9]

The Sadkers add that a sexist classroom atmosphere often is established by the typical behaviors of boys and girls themselves: "Almost all teachers we have talked with made it clear that relying on noisy students, the ones who volunteer, is a direct path to a classroom controlled by boys. Girls who know the answer are more likely to wait to be called on, while males are more apt to shout out." A teacher must actively intervene to keep this from happening—and often it's up to the parents to prod the teacher into an awareness of what's going on. Encouraging all children to wait and write down questions and answers instead of shouting them out is one way to free up class time for girls. The Sadkers cite the example of a Wisconsin teacher who used poker chips as a way of involving quiet girls: she gave her students two poker chips at the start of class and made them "cash in" a chip every time they asked or answered a question. Once the chips were gone, that was it; all students were required to spend both chips by the end of class period so everyone ended up participating.

Sexism is also evident in the administrative and teaching staff of the usual public school, which is overwhelmingly female with an occasional man teaching here or there, often in predictably "masculine" areas, such as science, shop, computers, and physical education. While no doubt it is often helpful for girls that many of their early examples of role models and authority figures are female, children are very canny about figuring out the real status of adults in their world. Thus, by third or fourth grade, many children will understand that while teachers are widely praised, they are poorly paid. Worse, since in the very early grades a young child often perceives her teacher as a kind of surrogate parent or caretaker, the experience of having so many women teachers may only confirm the child's perception that in our society women, and only women, take care of the children. Even when they work outside the home, that's their role.

Another disturbing finding is that the very qualities that teachers praise in little girls—their cooperativeness and friendliness, their ability to sit still in class, their eagerness to follow the rules—may stand in the way of their academic success in later years.[10] As the Sadkers put it in *Failing at Fairness*, teachers "do not realize the high academic and emotional price many girls pay for being too good." The Sadkers conclude that "girls receive less time, less help, and fewer challenges," than boys. "Reinforced for passivity, their independence and self-esteem suffer." Willingness to follow directions can turn into stifling dependency on an authority figure; quietness can conceal a lack of real intellectual participation; a desire to get the "right" answer all the time can deteriorate into a paralyzing fear of making a mistake. Seven-year-old Breah comes home from school worried and upset because her teacher said her paper was good but not great, while praise and criticism alike seem to bounce off her brother without making a dent. Why is it that the "good girls" of second and third grade turn into the apathetic, uninvolved girls of junior high, and lose their lead, particularly in math and science, when they get to high school?

One theory is that elementary school teachers actively work to remedy little boys' relative educational "deficits"—their inability to sit still, to control impulses, to use fine motor skills—while neglecting little girls' "deficits"—their comparatively weaker gross motor skills, spatial perceptions, willingness to explore and take risks. The teacher is often absent during recess and extracurricular activities, where these skills are most often developed.[11] The reason reading clinics abound, some argue, is that boys typically have far more trouble with reading than girls; far fewer clinics or special programs are available in math and science, problem subjects for many girls.[12] Later on, these deficits, which are not even perceived as such by teachers in the early years, may catch up and inhibit girls. As we discuss later, simply providing equal access to all activities may not be good enough if the little girls don't take advantage of them. While an adult may properly be faulted for failing to seize an opportunity, it is asking an awful lot of a seven-year-old girl to throw herself into the boys' football game (assuming they'll permit it) or to demand a turn at the classroom computer even though none of the other girls does. She may need some help and encouragement from the adults around her to do the unconventional.

It would be far too simplistic to place the blame entirely on sexist teachers. Little girls enter school with their own very firmly established attitudes, assumptions, and behaviors, learned from parents and television, among others. As we discussed in Chapter 3, children in nursery school spend a good deal of time developing their gender identity, which inevitably includes a lot of cultural baggage about what little girls can and cannot do. One of the few sex differences that teachers and school psychologists consistently mentioned to us was that girls ask for help more than boys. "Girls are the tuggers," as one teacher put it. "They very much want to do it right and they ask for help much more than boys do. Boys are not as insecure. Either the boys don't realize that they don't know how to do something, or they try to pass it off, a kind of macho thing." The boys we observed in classrooms projected an aura of "I know what I'm doing," even when they really hadn't the faintest idea, while many of the girls needed that little pat on the head. Studies have shown that such differences are already in place in preschools, and that they can be traced to a complex interaction between unconscious attitudes on the part of teachers and "preprogrammed" behaviors of the children learned at home. Preschool teachers claimed in one study that they objected to girls' "clinginess," but the researchers noted that the teachers failed to pay much attention to the girls unless they were close by.[13] In other words, the teachers were reenforcing the very dependency that they claimed to object to. In the same study, teachers were observed giving the boys step-by-step instructions that would enable them to learn to do things for themselves. Girls were left far more often to "pick stuff up on their own," forcing them to ask for help when they were unable to accomplish the task.

Some of the ostensibly sexist behavior that elementary school teachers display may in fact be an attempt to compensate for preexisting sex differences. For example, a teacher who made more eye contact with boys during "class meeting" might be trying to play fair, since she had just spent a good chunk of time helping out some of the more dependent, "tugging" girls. Or she might be trying to find out whether the boys' independence was a front for incompetence. Similarly, neatness is a quality that is important to many girls before they enter kindergarten. If the teacher does not praise them for neatness, girls may feel disappointed or wonder why their efforts are not being rewarded. Praising a boy for neatness, on the other hand, may leave him vulnerable to the teasing of his male classmates. Correcting sexism is not the only item on the agenda of today's teachers. Good teachers respond to the individual needs and gifts of each child; sometimes what looks like sexism may actually be a way of stimulating and involving a little girl in school.

Still another form of subtle sexism has been identified through the attribution theory. Dr. Gail Melson, a professor of child development and family studies at Purdue, explains: "Studies suggest that girls who succeed in science and math say they did well because they tried hard. Boys think they did well in these subjects because they are smart. Teachers also make these discriminatory attributions."[14] Carol Dweck, a professor of education at Harvard, offers another example: When girls make a mistake in class, the teacher is more likely to tell them simply, "That's wrong," whereas when a boy makes the same mistake, the teacher is more likely to say, "You would have answered correctly if you had done your homework."[15] Boys hear that they are capable and, if they work, they will succeed, while girls hear that they may succeed if they work very hard but that there is the possibility that they simply lack the ability. Thus a girl who begins to make mistakes is more likely than a boy to give up.

Finally, children themselves are powerful enforcers of sexist attitudes. "Males describe themselves as more powerful, ambitious, energetic, and as perceiving themselves as having more control over external events than females."[16] Girls' lack of confidence leads them not only to depend on the teacher for help more than boys do, but to concede defeat when faced with male competition. A recent study by the American Association of University Women reports that as girls approach adolescence their self-esteem dwindles even further.[17] This is one of the reasons that girls' academic performance, particularly in math and science, tends to slip later. (For more about girls and math, see page 120). According to one social psychologist, children of all ages tend to stereotype math and science as masculine pursuits.[18] Although this is unlikely to be an issue for your kindergartner, it will be soon.

In early elementary school, children's sex stereotyping comes into play more in social and play situations than in academics. Although in many cases the girls and boys part company by mutual consent, there is some evidence that boys' groups are more exclusive than girls' groups in elementary school.[19] Several parents have told us that their daughters came home in tears in first or second grade when their longtime male friends suddenly rejected them publicly. (For more about girls' and boys' attitudes toward each other, see pages 166–173). Girls, however, do seem to be winning acceptance on the playing field. A number of parents have told us stories about daughters determined to play soccer or T-ball on the playground during recess, which meant breaking into the boys' game. Often a teacher or school official had to intervene at first, but eventually the boys gave in. Once one token girl broke the all-male ranks, those with the interest and ability followed. One teacher recalled a girl's complaint that the boys would not let her play soccer. "The boys insisted that girls can't play as well as they could and she would wreck the game. We all went out on the playground to work it out, and she was *great*— ten times better than the boys. The boys just stood there with their mouths open. After that, she played whenever she wanted." In her study of elementary school children in the late '70s and early '80s, Raphaela Best confirms that a very determined, physically adept girl can break into the boys' games.[20] It's much less likely, however, that a girl with average physical skills will be welcome. Her skills and confidence in some sports will not develop, and may even atrophy.

The bottom line is that our elementary school teachers and principals have made substantial progress in identifying and trying to deal with sexism in the classroom, but there's still a long way to go. This goes for parents too. One study reveals that a child's self-concept has more to do with her parents' beliefs about her ability than with her own past performance.[21] In other words, if you think your daughter is going to have trouble with math, or science, or whatever, she is likely to agree with you, even if she has consistently done well in previous grades. If you think it's inconceivable that your daughter might ever work as a mechanic, pilot, or chemist, then it's unlikely to occur to her either. If we believe in our daughters, they'll believe in themselves. And if they believe in themselves, they will be well equipped to deal with whatever sexism they do encounter in school.

Helping Little Girls Succeed in the Classroom

The whole topic of sex differences, as considered in Chapter 1, opens up a morass of complicated, perhaps unanswerable questions about nature versus nurture, culture versus biology, conditioning versus innate abilities and predispositions, and so on. Putting this debate firmly to one side, and acknowledging the fact that there are more and wider differences within individuals of the same sex than between the sexes as groups, it is still worthwhile to discuss some of the typical behaviors and problems that arise for girls at school. These may not be issues for *your* daughter, but they are worth knowing about nonetheless, since they influence teaching methods and school policies.

One underlying difference between boys' and girls' behavior is illustrated by Marissa's behavior. A kindergartner, she reported to her parents one evening that Jeffrey had brought his magic kit to the classroom show-and-tell. One of his tricks was designed to produce an optical illusion that two objects of equal size were actually different sizes, but Marissa wasn't fooled. Marissa recounted, however, that she had only whispered her discovery to her friend because she didn't want Jeffrey "to feel upset." Marissa's mother commented, "Marissa has always been a kind child, and I am proud of her for that. Still, I couldn't help feeling a little twinge of disappointment that she hadn't spoken up and shown the teacher and the other children how smart she is."

Marissa's considerateness and her relative disinterest in scoring a competitive point are not unusual. As Carol Gilligan notes in her discussion of the games girls play, "Traditional girls' games like jump rope and hopscotch are turn-taking games, where competition is indirect since one person's success does not necessarily signify another's failure."[22] Gilligan notes that other researchers have found that when conflict erupts in the course of a game, girls are more likely to abandon the game apparently in order to preserve good relationships with other children, while boys are more likely to persist by relying on relatively elaborate rules to resolve conflicts—when fists don't, that is. Most researchers, and most parents, agree that boys seem more accustomed to dealing with head-on competition, and this significant social difference has an impact on the way they learn. In a school setting, girls often do better in small cooperative groups where they can trade information, share ideas, and work together as a team. Some boys, on the other hand, may learn better on their own because they prefer to come out on top all by themselves. A timid girl, who freezes up when asked to do a task alone, may be able to relax when she has the support of a small group. A boy working in a small group, however, might hoard information. In a less extreme example, he may simply feel less threatened by the competition inherent in many school assignments where each child is asked to come up with an answer alone. Finally, girls' relative lack of competitiveness may mislead some teachers into thinking that they are not interested in the subject or that they haven't figured out the answer yet.

Girls' reluctance to compete is not necessarily all bad, however. Competitive or not, most little girls do as well as or better than boys in elementary school. Many educators believe that all children learn better in cooperative, rather than competitive, atmospheres. Many schools are experimenting with teaching techniques that put less emphasis on speed and competition, particularly in math and science, where traditional teaching techniques have been blamed for generating needless anxiety for girls and boys. One lesson is that, while you should encourage your little girl to speak up for herself and to compete when appropriate, you should also value her cooperative nature. As Marissa's mother put it, "After mulling it over a bit, I finally realized that she had made the right choice. Show-and-tell is just a fun time for the kids; it's not the time to show the teacher what a genius you are. When Marissa decided not to burst Jeffrey's bubble, she really was just playing along with the game. Probably every kid in the room was too."

Learning to Read

"In first grade, one of the early reports we got about our older daughter was how well she was reading," reports a mother of two girls. "We didn't even know she could read. It turned out she was at the point where all the pieces fell together at the right moment. She picked it up without even trying. Now my younger daughter is teaching herself to read in kindergarten."

The stereotype that girls have an easier time reading than boys does have some truth in it.[23] Why should this be? There are no hard-and-fast answers, but we do have a number of theories. To the extent that girls have an edge over boys in verbal ability—one of the few consistently found sex differences (see Chapter 1)—it follows that reading would come more naturally. More controversial is the notion, also examined in Chapter 1, that girls are more aurally oriented and thus better able to learn to read by sounding out words through phonics—still the dominant method for teaching reading today. (On the other hand, more visually oriented boys should be better at whole word recognition, a technique in which children learn to recognize simple words and gradually build to bigger words by combining recognized words, prefixes, and suffixes.)

Studies have found that divorce has a more devastating impact on a boy's academic progress than a girl's (see Chapter 8), that first-grade boys from broken homes fall further behind in reading than girls do. Some studies report that girls read better because they are more interested in the subject matter.[24] One mother reports that her third-grade daughter loves to read novels about the lives of women—*Anne of Green Gables, The Secret Garden*, and the books of Laura Ingalls Wilder. Although the inner-city school she attends is deficient in many materials, these classics are readily available.

Our theory is that most little girls learn to read because they enjoy the activity itself. Reading is private time that lends itself to imagination and fantasy. The little girl who spent many hours talking to her dolls or coloring is likely to enjoy her books. Andrea, mother of eight-year-old Susannah, says that the first place she looks for her daughter is Susannah's bed. More often than not, Susannah is there, reading. Sophie, another eight-year-old, enjoys many of the books her mother remembers loving: *Peter Pan, The Wind in the Willows*. In fact, some parents we talked to reported that they actually felt their little girls spent too much time reading and urged them to go outdoors and play more.

Again, these stories are common, not universal. Although girls generally read sooner and more proficiently than boys, some little girls have trouble reading just as some little boys excel at it. It's a disservice to assume that just because she is a girl, your daughter will automatically become a good reader. If you want your daughter to be a reader, you should read to her frequently starting in infancy. One father gave his daughter presents only on birthdays and Christmas, but would always buy her a book she was truly interested in. "If you want your children to be bright and do well in school, there's one thing you should do every day—read to them," advises a nursery school director. Make a habit of visiting the local library, and ask the children's librarians for help with choosing age-appropriate books. You can find out how much your daughter is getting out of her books by asking her simple questions as you read. Ask a toddler to point to the green balloon or why she thinks the little rabbit is crying. Ask a preschooler what a cocoon is or why the little girl in the book wouldn't share her birthday presents with her sister. Many little girls love making books of their own. Emily used to dictate stories to us and then do the illustrations herself. Now that she can write all the letters of the alphabet, she writes the books herself, asking us how to spell the words. Just recently she started writing down the words by herself, making up the spelling as she goes along. Keeping your little girl well supplied with books, as well as with paper, pencils, crayons, and staples, will foster her interest in learning to read when she gets to first grade. You might also encourage her to "read" books to younger siblings: even if she is just making up words to go with the pictures or repeating text that she has memorized, she will feel proud, and little siblings will enjoy the extra attention.

Hilary, a seven-year-old girl now in second grade, shows signs of becoming a problem reader. A hesitant, quiet, rather nervous child, she withdrew in kindergarten partly because she was afraid of her overly controlling, perfectionist teacher. Although she felt a lot happier with her first-grade teacher, she was already well behind the other children in her ability to identify and write letters, and she still tends to say letters backward. Together, teacher and parents are helping Hilary overcome her disadvantage without undue pressure. Her mother spoke of Hilary's slowness in reading as "an area of concern" but not of alarm. Identifying the problem early and working on it calmly is the best thing that Hilary's parents and teacher could have done for her.

A little girl, who is a competent reader in first and second grades, can get "turned off" if she's bored by the materials used in school. One writer told that her daughter wasn't paying attention in her fourth-grade reading class until the mother suggested that the teacher include some stories about famous women. The little girl's interest picked right up, and the teacher was delighted with the addition to the classroom library. A child may also be bored by reading material that is either much too difficult or much too easy. If your daughter is ahead of her grade in reading, talk to the teacher to see if he or she can modify your daughter's lessons a little to keep her stimulated. And, of course, you should supplement your daughter's reading at home with whatever books would appeal to her. (For more about keeping tabs on your daughter's progress in school, see page 150.)

Girls and Math

About a decade ago a small storm of words whipped through the news media because of an article in *Science* called "Sex Differences in Math Ability: Fact or Artifact" by Camilla Benbow and Julian Stanley.[25] The article reported a study of seventh- and eighth-grade students (both male and female) who showed especially high abilities in math. These students were given the math college board Scholastic Aptitude Test (SAT), a test normally administered to students in the eleventh and twelfth grades. Girls scored 7 percent to 15 percent lower than the boys, and boys led girls in placing in the "very high ranges" by a margin of as much as ten to one. The authors concluded that boys have a genetic advantage over girls in mathematics.

The popular press picked up on the issue in a big way.[26] Follow-up studies showed that after seeing the news stories based on the *Science* article, parents (particularly mothers) whose confidence in their daughters' mathematical abilities was shaky to begin with had pretty much written their daughters off as math students. Why bother forcing girls to study math if even the gifted girls were easily outranked by boys? Girls are good at plenty of other things.

Feminists, as one might imagine, let out a howl of protest. Articles and studies poured out proving that girls are disadvantaged in math by prejudiced teachers and parents; that girls tend to take far fewer math courses than boys, and so are less well prepared for achievement tests; that from birth boys are showered with toys fostering visual-spatial abilities (blocks, trucks, baseballs, erector sets, gyroscopes) while girls are not; that as early as second grade teachers spend more time teaching math to boys and reading to girls; that starting in junior high, predominantly male math teachers use examples that predominantly boys can relate to—speeds of trains and rockets; gear ratios; fuel volume. Math, in short, argued the feminists, has long been a male bastion, and even gifted girls don't stand a chance. If you could find a girl whose mother and father both loved math and felt convinced from their daughter's birth that she would excel at it; if you could arrange to have her taught by women who made an extra effort to encourage girls to love math; if you could find her math books that used nonsexist problems; if you could encourage her to stick with math all through junior high and high school; then and only then could you hope to conduct a fair study comparing the math abilities of girls and boys.

One recent study indicates that the feminists may in fact be on to something. In an article published in *American Psychologist* in 1988, Alan Feingold concluded that, based on an analysis of PSAT and SAT scores from 1960 to 1983, "gender differences declined precipitously." Although boys had caught up to girls on the verbal section of the PSAT, girls were fast closing the gap in verbal reasoning, abstract reasoning, and numerical ability. Furthermore, they had reduced by half their lag in mechanical aptitude, space relations, and PSAT math scores. One stubborn and disturbing sex difference remained constant over the thirteen years of the study: boys continued to outnumber girls at the upper levels of performance on high school mathematics.[27] Even though high school girls are closing the gap in math, the question of why elementary school girls lose their lead in math performance after age thirteen remains unanswered. Nor have scientists come up with a persuasive biological explanation. It is primarily culture that holds women back.

In the meantime, however, your first- or second-grader is likely to do well at arithmetic. So why not wait until age thirteen to worry about these issues? The concern is really with the future—with attitudes and assumptions that may have a long-term impact on your daughter's performance in math. If teachers and parents actively encourage a girl's interest and mastery in elementary math, her self-confidence and genuine enthusiasm for the subject at age thirteen will help her weather the storm of peer pressure and other cultural forces. Even better, if her friends are similarly encouraged, this peer-group stereotyping is unlikely to prevail in the first place.

If a girl persists in math study through at least four years of high school, a world of career opportunities will remain open to her. Otherwise, the failure of girls to pursue advanced mathematics in high school and college "severely limits the career opportunities of females in exactly those areas of employment that offer some of the highest and least sex-discriminatory salaries."[28] For example, without four years of high school math your daughter will be ineligible for college calculus, a prerequisite for almost every major in the sciences, math, or economics. Even an interest in studying history would be hampered by this inadequate preparation for statistics.[29] Although girls are studying more math now than they did ten or twenty years ago, the latest statistics from the U.S. Department of Education show that on average girls still complete slightly less than three years of high school mathematics.[30]

Three key factors keep girls out of advanced math courses: anxiety that they will not succeed (math anxiety),[31] sex stereotyping of math as masculine, and an attitude that math will not be useful in future careers.[32] Parents of daughters believe that their girls had to work harder to succeed at math than did parents of sons, and parents of sons believed that advanced math was more important than did parents of daughters.[33] And of course parental (especially maternal) attitudes become self-fulfilling prophecies. As "mothers lowered their expectations for their daughters' math performance" after the *Science* article was widely publicized, "their daughters' math anxiety increased. Since math anxiety is directly related to scores, one may hypothesize that subsequent math scores declined."[34] Eventually, girls drop out of higher level math courses because the effort to succeed strikes them as overwhelmingly large. By high school, students are entrenched in the view that math is a masculine pursuit; girls who like and excel in math may be viewed as unfeminine.[35]

"Girls may receive no support for early interests in math and science from parents, little encouragement from teachers, and perhaps even antagonism from boys," sums up Joanne R. Becker, an associate professor of mathematics and computer science at San Jose State University.[36] The clear message for us as parents is to support our little girls' interest in math early on (kindergarten is not too soon), to help them enjoy math, and to let them know that we believe in their mathematical abilities.

One surprise hazard is the math "fast track," accelerated courses for gifted math students. The danger is for the girls who don't make it. As Dr. Edes Gilbert of The Spence School in Manhattan put it, "Girls who are perfectly good math students in eighth grade may be utterly defeated if they are not accepted into the accelerated program in high school. They just give up."[37] Part of the problem may be that many Americans believe that mathematical—and scientific—ability require some kind of special gift that few of us have. The flip side of that belief is that math, at least at more advanced levels, cannot be taught unless the student is gifted. Dr. Gilbert would disagree. "I believe that we can teach every girl in this school to be proficient at math, including calculus."[38] While the girls at an elite private school are no doubt unusually able, we think her point holds true for all schools. It is simply unrealistic in a society such as ours to think that mathematical proficiency is any less important than the ability to read and write proficiently. The lesson for parents, we think, is to support every child's study of math; don't give up just because your daughter doesn't seem to be a whiz.

"Parents should try to make math as much a part of their daughters' lives as reading," says Professor Elizabeth Fennema of the University of Wisconsin.[39] This means taking the time to introduce simple mathematical concepts into your daughters' everyday routines. Get her used to the idea of counting objects that she likes to play with—how many little Lego building squares will fit on the large rectangular piece; how many fish are in the fish tank; how many bunnies live under her bed. Introduce addition and subtraction using her toys, or by asking her to figure out how many years older than her little brother she is. Buy her games and puzzles that use numbers or simple math concepts. Provide construction toys to teach her about spatial and mechanical relationships. Encourage her to play active outdoor games, especially ball games, that teach the relation of distance, speed, and force. Again, it's not a matter of pressuring her into math, but rather of drawing on her interests and making her comfortable with the numerical side of things.

Lots of little girls like math. If you see a spark of enthusiasm, fan it—gently. You may be surprised how simple things can interest a child. Our daughter Emily has developed an interest in adding and subtracting, but her calculations were largely limited to counting on her fingers. Thanks to a friend's suggestion, we bought her a set of stacking cups that were graded by size and numbered from one to twelve. At first Emily was disappointed at receiving such a "baby" toy, but she was fascinated when I filled the four cup and the eight cup with Cheerios and suggested that she see if all the Cheerios would fit in the twelve cup. She spent another hour happily exploring which combination of cups would contain all the cereal. In the end, there were Cheerios all over the place, but the mess was worth the fun—and the learning.

Parents who suffer from "math anxiety"—those of us who have always felt inept with numbers and panic at the idea of computing a tip or balancing a checkbook without a calculator—may have an especially tough time conveying the message that "math is fun." But even the most mathematically incompetent among us can keep pace with elementary school math. If you give your daughter a positive send-off in the early years, she'll be that much more likely to hold her own later on. Try to avoid statements like, "I always *hated* math!" or "I was never any good in math!" You don't have to masquerade as a mathematical whiz, but try not to brag that you don't know what a slide rule is for.

One father reported, "I had always hated math in school, when I couldn't do the multiplication tables as fast as the other kids. Even though I use a fair amount of math on the job, I still get anxious if I'm confronted with a type of problem I'm not used to. The funny thing was that when Sandy started to ask for help sometimes with her arithmetic homework, I suddenly realized how simple and logical math is. She's doing geometry now. I'm enjoying it, and I think Sandy really gets a charge out of teaching me."

Too much help, on the other hand, can undermine a child's confidence. When she was growing up, Kelly, a mother of three, reported that the men in Kelly's family were all scientists. Although she was good at math, whenever she asked her father for help, he would insist on going back to the very basics. Not only was this boring and a waste of time, eventually she concluded that her father really didn't have any confidence in her ability. "I try very hard not to give that message," Kelly says now. "When my kids ask for help on their homework, I try just to answer the question they asked. Sometimes I bite my tongue, because I can see that they're going off on the wrong track, but it's better that they figure that out for themselves."

Dan, a New York City father, talked about how annoyed he felt when his daughter couldn't master simple math concepts in first grade: "I felt she was getting so much reading—maybe *too* much—and I wanted her to be rounded out, so I tried to help her with her math homework. But I quickly got frustrated. She just wasn't *getting* it, and I kept thinking, 'How can she be so stupid?' Finally I backed off. Her teacher is good, her attitude is positive. As long as the exposure is there, she'll get it eventually."

There are several excellent books that provide suggestions with math and math-oriented games that you can play with your child. Educational television shows, like "3-2-1 Contact!," may also help. (For a list of some resources on math, see the Appendix at page 265.) If your child's only exposure to math is via workbooks, don't be very surprised if she thinks it's boring. Give her a variety of contexts. If you are building a bookshelf or knitting a sweater, show her how to figure out how much wood or yarn you need. When you drive over a bridge, speculate on why it's holding you up. Point out women who use math: politicians, executives, school principals, bank officers. Your little girl should realize that math isn't just the province of brainy guys with glasses.

Some studies have indicated that girls do well in elementary math because they can use rote techniques that they have memorized. Boys, on the other hand, seem to be somewhat better at solving problems where no exact methodology has been taught.[40] This may partially explain why girls begin slipping behind in math as the problems become increasingly abstract. As one elementary school teacher put it, "Girls make the transition to abstract reasoning in math more slowly than boys. You have to give them more 'hands-on' experience, for longer." Show your little girl how math can solve a variety of problems in the real world, for example, dividing an apple so that three people all get the same amount. She should not go through elementary school equating math with multiplication tables or feeling that there is just one right way to solve a problem with math.

In this technology-driven economy there are fewer and fewer jobs that don't demand some facility with mathematical concepts. Indeed, many Americans worry that our children's relatively poor mastery of math and science may make this country less competitive in the world economy. And certainly, many of the highest paying and most prestigious jobs demand mathematical expertise. Girls, however, may not be getting a clear message that we, their parents, think they are going to need math. For example, in a recent survey by the Educational Testing Service, most seventh-grade girls thought that math was useful but only 40 percent of them thought that they would use it in later life. That percentage did not change for girls in eleventh grade. In contrast, 48 percent of the seventh-grade boys thought they would use math in later life, and by 11th grade 53 percent thought they would.[41]

Parents may also have to intervene at school. Will, a father of two daughters in Baltimore, says his third-grader, Kate, "has always done very well in math and last year she loved her teacher and that made it even better. But this year [third grade] she got off on the wrong foot with a diagnostic test and was put into the slower math group. It turned out, the slower group was using the same book that she had used in second grade, so essentially she would be repeating math. We saw the assistant principal and got her moved into the higher group, and it turns out she is doing just as well in the higher group. But the experience seems to have soured her on the subject. We tried to justify the move, but we were desperate not to make her feel pressured. I don't know if we've succeeded or not." Will's wife Kathy still remembers a math teacher who used to seat the children in rows according to how they had done on that week's math test. One day he stood a girl at the top of the bleachers and asked her whether she would bet her life on the right answer. All the girls in the class hated him from then on, and many ended up hating math as well.

Donna, a Milwaukee mother of three, reports seven-year-old Breah loves reading because she excels at it but already seems a little bit tense about math. "She comes home with stories about Nathan, the math wizard, who is super-quick at answering all the math questions. She has noticed boys seem to lead the class in math, and this disturbs her."

Patricia Lund Casserly of the Educational Testing Service in Princeton reports that since many girls are unaware of their talents in math, teachers have to inform them and remind them. "Teachers who identified their talent and encouraged them to 'do something important' with it as early as age eight or nine were important influences."[42] Julie Olson, the principal of Diamond Path Elementary School in Apple Valley, Minnesota, meets with students in groups of five and stresses the importance of math. "I was a math major," she notes, "and the kids know I love math. I have an eight-foot picture of Einstein in my office. In our small group meetings we discuss what it takes to be a scientist." The girls in Olson's school are doubly impressed that their principal is a woman and that she loves and uses math. The teachers at Diamond Path help their students see the usefulness of math in the "real world." In kindergarten, math is "hands on," with beads to string in patterns or buttons and bottle tops to arrange in multiples of various numbers. A favorite math game is to estimate the number of M&M's in a bag. Later, the children run a store in class, computing the transactions and keeping track of the accounts.

Casserly, Becker, and others offer these suggestions to stimulate girls' interest and performance in math:

• Screen math textbooks carefully for sexism.
• Whenever possible, use math problems drawn from social science or physical science or from everyday life.
• Offer role models of women using math effectively in everyday situations and at work, and talk about famous female mathematicians or scientists.
• Have the children work on math in small groups sometimes rather than always individually. As we previously noted, cooperative learning situations benefit girls. Grouping girls by math ability will give them class companions who work at their level and who will serve as future allies in combating the teasing of competitive boys. (Such teasing is generally at its worst in ninth grade.)

You might want to discuss some of the suggestions with your daughter's teacher or bring them up at a PTA meeting. A number of parents mentioned to us that their daughters' first experience of the "pop quiz" or weekly test was in math in third grade, and this really turned them off the subject. "My daughter reacts badly to math tests," complained one mother. "The pressure really makes her panic." Talk with your daughter's teacher about ways to eliminate the pressured, competitive atmosphere that often pervades math instruction. You'll be doing the boys a favor too.

Some studies suggest that girls do better at math when they are taught by women, but the parents and school principals we spoke to all rejected this notion. One father reported that his daughter really flipped for a male math teacher in second grade. "He was different. The women teachers were into establishing rules and keeping a controlled and quiet classroom. This male teacher walked into class the first day bouncing a basketball and put his feet up on the desk. She thought he was funny and she did very well in math." Julie Olson says that the science teacher in her elementary school is a man and he's worked out wonderfully for both girls and boys: "The kids really relate to his enthusiasm. The girls get into science because of him. It's the first time they have a male teacher, and it's really a thrill for them."

Girls Incorporated, a nationwide organization, runs Operation SMART through its local affiliates and community-based organizations to encourage girls to get more involved in math and science. The after-school program, which is for all ages, emphasizes hands-on experimentation and exploration using computers, tools, and building projects. Career development is also part of the program, even for younger girls. Ellen Wahl, the project director, notes that Operation SMART has succeeded in changing the educational and career paths of many girls. "We've seen girls enter the program thinking they would be cosmeticians who ended up going into environmental science instead," notes Wahl. For more information about the program, contact Girls Incorporated, Operation SMART, 30 E. 33 St., 7th floor, New York, N.Y. 10016, (212) 689-3700.

Making Science Fun

With a little extra effort, you can find ways to make science, like math, fun all through the year. One father described how a family vacation to the seashore turned into a wonderful introduction to marine biology for a five-year-old girl, with after-dark observations of luminescent algae, seashell collections, and readings of simple picture books about the characteristic plants and animals of the shore, the sea, and the salt marsh. Similarly, visits to mountains, canyons, and deserts can be used to discuss simple concepts of geology; books and pamphlets written for children are available at the visitor's centers of many national parks.

Parents have shared some other good suggestions with us:

One day my second-grade daughter brought a box of rocks to school, and her teacher started a discussion about rocks—how they're formed, the different types. Out of this discussion grew the idea of the kids working with the teacher on writing a book about geology. Then the teacher had a weekend at the shore and brought back rocks for every child in the class. It turned into a big project and my daughter really enjoyed the whole thing.

My father-in-law is a physicist and he talks to my kindergartner, Amanda, all the time about what he does. Astronauts, planets, and rockets are her major interests.

My daughter collects rocks and seashells, and we talk about what she finds. Identifying a new rock can be the highlight of her day.

I have always loved botany and I talk about trees and leaves to the girls (aged eight and six). Hilary, who's eight, was fascinated by a unit on rocks and minerals she did at school. She talked a lot about classifying rocks by their hardness and glossiness.

My third-grader became fascinated by volcanoes, and her grandparents sent us all sorts of photos of volcanoes from their trip to Hawaii. She was in awe when I told her that I climbed Mount Saint Helens. We've done a lot of reading about it together.

Our third-grade daughter gets very little science in school, but she shows a lot of interest in earth science and biology. We have signed her up for Saturday morning courses at the city's science museum. In one course they studied water, and I remember her talking excitedly about how a plant draws water up through its roots and stem. When she was six she loved the course on dino-saurs. In the earth science course they talked a lot about the structure of the earth and they built a volcano. That was a big hit with all the kids.

My third-grade daughter just finished a big report on porcupines, and she really threw herself into it. It was quite elaborate. She wrote about their habits, their ene-mies, fun facts. The teacher sent her home with some quills to examine. She talked about things that are like porcupines, like spiny fish and cactus. I learned a lot. . . . They also did a school project in which they had two rats and they fed one cola and the other one milk and studied the effects. She got to take home one of the rats one weekend. She thought it was great, but I wasn't too thrilled. . . .

Girls' relative lack of proficiency in science, particularly by junior high school,[43] seems to have its source in many of the same cultural factors that undermine girls' ability in math. One writer and science teacher asked a group of little girls to draw a picture of a scientist: without exception, each produced a picture of a male figure with glasses, the classic image of a male "brain."[44] School and TV provide very few examples of female scientists. An occasional pi-ous reference to Madame Curie is overwhelmed by males, from Galileo to the Ghostbusters. Particularly as she ap-proaches adolescence, your daughter may perceive being "scientific" as unfeminine and uncool—something for those weird boys with glasses. Science instruction in her elemen-tary school may consist of boring classes devoted to read-ing out loud from a science textbook, with little or no hands-on experience. Your little girl may gain the impres-sion that science is about "things," permits no room for emotions, and has very little relevance to anything she really cares about.

What can you do? A starting point is to realize that in elementary school imparting specific factual information is much less important than developing a zest for scientific inquiry and some basic skills for examining the physical world in an orderly, rational manner. As we've said before, school is important, but your attitude is even more so. You can begin by generating some curiosity about phenomena right under your little girl's nose. Does your little girl realize that her pediatrician is a scientist? How does the doctor know when that sore throat needs an antibiotic and when it will go away by itself? You might suggest that your daughter ask at her next checkup. If the doctor has the time, it would be wonderful if he or she would describe when she decided to be a doctor and what she had to study to be one. To a very young child, you might talk about nutrition. What happens to that peanut butter after you eat it? Where does it go in your body? What does your body do with it? Is there peanut butter in your toes? How could you find out? What about that TV set that your daughter is so fond of, or the computer? How does it work? Could she open up the back and look inside? Why do all the leaves fall off the trees in autumn, and what makes them come back in the spring? How come that fly can walk on the ceiling? Bugs and worms aren't yucky, they're interesting. Let's watch them! Why do some toys float in the bathtub and others sink? Can your daughter form a hypothesis and test it? For more ideas on simple science projects for young children, see *What Will Happen If . . . Young Children and the Scientific Method* by Barbara Sprung, Merle Froschl, and Patricia B. Campbell (New York: Education Equity Concepts, 1985).

You should make a conscious effort to provide toys that expose your little girl to spatial and mechanical concepts: bowling and basketball games, construction toys, science experiment sets for older girls. Make use of facilities in your community, libraries, zoos, natural history and science museums. Try to point out people, particularly women, who use science in their work. Do you use science at work? At home? Make sure your little girl knows that. So many little girls say things like "Boys are doctors, girls are nurses," even when a woman in the family, sometimes even Mommy, is a physician.

Pay attention to the quality of the science instruction in school. At one elementary school, the teachers themselves complained about the quality of the available science texts and won a small grant to write their own textbook, which the children seem to like a lot. This is a rare success story. Curricular changes are often slow and may not do your little girl any good. In the short term you can try to enhance the science teaching by raising the issue with the PTA and the principal, volunteering your services, or enlisting help from friends who have some useful scientific background. One mother offered to do a demonstration of how yeast works; a grandfather led a nature walk identifying different species of trees; a father built an electric circuit in class with a light that would indicate when the bathroom was occupied. These are just the kind of hands-on "real world" science projects that girls respond to most enthusiastically.

Computers in the Classroom

At the school orientation meeting we were excited to learn that there was a computer in our daughter's kindergarten classroom for playing letter and number matching games. But a month into the school year, she still hadn't used it. "Computers are boy things," Emily reported. "They *really* know what to do with them." Maybe the boys had taken over control of the computer and weren't letting the girls use it, we suggested, imagining a gang of leather-clad, pint-sized male hackers standing shoulder to shoulder around the terminal. "Nah," Emily answered, already bored with the subject. "I just don't feel like using it."

Emily's indifference is not atypical. In a second-grade class, we observed exactly the same phenomenon. The half hour before gym was designated a quiet work period in which the children were to operate, without direct guidance from the teacher. After explaining their options, the teacher mentioned, almost as an afterthought, that they should take turns on the computer and she asked Katie to begin. The program was a computer game in which the children used the directional keys to hunt for a number hidden within a checkerboard pattern. Katie spent about five minutes at the computer, playing the game with quiet absorption. When Katie got up, Keith and Jeffrey sat down at the computer together, talking and playing the game quietly, but with more enthusiasm than Katie showed. Keith was called to his small group reading instruction, and Michael took the next turn at the computer. Then, when his reading group broke, Keith returned to the computer. Next Scott sat down, then Eric, then Spencer. Spencer had been bored and restless during most of the quiet work period, but he settled down intently at the computer for five minutes.

When the quiet work period was over, the teacher asked whether everyone had taken a turn on the computer. Nearly all the boys nodded yes. Aside from Katie, not a single girl had used the computer; they simply had no interest in using it.

Studies back up this impression. Junior and senior high school girls were found to make much less use of optional computer time in class than boys. Boys were also more likely to have access to home computers.[45] Although nearly every public elementary school in the United States now provides some computers for the children,[46] access alone may not be adequate. Rather, teachers and parents need to demonstrate appealing uses of the computer to girls, get friends to use the computer together, and work to counter the stereotype of the computer as a "boy thing," as our five-year-old put it. If you can afford to buy a home computer that your daughter could use, do so. However, Elizabeth Fennema cautions that "just buying a computer is not going to make a big difference. It's what you do with it after you have it that is important."[47] Take the time to teach your daughter how to use the computer, find out what sort of software she finds most appealing, and try to match the software to her level of ability. Too often home computers are used almost exclusively for competitive and violent video games which turn a lot of girls off. Try to get your daughter to mix fun and learning by buying age-appropriate software. There are programs that are traditionally educational and others that have applications your daughter may find fun as well as educational, such as graphics that will allow her and her friends to make designs or print a newsletter for the kids on your block. Your school district may subscribe to a listing of educational software which you can consult, or a good computer store may have some helpful suggestions.

Put the computer in a room where all your children have equal access to it. Be aware of the kind of models you, as parents, provide. If Daddy loves to fool around with the computer, but Mommy always says she's too busy or hasn't learned how to work it yet, this, more than anything else, will reinforce a perception that computers aren't really for girls. One mother reported that her eight-year-old daughter was not really interested in a bedtime story now that she read so much and so well to herself, so the father had taken to playing a computer game with his daughter before bed. But the mother, an artist, admitted that she had never learned to use the computer, even for games. While this new twist on the bedtime routine may fuel and sustain the girl's continuing interest in computers, there is some risk that this little girl will eventually conclude from her parents' example that computers are a "male" thing. It would be nice if this mother would take a crack at the computer. She might be pleasantly surprised.

Most of the parents we spoke to painted a slightly more encouraging picture. "The computer is available during free period," said one mother of two daughters, in second grade and kindergarten, "and from what I've seen the kids trample each other to get to it. The children who are fastest get to use it most—it doesn't have anything to do with sex." Holly, the mother of two daughters, one in fifth grade and one in second, said that last year she went to their school every Wednesday to work on the computer with the children in a computer lab. "We wrote stories on the computer, and used it as a tool in creative writing. I found that the girls liked it even better than the boys." "My daughter is definitely interested in using the school computer," noted a mother of a third-grader. "It's both the games and the way she can use it to retrieve information. She really seems excited by it." Mary, the mother of five (two sons and three daughters ranging from fifteen months to nine years), feels that her girls use the home computer in different ways from the boys. "Both the boys and girls like to sit at the computer, but the boys really go for the games. The girls use it to figure out how to spell and to play around with the wording of a sentence."

Computers are proliferating in America's classrooms, but in many cases our teachers and students have not caught up with the technology at their disposal. A recent survey by the Educational Testing Service (ETS) found that most third-graders could identify the parts of a computer, but could not tell it how to perform its functions.[48] In our local school system, all classrooms are equipped with a computer terminal, but the computers are used primarily for learning games on an optional basis until third grade. At that point, children receive short weekly periods of special instruction to help them incorporate computers into their classwork. However, the advantage of computers over traditional teaching methods in elementary schools has by no means been conclusively established, nor is it clear that elementary school students of either sex are really making much use of in-class computers.[49] The ETS study found that computers are often taught about instead of being used as tools. That's like describing a ruler instead of letting a child use it. The study also reported that many teachers, educated before personal computers were widely available, are themselves minimally trained in the use of the computer and are, as you might expect, ambivalent about their value in the classroom.[50] The result may be that many children are not receiving very meaningful instruction on the computer, leaving them with the impression that computers are mainly a kind of high-tech toy. This, in itself, may discourage girls who may be less interested than boys in Nintendo and the like. As Jo Sanders of the Women's Action Alliance points out, girls seem to be more interested in computers as tools for performing useful tasks: writing, spelling, computation, graphics.[51] In a recent study entitled the Computer Equity Expert Project, Sanders found that girls responded very favorably to applying computers to robotics because they were able to see concrete results of their programming. She also recommends that schools (or parents) set up mentoring programs in which older female students take younger girls under their wing in the computer lab and that girls-only days or periods be established in computer labs so that girls don't have to compete with boys for time on-line.

While computer use is only one aspect of a good elementary education, we think it is now generally underutilized and will gradually increase, as more teachers and parents are themselves products of the computer age. At present the major benefit to our young children from classroom computers is familiarity—what computers look like, some conception of what they can do and how to make them do it, what sort of schoolwork they are most helpful with. But even if this is the only benefit, it will stand them in good stead in high school, when computer use really does become important.

Girls at Work and Play: Snapshots from a Second-Grade Class

Psychological studies, interviews with teachers and parents, even conversations with your own children can only tell you so much about what *really* goes on in school. We thought it might be fun—and instructive—to join a class and see for ourselves. It was both. Here are some of the more memorable "snapshots" we took away with us of girls at work and play at a local second-grade class.

First impressions. The classroom is bright and cheerful, with big windows opening onto the playground, a computer terminal at the front, the inevitable blackboard, cubbies along the side wall, and the walls fairly rioting with student projects. Desks are not lined up in rows but pushed together into little "islands" composed of four or five desks, so the students sit in small groups facing each other. When we first walk into the class, the children are very curious about who we are and why we are here, and they keep glancing over at us. But they quickly forget about us and go about their normal routines.

We notice right away that, unlike our daughters' preschool and kindergarten classes, all the girls here are wearing trousers—rather simple corduroy or blue jean trousers at that. Most of them have very long hair done up with barrettes or clips; but as far as dress code goes, they are pretty much indistinguishable from the boys.

Morning meeting. The children all sit on the floor gathered around the teacher, who sits on a rocking chair and leads a kind of freewheeling discussion of current events, the weather, the class schedule, and so on. Katie, Maria, and Erin, who strike us right away as class leaders, sit as close as they possibly can to the teacher (we'll call her Ms. Barnes) without being in her lap. Erin, we later learn, is the class president, a tall and pretty girl with long glossy chestnut hair and a clean-scrubbed, open, friendly face. She has a calm, self-assured manner and seems popular with both girls and boys. Katie is blond, freckled, a bit on the chunky side, and big for her age. She wears thick glasses. She seems like a serious, rather competitive student, eager to please the teacher and to be praised for giving the right answers. Maria has curly, sandy blond hair, a big smile, and tons of confidence. She is not scared to volunteer an answer even when she's wrong. Katie, Maria, and Erin shoot up their hands just about every time Ms. Barnes asks a question, and sometimes they leave them raised even when someone else is called on.

Ms. Barnes is both relaxed and animated, warm and caring and totally in control of the class: she strikes us as the ideal second-grade teacher. She starts by explaining the schedule for the day, discusses the upcoming Halloween parade, and then moves into a discussion about Leonard Bernstein, who has just died. All the children listen quietly, though the girls fidget less than the boys. Ms. Barnes asks the class whether they know what Bernstein did, why he was so famous, and why he is suddenly in the news. Maria and Katie shoot their hands up. They explain that he was a composer and that he has died, but a boy volunteers the exact time and cause of his death. Terryl, a curly-haired, very soft-spoken girl, talks about how famous he was; Erin says her parents thought he was special. Then one of the boys asks whether he's in the book of world records.

We notice that the two Asian girls in the class—Abigail and Wakako—say nothing, but all the other girls participate. About half the boys remain quiet, but two or three of the same boys raise their hands every time there is a question. Ms. Barnes shows no obvious preference for one sex or the other.

Katie mentions that she has brought a clipping in from the newspaper. Although her voice is very soft, she does not seem in the least bit shy. She basks in the attention she is getting from Ms. Barnes. The clipping is about a pitcher on the Boston Red Sox who was thrown out of a game for using abusive language. Ms. Barnes exchanges a twinkling look with us, as if to say, "See what a nonsexist class I run: a *girl* is the one who is up on baseball news!" Both girls and boys participate eagerly in the ensuing discussion of baseball and the World Series (which started that day). The girls are interested and well informed, but the boys really spring to life, showing off their precise (though not always accurate) knowledge of baseball statistics, talking loudly and with animation, arguing about scores, starting lineups, and the like. Maria knows the opposing teams will be the Oakland Athletics and the Cincinnati Reds. "Who won the Series last year?" asks Ms. Barnes, a self-described sports enthusiast. Two girls and four boys raise their hands. "Who do you think will win this year?" she asks. All the boys vote for Oakland, all the girls vote for Cincinnati. (As it turned out, the girls were right: Cincinnati swept the Series that year, much to the surprise of sportscasters, bookies— and Ms. Barnes's second-grade boys.) "What is the magic number of games it takes to win the Series?" Ms. Barnes asks the class. Most of the boys know instantly that it's four.

They move into a discussion of numbers as they fill in the class calendar and figure out how many days they have been in school so far. Ms. Barnes has decorated the October calendar with a repeating pattern of pumpkins placed on each day: first four days with pumpkins facing up, then two days with pumpkins facing down. "Which way should the pumpkin be put today?" she asks. No one really knows the answer. All the numbers on the calendar that are multiples of five or ten are circled. "Should we circle 26?" Maria answers no and explains why not.

Quiet work time. The children have about half an hour of quiet work time before gym, and Ms. Barnes instructs them that during this period they are to write in their journals, read a good book, meet with her in small groups to work on spelling, and use the computer (see above for a discussion of how boys and girls in the class make use of the computer). In general, the girls seem to use the free time more productively than the boys. They waste less time wandering around the classroom; they either find activities quickly or ask Ms. Barnes to help them; they spend less time whispering and daydreaming and more time concentrating on the task before them. The boys seem to concentrate in bursts, the girls in more prolonged stretches of time. Tara, a small and delicate girl with flowing brown hair, spends almost the entire quiet work period reading and writing with intense concentration in her journal. Michael, who sits next to her, can't find anything to do and occasionally interrupts her to ask questions. Abigail reads quietly. Wakako flips through a book but doesn't really read it. Jasmine, a large, olive-skinned girl with thick black hair, reads for a while, whispering the words to herself, and then wanders around the room.

Ms. Barnes had told the children at the start of the quiet work period that they could have their snacks at 10:30, but no one notices the time. Then, around 10:35, they remember and they walk to the back of the room in groups of two and three to get their snacks out of their backpacks. "Make sure to put in your book that snack time is the high point of the second-grade day," Ms. Barnes whispers to us, smiling. They eat their snacks quietly, and most of them return quickly to work. The entire class breaks for gym.

Gym. Gym is coed, and Coach Schwartz comes up to the classroom to take the girls and boys down to the playing field. They file out, girls in front, boys behind. The coach sits them down in a big circle (they sit, by choice, in sex-segregated clumps) and explains that they're going to do preparation for soccer. First they warm up by running around the circle one by one: as the coach calls each child by name, he or she gets up, tears around the circle, and plops back down in his or her place. The boys are generally faster than the girls, and some of them yell excitedly while running; however, Kelly and Pam are very quick and coordinated. Some of the girls busy themselves sweeping away the pine needles that have fallen on the field. When this exercise is over, a few of the boys chat with Coach Schwartz about the swimming meet yesterday. Already there is an easy male camaraderie over sports from which the girls are excluded—or at least the girls show little interest in joining in.

Coach Schwartz now lines the children up in four squads, carefully mixing them by sex and, as far as we can judge, by ability. Maria is the only girl asked to head a squad, which fits with her bubbly self-confidence. Coach asks the class to review some of the basics of soccer and to define the terms used for its play—dribbling, shooting, trapping, passing. Only the boys raise their hands to answer, although the girls seem interested. Now the class begins an exercise in which four children at a time, one from each squad, dribble the ball across the field, keeping it under control, stopping and starting at commands from the coach. Maria has nice control, but she is far slower than the boys who head up the other squads. Pam is quick but has no control. Jasmine, who ran around the circle in a sluggish, shambling way, is surprisingly adept at dribbling. Katie is slow and awkward at first, but she improves as she warms up. Tara gives the ball a mighty kick and sends it flying. Keith, a smallish, cute, bright-eyed boy, is clearly heading for soccer stardom—he's both quick and totally in control. Coach shouts out praise and criticism: "Good control, Maria!" "Very nice, Matthew!" "Don't let it get away from you, Pam!" "Superb, Keith!"

In general, the boys seem to throw themselves into the exercise more enthusiastically, but many of them are rather sloppy. The girls are a bit more cautious about keeping control of the ball; their faces look a little tenser than the boys' faces, many of which wear expressions of pure joy. In terms of ability, the best boys—Keith and Matthew—are well ahead of the best girls—Jasmine and Maria. And the worst girls—Raina and Tara—are worse than the worst boys—Spencer and Michael. But the majority of children of both sexes seem pretty evenly matched, as one would expect from the literature on sex differences. The girls all participate willingly and in most cases happily. They seem to take it for granted that sports are part of their life at school.

Quiet work time resumes. The kids return to the class red-faced and winded and resume the quiet work activities they set aside for gym. In the last twenty minutes or so before lunch, more of the girls get restless. Several of them now approach Ms. Barnes for help. Wakako does not know what to write in her journal. Erin needs help with the spelling page of her workbook. Pam needs help opening her cereal box. Now Erin, Maria, and Pam ask permission to go to the back of the class together to read the James Stevenson story Ms. Barnes has assigned. They plop down on the floor together in a hidden corner and whisper for a bit; then they settle down to read. None of the boys has come to Ms. Barnes to ask for help, but she notices now that several of them are just staring into space or wandering around. She gives them a few suggestions for what to do, what to write in their journals. Matthew decides to write about China and Japan. Erin, Maria, and Pam return quietly to their desks. Katie has spent the last ten minutes reading with total absorption, utterly oblivious to the comings and goings of her classmates. Keith has gotten bored with the computer and starts bugging Erin. Keith strikes us as Erin's male counterpart—a natural leader, friendly with most of his classmates, well coordinated, and genuinely interested in learning rather than just pleasing the teacher. Ms. Barnes had suggested earlier that Spencer find a book to read, but he poked around the bookshelves in a halfhearted way, came away empty-handed, and is now at the computer. Jeffrey has stopped reading and is chatting with Maria. Tara has finished her monumental journal entry and is now chatting with her neighbor Matthew, who seems glad of the opportunity to lay aside the work he just took up two minutes before.

Outside the hall fills with the noise of children on their way to lunch, and Ms. Barnes's class grows restive. Maria and Jeffrey are talking animatedly about chicken pox. Pam is having trouble getting started on her journal: having written the date at the top of the page, she seems stumped. Keith is rifling through his desk. Michael is resting his head to one side. Erin is writing rapidly in her journal. Maria and Pam start to tease Jeffrey. Tara wanders over to join in.

Ms. Barnes asks a few kids what they've written about in their journal. Michael wrote about "Star World," which appears to be an attraction at a local amusement park. Tara's epic journal entry turns out to be about going to first holy communion and attending religious classes after school and the visits her cousins paid recently. Her entry is one long, stream-of-consciousness sentence with no punctuation. Wakako wrote about playing hide-and-seek with her brothers. Erin wrote about going to her friend's birthday party. Ms. Barnes tells us that boys tend to write about sports, especially when the baseball season is in full swing and the Mets are playing. The girls might write about ice skating or gymnastics, but they're more likely to write about family activities, what they did at home, visits from relatives.

As the children line up to go to lunch, the boys, who had been drooping toward the end of quiet work period, seem to rekindle with explosive energy. They ask Ms. Barnes for the soccer ball. Clearly, they are eager to be outside and running around.

Lunch. The sex differences that were muted in the classroom and in gym emerge sharply and abruptly at lunch and recess. Having been supervised closely all morning, the children are now free to sit where they want, talk with whomever they choose, and, during recess, wander at will over a huge play area that includes jungle gym, sandbox, grass and paved playing fields, stands of trees, little fenced-off enclosures, and a separate kindergarten playground, which the older children can use if they want to. The teachers take their break during recess, and the nonprofessional aides keep track of the children; they really don't supervise or organize the play so much as monitor the kids, break up fights, keep strangers from wandering in and children from wandering off. What the children do during recess is pretty much up to them.

We eat lunch with the children in the cafeteria, to a background of noise that escalates from a dull roar to a deafening cacophony. At the start of the day, Ms. Barnes had told the class that we were writing a book about children, deliberately leaving out the fact that we were interested primarily in girls; nonetheless, the only children to approach us in the cafeteria are girls. The boys are either not interested in the adult strangers or too shy to engage them. We chat with Erin about her duties as class president and about her favorite activity at school (recess). She points out her best friend, from another second-grade class, and talks about her birthday party, which was held at the local ballet center. The main entertainment was improvising ballet dances to music from *The Little Mermaid*. Like almost all second-grade birthday parties we've heard about, this one was single-sex.

Jasmine comes up to tell us how much she likes the monkey bars; her cousin is teaching her how to climb on them. Wakako says she likes to play baseball with the boys. English is her second language (she speaks Japanese at home), but she is not at all shy or self-conscious about her heavy accent and halting grammar. She seems determined to make contact with us and ask us questions. She, Tara, and Raina, the only Hispanic child in the class, seem amazed that we've brought only one little sandwich for lunch. They seem to take an almost maternal interest in our well-being. Erin, Maria, and Abigail are talking in a tight little cluster. Pam shows off her book about the pop group New Kids on the Block. Erin goes over to join her best friend, and Maria walks over to the door to be the first in line to go out. As the line forms, snaking back through the cafeteria, there is much pushing and shoving, most of it instigated by boys. Spencer knocks over Raina, but she laughs it off. The aides start to shout at the children to quiet down, but it has no effect. Suddenly, the aides open the door to the playground and the children burst out of the cafeteria and zoom off to freedom.

Recess. As soon as they're outside, the boys, led by Keith, Michael, and Jeffrey, head off to the grassy playing field. They practice karate kicks for a few minutes and then launch into a soccer game, which goes on for the duration of recess and involves most of the boys in Ms. Barnes's class. The boys who don't play soccer join a male group that is frantically digging an immense trench (which they dub a "corridor") through the sandbox. This group also remains fixed and focused throughout recess.

The girls, on the other hand, separate into small groups and drift dreamily and rather quietly from one activity to the next. The play area is studded with pairs and trios of girls, strolling around together, chatting, sometimes sitting in the shade, sometimes swinging gently from the monkey bars or straddling the parallel bars. None of the girls joins the boys' soccer game, but some of them do sports activities on their own. Three girls play a kind of scaled-down version of basketball. Five girls, including Katie, are playing tetherball, and Matthew plays with them in a half-hearted way, constantly eyeing the boys' soccer game but never joining in. A group of five girls, led by Maria, has formed at the far end of the playground, thirty or forty yards away from all the other children. They balance on some posts that have been sunk into the ground. We're too far away to hear what they talk about, but we gather they are an exclusive clique and that nonmembers would be shooed away. Erin goes off with her best friend from the other class. Later Tara and another girl join them, and the four talk while swinging from the monkey bars. Wakako and Raina, both of whom are loners who have not yet made close friends or been accepted by one of the girls' groups, hang around the fringes of the boys' group in the sandbox. Occasionally, they join in the digging, but the boys take no notice of them.

Three girls from another class walk by, talking in a "nyah-nyah" tone about being in the club or out of the club. They stop a boy and ask him whether he would pick up a dead mouse. Apparently they have found one in the kindergarten playground. The boy is noncommittal, so the girls ask an aide if she would take care of it. Now that an adult is involved, they've become slightly more shrill and whiny about it, insisting that if the aide won't pick it up she should at least call a janitor. The aide can't be bothered about it, so the three walk back to the kindergarten playground to reconnoiter. Erin runs to catch up with them and to see what it's all about. Meanwhile, Maria's group at the far end of the playground is having a huddle. These "in-crowd" girls are as intent on the secrecy and privacy of their little club as Keith and Jeffrey and their boy pals are on keeping the soccer game going smoothly. And so it goes for the duration of recess.

Our time with Ms. Barnes's second-grade class confirmed some of our preconceptions and overturned others. The girls did tend to stick closer to Ms. Barnes than the boys did, as several research studies suggested they would; and the girls who did not stay close to Ms. Barnes tended to be left out of the "action" in class. Girls also asked for more help and tended to avoid using the class computer. Otherwise, there was very little sign of sexism in the classroom. Ms. Barnes noted that on the first day of school she told the children to sit anywhere they liked, and girls and boys promptly grouped themselves by sex. Ms. Barnes just as promptly reshuffled the children into "people tables," mixing boys and girls, and she has made sure the children understand that all activities in school are "people activities," not things for girls and things for boys. Her nonsexist policy seems to be paying off. Girls are just as likely to lead discussions, raise their hands, and bring in clippings for current events. We laughed with Ms. Barnes after class about how perfect it was for our book that Katie brought in a clipping about a Red Sox pitcher—but it really wasn't anything out of the ordinary. Girls today are interested in all sorts of sports. It's no longer a matter of a few girl jocks or superstars per class, but a widespread enthusiasm— seemingly just as widespread, though perhaps a bit less fervent, among girls as among boys.

However, when you move from the classroom to the school yard for recess, you seem to be leaping from the 1990s back to the 1950s. True, girls are no longer jumping rope or playing hopscotch, but the sex segregation and the sharp differentiation between the girls' activities and the boys' activities remain very much as they were a generation ago. Katie might be tuned in enough to baseball to clip an article for class use; but neither she nor any of her female classmates played a team sport on the playground (the girls playing basketball were just shooting hoops, whereas the boys playing soccer had organized themselves into two competing teams). It's not that the boys were deliberately excluding them, but rather the division of sexes and activities seemed to have come about by common consent. Both sexes were happy doing what they were doing.

The behavior of Ms. Barnes's second-graders very much accords with recent studies of how children act as powerful agents in reinforcing sexual stereotypes. On the playground, the girls and boys seem to divide "naturally" and uniformly, but actually there are all sorts of subtle pressures, cross-currents, shifting alliances, and fashions. The most popular and assertive members of both sexes seemed to lead their same-sex friends as far from the other sex as possible: Keith organized his male pals in soccer; Maria took her female pals off to the far end of the playground where they could play undisturbed in an exclusive all-girls club. The unpopular, loner girls gravitated to the fringes of the group of unpopular boys who were digging in the sand. Maria and her crowd probably would have chased Raina and Wakako away; but the clump of boy diggers didn't care—none of them was interacting much anyway, except to shout an occasional command. The group of girls playing tetherball on the fringe of the boys' soccer game seemed to act as a bridge between the two camps: the more active girls could play a low-level, nonteam sport and keep an eye on the boys; the less active boys, like Matthew, could play with the girls and still keep one foot in the boys' camp.

In the future, no doubt, Maria and her crowd and Keith and his crowd will start moving closer and closer together as it starts to become "cool" to hang out with the opposite sex. But in second grade, "cool" for a girl means boys are yucky. The uncool girls either haven't figured this out yet or don't care. Some of them never will.

Parents sometimes lament the fact that once their children go off to school they have pretty much lost control of them. The kids come home spouting new rules, new facts, new attitudes, and new opinions that they have learned from teachers, picked up from school movies, read in school texts. But teachers and the materials they use are only one influence on our children at school. In some basic social sense, the *real* action happens during recess when our children come in contact almost exclusively with each other. As much as the Ms. Barneses of the world are doing to stamp out sexism among their seven-year-old pupils, once they hit the playground, the girls and boys are doing their best to keep the old flame blazing. During recess, to judge by Ms. Barnes's class, as well as a number of studies and observations by teachers, our daughters are busy proving to themselves and to each other how different they are from the boys. All by themselves, with no special instruction or adult incentives, our girls are doing a bang-up job of teaching each other how to be girls.

Parenting Tips: Keeping Tabs, Getting Involved, Dealing with Problems

"I'm up at my daughter's school all the time," Heidi, a Midwestern mother of two, told us with a touch of pride. "I do class parties, I go in to read to the children. I correct papers and spelling tests. I did a big science bulletin board last year. This has definitely benefited my daughter, and it makes my husband and me feel more relaxed. If there is something going on at the school, we know about it."

Holly, who has daughters in fifth and second grades, said she volunteers on a weekly basis to work at the school, helping out in the library or working in the computer lab. "I know what the issues and complaints are as they arise," she noted. Holly has found over the years that most of her daughters' teachers appreciate her interest and are eager to listen to her suggestions or handle any complaints.

Sarah and Driskin, who recently moved with their daughters from Baltimore to Chapel Hill, North Carolina, made an extra effort to make themselves known to schoolteachers and administrators. "I check in regularly," says Sarah, who teaches part time herself. "I work in the library, help with the book fair, and play guitar. As a teacher, I know that when parents are involved, it really can help you figure out the children's needs."

You may not have the luxury of time that Heidi, Holly, and Sarah have (none holds a full-time job); but even if you can't be at your daughter's school "all the time," it's wise to take as much time as you can for getting involved, meeting with teachers, and generally keeping tabs on the school situation. Your expectations for and support of your little girl are probably the single most important factor in her happiness and success at school. And one of the best ways to show your support is to participate as often as you can in school projects, outings, or special events. "Parents who spend more time at school will receive better treatment," summed up one mother of three. "I feel guilty about not being there more often." Another mother commented incisively, "It's important to get the message across that you care. Being present at school is a way to say, 'I'm interested in you, your teacher, and your friends.'"

Many of us worry that we'll be perceived as meddlesome if we try to get too involved in elementary school activities, but in fact many teachers, especially in the early grades, encourage parental participation and assistance on field trips and welcome parents into the classroom as observers or as "guest speakers." Doing a special project at your little girl's school can also be a good way of illustrating career options for women. A woman obstetrician did a little presentation for her daughter's kindergarten class about how babies are delivered; the powerful subtext was that women can be doctors too. Feminist Letty Cottin Pogrebin tells of an attorney who organized a day of moot court for her daughter's third-grade class. Mothers who are scientists and mathematicians can really get girls excited about these subjects and prove to them that women can succeed in these fields. Chat with the teacher beforehand about age-appropriate projects, and bring in as many visual and hands-on materials as you can. "Madame Curie, the only person to win the Nobel Prize twice in science, has less impact on the lives of girls

than does Mae West," notes a woman educator.[52] Women
working in the sciences can do something to change this.

Fathers should also make an effort to participate in
school events. Fathers' interest and support particularly enhance young girls' self-confidence and motivation.

Teachers usually welcome information that helps them
understand their students and teach them more effectively.
They also appreciate parents who listen to their comments.
Parent-teacher conferences provide a good opportunity for
parents and teachers to exchange information about the
children. Bring in specific questions you have about your
daughter's progress in school, and offer the teacher any insights you have about her special strengths and weaknesses
in learning new concepts, making friends, using materials,
or participating in group activities. Don't feel obliged to
limit your contact to parent-teacher conferences. "If you
have any question, always go in and talk about it as soon
as it comes up," advises a mother of two, who teaches remedial reading. "You can't count on things being the way
they should be." Some parents assume that there is little
they can do to influence the curriculum or teaching techniques, but this is not necessarily so. Most teachers welcome parents' insights that may help them capture a child's
imagination.

A number of teachers report that many parents still seem
more preoccupied with their daughters' social success than
their academic achievements. As one teacher put it, "Parents still sometimes come in with the attitude that their
daughter doesn't have to be in the top reading group because she's a girl." One school principal noted, "When I'm
talking with parents of girls, I often hear complaints like,
'The other girls won't play with my daughter,' or, 'My
daughter keeps hounding me to get her the same clothes as
the cool girls.' Parents of boys don't worry about these
kinds of issues as much." Some studies back up this perception, finding that parents of boys tend to be more vigi-
lant about their sons' academic progress in school than
parents of girls.[53]

To the extent that this is true, it may be because boys, at least in elementary school, generally have more academic and behavioral problems than girls do.[54] But it is precisely this focus on fighting and class disruption that sometimes leads teachers and parents to overlook the school problems of little girls. "If a child is behaving badly and hitting other children, you'll notice it faster than if the child is sullen and depressed," notes one Minnesota elementary school teacher. "This withdrawn effect is more typical of girls. It's harder to get a handle on the shy and quiet problem child." The authors of another article feel that boys suffer unduly in school because they are targeted for more frequent and harsher discipline; but girls suffer because their problems are often not identified as problems—or worse, misinterpreted as compliance. The authors speculate that this neglect of girls' problems in elementary school may explain why by age eighteen, females outnumber males as the primary clients of mental health professionals, while the reverse is true before age eighteen.[55] Interestingly, several principals and elementary school social workers we talked to noted that they are seeing an increase in aggressive and disruptive behaviors among girls in school. One principal speculates that pressures due to dual-career marriages and single-parent families may be taking their toll.

Even if your daughter is not having a problem at school, she still may not be getting the personal attention that the louder and more aggressive children (often boys) are getting. "My daughter is a good student, but she's withdrawn," said one father. "She's in a class with thirty kids, and it wouldn't surprise me if she wasn't getting a lot of individual attention. I wonder if it would be different if she were a boy? I am inclined to believe that well-behaved, high-achieving girls don't get much attention."

In the case of girls who are not high achievers, the neglect of their social problems is directly linked to the neglect of their academic problems. A number of researchers have pointed out that schools nationwide have remedial reading programs because difficulty in learning to read is primarily a male problem. Math and science clinics are far less common for the simple reason that girls need them most. "The academic needs of males are systematically addressed; the academic needs of females are systematically ignored."[56]

In discussing your daughter's school performance with her teacher, you might want to pay special attention to these potential problems. How actively is she participating in class? How dependent is she on the teacher's approval and direction? Is it possible that her model behavior in class really masks a deep-seated alienation or defeatist attitude? Does she feel excluded from certain activities or pieces of equipment by aggressive or hostile boys? Does she lack the assertiveness to join in the most desirable games or activities? One kindergarten girl, when her mother asked her what she had done in school that day, replied with a sigh, "Color, color, color. That's all I *ever* do." From the teacher's point of view, this girl was behaving perfectly—coloring quietly for hours with apparent absorption and expertise. In fact, the girl was too timid to approach the block area, which was dominated by boys, too insecure to sit down at the computer, and too shy to join in the doll play with the other girls. Lots of little girls "color, color, color" when, with a little extra push from teacher or parent, they might engage in something more challenging and more stimulating.

Persuading a teacher that a child who is not causing *the teacher* any problems needs some special help may require a little skill. Obviously, if you go tearing into the classroom shouting, "You're ignoring my little girl!" you are unlikely to win any friends. On the other hand, mothers in particular may be hesitant to second-guess a female teacher, almost as if they view the teacher as another mother. Just as you wouldn't criticize another parent about the way she raises her children, the feeling seems to be that you shouldn't intrude on the way the teacher handles "her" children. A better approach is to remind yourself that the teacher is a professional who is, more likely than not, interested in any information that will help her teach more effectively. Thus, your first approach should be simply to describe the problem that you have identified. The teacher may surprise you by having some suggestions; in case she doesn't, it's a good idea to have a few constructive suggestions of your own.

As we noted before, girls tend to underrate their abilities while boys overrate them, and parents also tend to rate their sons' abilities, particularly in math, higher than their daughters'. The typical problems of girls in school are really a series of linked problems: low self-esteem causes girls to withdraw; dependence on teacher or parent makes them passive; neglect by school (and parent) makes them fall even further behind in math, science, and social adjustment; lack of success reinforces low self-esteem, causing even deeper withdrawal. We as parents are often in a better position than teachers to identify this vicious cycle quickly and try to nip it in the bud. It's our job to figure out when our little girl's quiet compliance is really "good behavior" and when it's really bad, most of all for her. And, if we suspect that it is negative, then we need to work closely with her teacher in helping her come out of her shell.

Single-Sex Schools: The Pros and Cons for Girls

Most of the debate on the merits of single-sex versus coed schools—and there's been a lot of it—has centered on college and, to a lesser extent, on high school. The argument for single-sex education, at least in high school and college, is that it provides girls and women with an environment dedicated to their interests and needs where they can develop to their full potential without the distractions and sex stereotyping that may occur in coeducational schools.

If you have a girl in elementary school, you may be thinking, "Well, we'll think about sending her to an all-girls college when the time comes, but what difference does it make whether there are boys in second grade?" Some people think it *can* make a difference right from the start.

As one kindergarten teacher at a girls' private school, whose previous job had been at a coed school, put it, "When you have boys in a classroom, you spend a lot of your time just trying to get their attention. But the girls just eat up the instruction. They want to read. They want to write. You can do so much with them." Certainly, the classroom dynamic confirmed this: for a full half hour, all eighteen little girls worked intently, at constructing and designing a stage set out of cardboard boxes, chatting comfortably with each other and with the teacher. Nobody left the group; nobody seemed restless or bored. There were no squabbles over the glue or the colored ribbons.

The head of the lower school at an elite girls' school pointed out that teachers at a girls' school can't discriminate between the sexes, consciously or unconsciously. The school can also deliberately compensate for little girls' relative deficits, particularly with games and tools that build spatial skills, and tailor activities to their relative advantages, particularly in verbal skills. Finally, she said, "We start building their self-esteem from day one."[57]

Some researchers believe that single-sex education allows girls to develop their natural abilities and personalities more fully because the girls cannot take a backseat to the boys. In her college-level study, Dr. Katherine Canada found that students and professors interact with each other with approximately the same frequency regardless of the number of students or of professor-initiated interactions. Since boys (or men) tend to dominate and interrupt more while girls (or women) tend to agree and open the way for others to speak, boys force girls into silence by locking up most of the student-teacher interactions. In all-girl classes, though, girls will fill both active and passive roles. Dr. Canada concludes that "girls in single-sex classes take a broader role. This is why we see single-sex colleges generate so many more career-dynamic women than coed colleges."[58]

An all-girls school may have some subtler, but even more important, effects. In all-girls schools, the girls may feel freer to be interested in math, computers, and sports because those areas are not "occupied" by the boys. One administrator of a girls' school noted that "kindergartners believe they can do everything, but by the time they reach age seven, little girls begin to 'self-select' out of certain activities, announcing that 'I'm not good at that.' "[59] We don't have any studies to prove it, but it's possible that a girls' school may be better able to help a young student accurately assess her abilities and not automatically "self-select" out of "boyish" subjects. In addition, as a girl enters adolescence, a good girls' school may be able to bolster self-esteem by making it clear to her that her learning, her skill at sports, and her abilities in the arts are important. After reviewing the available literature on the subject, the Sadkers conclude that "girls in single-sex schools have higher self-esteem, are more interested in nontraditional subjects such as science and math, and are less likely to stereotype jobs and careers. They are intellectually curious, serious about their studies, and achieve more."

Recently, a number of coed schools have begun experimenting with single-sex classes in math and science. Girls in such classes for the most part seem delighted to be rid of the teasing and pressuring of disruptive boys, and they thrive in academic situations that stress cooperative learning rather than competition. "It may not be the solution to the world's problems, but it seems to be serving our young women," commented the assistant principal at Marin Academy, a California school that pioneered an all-girl algebra class. Marie Wilson, president of the Ms. Foundation for Women and co-author of *Mother-Daughter Revolution*, wholeheartedly agrees: "All girls classes are the way to go. . . . People need their own caucus first to figure out who they are." Critics, however, warn that these experiments may end up segregating girls as second-class citizens, and further that cooperative learning techniques need not be restricted to girls but could just as effectively be incorporated into mixed-sex classes.

Of course, just because a school is for girls only does not

necessarily mean that it is a good school, that it provides the most stimulating environment for girls, or that the faculty and administration do not harbor sexist attitudes. Moreover, parents should consider whether the possible academic advantages of single-sex education—and they seem modest in the primary grades—outweigh the social drawbacks. Single-sex schools reinforce the attitude that girls and boys are fundamentally different and that sex segregation is proper. Particularly if your little girl has no brother, sending her to an all-girls school may prevent her from having friends who are boys. Parents should also consider whether they wish to shelter a little girl from the competition, distractions, and possible sexism of a coed environment in the hope that she will develop skills and confidence that will enable her to deal with such problems later, or whether they prefer to expose her to "reality" right away in the hope that they and the school can help her develop skills and confidence despite, or perhaps even as a result of surmounting, these problems.

So, what should you do? We think that if you have the option of sending your little girl to a good girls' school, you should consider it. The available evidence suggests that she is likely to emerge from it slightly better educated and more self-confident, but single-sex or coeducational is only one factor to weigh in trying to ensure a good education for your little girl. For example, the school's distance from home, its "fit" with a child's temperament and interests, whether other neighborhood children attend, are all equally important considerations, at least in elementary school. And, of course, a school's quality should be the overriding factor. As Valerie Lee, a University of Michigan researcher on the impact of single-sex schools, says, "I can't conclude that all you need to do is send your girls to an all-female school and your problems will be solved. It really depends on the school. You have to sit in on the classes and find out what's going on there."

5

♥

The Social Life of the Schoolgirl: Sports, Friends, and Boys

Socially, our daughters take a quantum leap forward during the early elementary school years. As they turn their sights more and more on the world outside of home, their friendships become increasingly important, particularly friendships with one or two best girl friends. As girls and boys mature, their styles of social interaction diverge: the way girls and boys play with friends, their preferred activities, even the way they speak become markedly different. Sex segregation tends to solidify during first and second grades, especially in school. But very often girls maintain "underground" friendships with boys after school, in the more relaxed environment of the neighborhood or during summer vacation. In this chapter, we'll take a look at the way all of these social issues affect girls from age five through age eight. We also take a peek into the future at how friendships and social patterns change as girls enter late elementary school.

In the past few years, elementary school girls have become increasingly active in all types of sports, from soccer to basketball. Sports can often provide an avenue of contact between the sexes, though single-sex teams have certain advantages for girls as well. We'll close the chapter with a discussion of the new excitement of young girls' participation in sports, and we'll answer the questions that parents have about the merits of mixed-sex versus single-sex teams.

Talking, Playing, Hanging out with Friends

When our first daughter was born, one of our aunts joked that we'd have to go out and get another telephone. "You know girls—gab, gab, gab. You'll never get her off the phone!" As it turned out, Emily does love to talk, but then so do her male cousins and most of the little boys she hangs out with at school. Actually, judging from our experience and that of other parents and teachers, it's not so much the quantity of talking as the content that distinguishes girls from boys. "Girls talk more about their feelings than boys do," said Dr. Ana Dybner, a psychologist with the Great Neck Public School system on Long Island. "They make more declarative statements about how they look, how they feel, how something affects them. Boys are conditioned not to focus on feelings, so they act out more. Movies and books and other cultural stimuli give girls the cue that it's okay to express themselves. They pick up on the dramatization associated with women in our culture."

On the positive side, parents have pointed to their daughters' ability to empathize with the feelings of other family members and friends and to put their feelings into words. On the negative side is the tendency of little girls to become hypersensitive to the smallest emotional disturbance. One mother of a son and a daughter said that when boys have an argument, they blow up, hit each other, and are back playing happily two minutes later; but girls can carry on a dispute for weeks, dwelling on the fine points of who offended whom, holding grudges, endlessly and volubly mulling over their sense of injury.

In exploring the reasons why children segregate themselves by sex, Eleanor Maccoby points out that girls and boys use language in very different ways. Whereas boys tend to make direct demands, to issue commands and interrupt, girls rely more on polite suggestions; they tend to agree with each other more, and they pause more often to let another girl speak or acknowledge what she has said. "Speech serves more egoistic functions among boys," writes Maccoby, "and more socially binding functions among girls."[1] Other researchers note that girls devote a great deal of time to discussing who likes whom and "continually negotiate the parameters of friendship."[2] Girls seem to share secrets more than boys do, and girl friends confide in each other their emotional ups and downs far more than do boys. Giving voice to feelings, even the negative feelings of a complicated falling-out, helps girls direct combative impulses into socially acceptable channels. Boys may clear the air faster by belting each other, but they also learn far less about the nuances of relationships.

As noted in Chapter 4, girls and boys inhabit entirely different social worlds when left to their own devices on the school playground, girls hanging out in groups of two or three and boys in considerably larger groups. After spending several years observing hundreds of girls and boys interact in various schools around the country, psychologists Barrie Thorne of Michigan State University and Zella Luria of Tufts University found that both the playground and the school cafeteria were sex-segregated, with male and female tables in the latter, and boys and girls "controlling" different areas in the former.[3] They found gender segregation to be even more prevalent than race segregation.

Not only do boys form larger groups, but they take up more space on the playground, fight more, and their social relations "tend to be overtly hierarchical and competitive." Girls, on the other hand, interact in "small groups or friendship pairs, organized in shifting alliances." On the playground, they take turns on equipment more amicably than the boys, and often seem to be performing for each other, doing tricks on the monkey bars or executing elaborate pantomimes or, in the later grades of elementary school, imitating cheerleading routines. Often what appears to be a female threesome—or triad as psychologists refer to them—is actually two dyads with one girl in a pivotal position. Thorne and Luria discuss how complex this network of dyads and triads can become among school girls: one girl might be a member of several pairs at the same time, and friends often switch allegiances abruptly and cruelly play off one "best friend" against the other. Several parents have spoken to us about the problems inherent in this grouping. "She has two best girl friends," said one mother of her eight-year-old, "but when all three of them try to play together it's awful. There's always one who feels left out." Our older daughter Emily has developed an intense aversion to "double play dates"—two girls visiting a common friend at the same time. The two girls who are bigger, older, wearing the same color, or whatever invariably gang up together against the third.

In the final years of elementary school and the first years of middle school, the fluid dyads and triads of girl friendships often merge into rigidly defined and jealously guarded cliques. You may remember such cliques from your own childhood: the "cool crowd" of girls who had the right clothes, the right shoes, who carried their books in a certain way, who walked to school together in almost military formations, who ate lunch and jumped rope together and who would sooner die than be caught playing with an uncool girl. There are cliques of athletic girls who play soccer together after school and bookish girls who study together and girls who are into horses or ballet. "I see the cliques forming in fifth grade," said a mother whose daughters are in fifth and second grades. "They go around saying 'she's cool, she's in, she's not cool, she's out.' The girls do it more than the boys. I'm concerned that my daughter's self-image is going to be based on what these cool girls think of her." One mother of a fourth-grade daughter told us with relief that her daughter was in the "good crowd" and was totally uninterested in joining up with the "cool crowd." "I told her how the cool group is just a bunch of snippy kids who have to wear certain things and who are ahead of themselves in showing interest in boys. I told her she didn't have to be like that, and she isn't. She knows that their snobbishness is hurting other children." A father from Baltimore said his daughter's inner-city school is about half white and half black, and even in the early grades the children tend to segregate themselves by race. At first, the segregation may have as much to do with geography as race, since the children form the tightest friendships with those who live in their neighborhoods and the neighborhoods tend to be segregated. But eventually, the children become aware of the differences in the color of their skin; unfortunately, unlike other elementary school cliques, the racial cliques don't fade away as the children grow up.

There is seldom much that we as parents can do to get our daughter into a desirable clique or out of an undesirable one. Probably the best approach is to talk with her about why the "cool crowd" is behaving in such a hurtful way and to remind her of how important her other friendships are. One father told his daughter that she wouldn't want to be like the cool girls because they're mean and she's not. Sometimes cliques become so deeply entrenched and their exclusiveness becomes so damaging that it makes sense for parents and teachers to step in and talk to the children. Children sometimes relax the rules of their groups if they see how they are hurting their classmates. Barbara Raber, an elementary school principal in Great Neck, New York, has seen years when cliques have become a serious, schoolwide problem, particularly in third and fifth grades. "I speak to small groups or meet with an entire class or even the whole grade," she says. "We talk about hurt feelings and how it feels to be the victim or the outcast. I try to get the children to understand how their classmates are feeling."

Since for boys the primary social medium is sports, the rules of "who's in and who's out" depend largely on athletic prowess. As Mary, the Milwaukee mother of five, commented, "Boys are easygoing in the way they play in groups. They'll be playing soccer together, and another guy will come along and join up in the game, and they will all be totally relaxed about it. With girls it has to be a best friend."

Other sex differences in social behavior become apparent during the elementary school years. One researcher who studied a small New England town found that parents give boys a far larger range of territory when they play outdoors.[4] In addition, boys invested more energy and ingenuity in "manipulating the environment," building tree houses, forts, and playhouses, while girls never built any structure with fixed walls or a roof. In a mixed-sex group of children engaged in a big dam-building project, the boys acted as the bosses and main workers, digging and "engineering," while the girls were consigned to the sidelines, either as passive spectators or water carriers. When girls did use outdoor structures, they tended to turn them into kitchens and stock them with play food and cooking utensils. One school psychologist noted that girls seem more aware than boys of the importance of money and economics, both in their play and in their serious exchanges. One is more likely to hear a girl than a boy say, "I can't afford that" or "I wish I had enough money for that."

One largely undocumented social behavior among girls in middle elementary school is an interest in "adopting" younger girls as surrogate little sisters. On several occasions in parks, seven- and eight-year-old girls have befriended our two- and five-year-olds, pushing them on the swings, helping them dig in the sandbox, laughing (in a nice way) at the two-year-olds' mispronunciations. One mother reported that her two daughters, ages eight and six, love helping out with younger girls; they seem to get a kick out of showing them the ropes in the playground and instructing them about where it's safe to ride a trike. It may be that these older girls are flexing their maternal muscles or practicing for future jobs as baby-sitters. It's also possible that having just graduated from the ranks of little girls themselves, they are now eager to show off their relative maturity while regressing into the safe world of early childhood.

Thorne and Luria, in the study mentioned on page 161,

confirm Maccoby's belief that schoolgirls and boys use language differently. "While boys use a rhetoric of contests and teams," they write, "girls describe their relations using language which stresses cooperation and 'being nice.' " Nonetheless, they point out that recent research has added some shading to the stereotype of the goody-goody girls. Girls break rules too, though they do it in subtler, quieter ways than boys (partly because their friendship groups are smaller), and they compete with each other using verbal sparring and comparisons. Girls also display greater physical intimacy with each other. In kindergarten and first grade, boys still hug each other or drape their arms around each other without a trace of self-consciousness, but gradually such behaviors taper off, until by fifth grade they are completely absent. Girls, however, continue to hold hands, stroke and comb each other's hair, lean up against each other, and use "cuddly touch" throughout elementary school.

As part of the intimacy they share, girls tend to notice the appearance of friends and to comment on each other's clothes and haircuts. Well before the issue of appearing desirable to boys arises, girls begin striving to look attractive for each other. Actually, many adult women frankly admit that appearing attractive to other members of their sex never stops being important. And certainly in our own experience, women are more apt than men to notice that a female friend has lost a few pounds or bought a particularly flattering outfit. Looking good and "put together" is both a pastime that girls share and an arena for competition—a bit like sports for boys.

Thorne and Luria perceptively point out that in discussing their one-on-one friendships, commenting on each other's appearances, and sharing secrets, girls are in a sense rehearsing for the intimate relationships that they will hope to form with boys once they reach adolescence. Boys, however, approach adolescence from an entirely different direction. In middle and late elementary school, boys begin to use dirty words, especially words associated with sex acts,

and to tease each other about being "fags." Later, on the
threshold of puberty, boys begin passing around pornographic magazines and fantasizing together about women's
bodies. As Thorne and Luria put it, for boys the "commitment to sexual acts precedes commitment to emotion-laden,
intimate relationships," whereas it is just the opposite for
girls, who have been talking about emotions and "constructing intimacy" for years. When adolescent boys and
girls begin dating, tension frequently arises from the radical
differences in the expectations and needs of the two sexes.
To put it bluntly (and a bit oversimplistically), the teenage
girls want romance and the boys want sex (or at least think
they *should* want it). Thorne and Luria believe that this dis-
crepancy between the sexes, which originates in the friendships and games of elementary school, often persists in the
adult relationships between men and women.

Dealing with Boys

"What do you think about boys?" Chances are your elementary school daughter will have *a lot* to say on this
topic, some of it rather surprising. Little girls run the gamut
from dyed-in-the-wool boy haters to flamboyant tomboys
who would much rather kick a soccer ball around with the
guys than pick up a Barbie doll or a pretty pony. One common thread is that boys are very much on the minds of elementary school girls and, if anything, the girls become
more preoccupied with boys as the years pass and contact
diminishes.

Most parents and teachers report that in kindergarten the
sexes still mingle to some extent, but that sex segregation
really solidifies in mid-elementary school. Your kindergarten daughter may bring home amazing tales of the
naughty pranks of her male classmates—raids on the art
supplies, transformations of playground equipment into
prisons or caves, elaborately planned humiliations of an
outcast boy or girl—antics that she would only perform in

her wildest dreams and in which she clearly takes a vicarious delight. We overheard a conversation about boys between our older daughter and her best (girl) friend that went something like this: "Michael is the worst boy in my class." "All the boys in my class are the worst." "Yeah, but Michael is the worst worst. He tied up Nan in prison and wouldn't let her out. I hate him." "There's a boys' club in my class. They're always doing crazy things. All the girls hate them." "All boys are dumber than girls." "Boys are always in trouble and girls are never in trouble." "Let's pretend the boys are being pirates and we're running away from them." "Yeah!"

We knew that Emily's rigidly anti-male stance was partly a front, assumed for the sake of female solidarity. In truth, she likes lots of boys, plays with them happily, and shows a bolder and zanier side of her personality when she is with them. She reports that there are several different categories of males in her kindergarten class: the wild boys, who never play with girls; the quiet or "girl-type" boys, who share the girls' enthusiasm for coloring, talking, and nonaggressive play; and the "in-between" boys. Emily is lucky that she can move back and forth between the boys' camp and the girls'. We've heard several stories of kindergarten girls who were so terrorized by the rougher boys in school that they developed something of a phobia about boys in general. On the other hand, some kindergarten girls prefer the company of boys. Julia, a New York City tomboy, *only* had boy friends in preschool, and she was totally unprepared for the sex segregation of kindergarten. "It was very upsetting to her when boys would no longer play with her," recalls her father. "It really gave her a lot of trouble at the beginning of school." Melissa, a vivacious kindergartner with two older brothers, gravitates toward the boys because she's more accustomed to their rough-and-tumble style of play. So far, they accept her as "one of the guys."

As noted earlier, sex segregation tends to become more and more deeply entrenched each year, and boys are usually more rigid about enforcing it than girls. By first or second grade your daughter may become painfully aware of being shut out of boys' games and "clubs" at school. Parents have noticed that long-standing, mixed-sex friendships sometimes go "underground" in school: the children continue to play together when no classmates are around to tease them, but in school, the little boy and little girl who have known each other since infancy pretend they are strangers. On the other hand, some children continue to carry on their mixed-sex friendships openly, either not noticing the ridicule of classmates or not caring about it.

Girls very often retaliate for exclusion from all-boy "clubs" by excluding boys from their own activities. "There's no way she would have boys to her birthday party," said Holly of her seven-year-old daughter. Erin, in Ms. Barnes's second-grade class, gave us an "are-you-crazy?" stare when we asked if there were any boys at her best friend's Little Mermaid birthday party. Meredith, age eight, doesn't exactly dislike boys, but she doesn't really enjoy playing with them. "She knows what to do with girls," says her mother, "but with boys she's at a loss." Her six-year-old sister Christina, on the other hand, has lots of boy friends and does not yet feel self-conscious about playing with them. "I hear from Micky's mother that he's crushed if Christina doesn't talk to him," reports her mom. "He'll even play with Barbie as long as he can get her to come over to his house." Another mother notes that her daughters complain about how rough and awkward the boys are in school: they're always pushing and jostling the other kids on line, they get attention by crashing around and yelling, and they seldom resist the temptation to pull her daughters' long braids.

Gradually, as your daughter advances through elementary school, you may begin to detect a certain thrilled fascination behind the outward contempt. "She thinks boys are icky," one mother said about her fourth-grader, "but I get the feeling that a lot of the boy hating at this age is a form of curiosity." Will said his eight-year-old daughter Kate insists she can't stand most boys, but "within the last year she's become very interested in romance and the life that is awaiting her. Last summer we hired a teenage girl to mind Kate and Molly [his four-year-old] in the afternoons. Kate would usually have a friend over, and it turned out she and her friend were peppering the baby-sitter with questions about sex." Another father said of his two elementary school–age daughters, "In their opinion, boys are rude, destructive bullies, but they are fascinated by them too. I think what they admire most is that boys can be so ill-behaved and get away with it."

"By third and fourth grades, girls spend a lot of time talking about boys," noted an elementary school psychologist. "They say they hate boys, but this is how they show their interest. By fifth grade you start hearing, 'Hey, he's cute!' " Vociferous boy hating is also a way for girls to protect themselves from teasing about secretly liking one of the boys or having a boyfriend. One mother described how upset her daughter became at such teasing. She retained a few male friends into third grade, and enjoyed playing sports with boys now and then. It was no big deal to her, but the other girls wouldn't let her alone. Why, she wondered, couldn't she be friends with a boy without everyone saying she had a "boyfriend"? Will has noticed that when a group of Kate's third-grade friends gather at the house, they frequently accuse one another of liking a certain boy. The response is either a vehement denial or retaliation by accusing another girl of the same crime. Such teasing and self-consciousness often rise to a fever pitch as the children approach adolescence.

Eleanor Maccoby believes that elementary school children are conscious of the romantic implications of boy-girl encounters and "intensely aware of one another as future romantic partners."[5] But such awareness only heightens the risk of being caught out talking to a boy "in public." Raphaela Best has noted that teachers (and probably most parents) rarely give elementary school children any real information about love, sex, or sex roles, so sex education is largely self-taught.[6] Because children may have few, if any, friendships with the opposite sex to give them a more balanced understanding, they often have only two models for relations between the sexes: love, which they equate with sex, and hate.[7]

Occasionally the two sexes emerge from their self-imposed isolation to join in quasi-sexual, quasi-combative "chase and kiss" games. The third-grade girls may initiate the game one day by pursuing stray boys on the playground, grabbing them and planting kisses on their cheeks or mouths. The next day the boys may launch their retaliation. Parents should realize that both sexes play these games, though adults may be more likely to label the girls' pursuit as sex play, while shrugging off the boys' pursuit as boyish high jinks.[8] As one mother of four daughters put it, "The girls chase the boys. Then the boys chase the girls. They both discover how it's okay to be with one another. Pretty soon they start talking about, 'She likes so-and-so.' They're teasing, but also looking around." Some psychologists see these chase games as the first breaching of the elaborate defenses between the sexes; they're a kind of primitive rehearsal for the dating rituals of a few years hence.[9]

Chase and kiss games and inter-sex teasing are one thing. But sexual harassment is in another category altogether, and disturbingly, it seems to be on the rise in America's schools, even elementary schools. More and more school-age girls report incidents in which boys flip up their skirts, pull down their pants, poke and squeeze their private parts, and make lewd comments to them. As Myra and David Sadker write in their recent book *Failing At Fairness*, "Sexual harassment is a way of life in America's schools. While teachers and administrators look the other way, sexually denigrating comments, pinching, touching, and propositioning happen daily." Louis Harris and Associates found in a recent survey of kids in grades 8 through 11 that 81 percent of girls and 76 percent of boys have been the target of some sort of unwelcome sexual behavior. The Sadkers note that these statistics are somewhat deceptive, because girls are "far more likely to have been harassed repeatedly and at younger ages" than boys and they are "far more likely than boys to report feeling embarrassed and upset, self-conscious and scared as a result of the experience." Minority girls are significantly more likely to be harassed in elementary school than white girls.

Dr. Nan Stein, director of the Sexual Harassment in Schools Project at the Wellesley College Center for Research on Women, advises children to report instances of sexual harassment in school to teachers, guidance counselors, or school principals. "Find a person who believes you," says Dr. Stein, "and who will do something about it." If your daughter tells you about incidents of sexual harassment, take her seriously and help her bring the problem to the attention of school officials. If the school tries to deny or hush up the problem, you can file a complaint with the department of education in your state.

A number of teachers and parents have reported that now and then a precocious girl and boy or even a group of girls and boys will start to act out romantic scenarios years before anyone would expect such behavior. One New York City dad reported how upset his seven-year-old daughter became when her best friend, a former tomboy, started to hang around with the coolest boy in the second grade: "They acted almost like teenagers in love. She draped herself around him and gave him all the power. The other children were titillated by the whole thing, but also disturbed. My daughter kept saying that her friend was acting like a jerk. It was a major social issue all year." A second-grade teacher reported that in most of her classes the boys and girls keep pretty much to themselves on the playground, but a few years back she had a class in which the boys and girls were playacting all sorts of romantic situations and talked a lot about dating. Although she felt it was inappropriate, she tried to deal with it positively. She organized a few dances for the class, and they talked about the group dynamic. She later heard from other teachers that the same group continued to be socially precocious throughout elementary school.

It's interesting to note that children sometimes relax their rigorous sex segregation when they are away from the highly ritualized and pressured school environment. Denise said that her seven- and ten-year-old daughters think that boys are neat and enjoy playing with them, though her seven-year-old found it hard to sustain school friendships with her two favorite boys last year because of the teasing. During the summer, however, when the family rented a cottage in Maine, the girls became very close to two brothers who were staying in the neighboring cottage. "They liked the boys' games," said Denise, "and really enjoyed playing baseball and soccer with them. But they also brought the boys into their fantasy play." Both sexes seemed to enjoy the opportunity to hang out together without worrying about whether or not it was cool.

Many adult women who grew up with sisters or as only children speak of the social disadvantages they felt in adolescence because of their uneasiness around boys. Having viewed boys as "the enemy" or as blundering alien creatures throughout elementary school, they were totally unprepared for the major changes of adolescence. You can help your daughter avoid this dilemma by trying to keep up some sort of positive contact with boys during the boy-hating years of elementary school. Talk with her in an age-appropriate way about how limiting sexual stereotypes can be. Try to arrange play sessions with boys on neutral territory away from school. Ask her teacher if she shows an interest in any of her male classmates. Encourage her to participate in coed sports or after-school activities. Our own daughters have seven male cousins who run the gamut from gentle souls to macho sword-and-gun freaks to serious sports fanatics to budding scientists. The girls get a crash course in weaponry, hockey, rocket launchers, and Nintendo whenever they visit, and they love it. Some of the cousins also seem intrigued by our girls' fantasies about Rainbow Bright, Sleeping Beauty, and their herd of Little Ponies. It remains to be seen whether contact with their cousins will ease our daughters' transition to adolescence—but it certainly can't hurt. If nothing else, they are learning how much fun boys—and their games—can be.

Girls and Sports

The triumphant 1994-95 season of the University of Connecticut women's basketball team marked a symbolic turning point for girls and sports in America. It wasn't just that the U. Conn. Huskies had a perfect, undefeated record that year, culminating in their victory over the University of Tennessee Lady Vols at the NCAA tournament in January, 1995. It wasn't just that the Huskies' dynamic 6 foot 4 inch center Rebecca Lobo swept up every honor and MVP (most valuable player) award available for the sweeping. These were certainly memorable, exciting events. But the real clincher was the frenzied national attention focused on the team. Live television coverage; screaming fans; coveted tickets scalped at exorbitant prices; morning headlines; big splashy stories in *Sports Illustrated*. When Lobo attended mass at a Connecticut church at the height of the season, *Sports Illustrated* reported that a nun told her, "You caused more commotion than if Jesus Christ had walked in here himself." Hot male teams have come to expect this kind of hero worship—but this was something entirely new for a female team. Yes, female ice skaters, gymnasts, golfers, and tennis players have been superstars, but never before female basketball players. Women's sports—women's team sports—had arrived. As *Time* magazine reported, "23 years after Title IX mandated equal opportunities for women," female participation in sports "has come into its own without sacrificing ethics."

The triumph of the U. Conn. Huskies was a generation in the making—a generation in which girls were finally given access (if not always equal access) to school athletic facilities and resources. Title IX (see page 106) may not have completely evened the score between the sexes, for at many schools the lion's share of athletic resources and attention still goes to boys and the law is seldom, if ever, enforced. But there is no question that it has been, and continues to be, a boon to girls who want to play sports. Participation of girls in high school sports skyrocketed from 294,015 in 1971, the year before Title IX was enacted, to 2,124,755 in 1993-94. And the signs are good that the numbers will continue to surge. The future Rebecca Lobos are playing ball right now on basketball courts, baseball diamonds, and soccer fields all over America. Already women are closing the gender gap on athletic records and endurance tests. It's more than likely that our daughters will pull ahead of boys once they hit their prime.

The participation statistics and new records are impressive. But statistics alone do not fully reflect the shift in girls' attitudes toward sports, especially the attitudes of little girls. These days, the big question for many kindergarten girls is not *whether* they're going to be on a soccer, T-ball, basketball, or swim team, but *how many* they can fit in. Third grade girls wear their satiny team jackets as badges of honor. First graders huddle over school lunch on Monday comparing how many soccer goals they each scored at the game that weekend. Team sports are the glue that binds together the social lives of elementary school girls. It's not just that sports are cool for girls: sports are taken for granted, just as they are for boys.

Listen to some of the comments we've been hearing from parents all over the country about their daughters' involvement in sports:

- A North Carolina mother comments that even though her third-grade daughter is almost painfully shy, she loves physical education in school. "She plays football, runs track, she's learning to juggle and jump rope. The sports are not divided by sex. The Rainbow League flyer for soccer and track went out to all the kids, boys and girls alike."
- A Maryland mother of four daughters notes that two out

of the four love sports, and her oldest in particular is passionate about soccer, softball, and T-ball. Her husband, though disappointed not to have a son, has discovered how much fun it can be to play ball with his daughters and has started coaching the local softball team.

- A Minnesota mother of two says that both she and her husband like sports, and both their children share their interest: their eight-year-old daughter loves softball, volleyball, soccer, football, and ice skating; though she won't go hunting with her dad, she does join him on his fishing trips. "Jamie looks for things that boys can do like running fast and playing catch, and then does them better," says her mom. "When boys tease her about playing sports, that really sends a flag up. She sets out to prove she's better than they are."

- A Massachusetts mother of two daughters praises the local school system for encouraging girls to get involved in sports and for offering a broad range of after-school programs. "They have everything from karate to quilting," she said. "Though the boys dominate the karate class, there are some girls in it. There still aren't any boys in quilting, however."

- A Wisconsin mother of five admits with a laugh that she once told her five-year-old daughter, "When you get to high school, you'll go and cheer for your brothers on the basketball team." "No I won't," Sarah shot back. "I'm going to play basketball myself." Sarah isn't waiting for high school, either. She already plays on a girls' pee-wee basketball team.

- The school psychologist of a large suburban elementary school commented, "Girls are more involved in sports than they used to be, especially soccer. They used to play jump rope, hopscotch, and jacks during recess. Now they are using more energy and taking more of a place beside the boys."

We've certainly seen our own daughters thrive in team sports, especially soccer, though all three were somewhat reluctant to join in at first. Our local league starts up at age five, and the girls were dubious whether they were big enough or "good" enough to sign up that young. We have to take some of the blame, for before soccer season began we had only made a few half-hearted attempts to kick a ball around the yard, and we quickly gave up when the girls began to quarrel. Nonetheless, Emily joined a team and she stuck with it for the first season largely out of peer pressure. She improved steadily season by season in skills and confidence, and when she booted in a crucial goal at age eight, it was a personal as well as a team triumph. Sarah and Alice, quick to master new skills and highly competitive with each other, emerged at age seven as the "stars" of their micro-soccer team—in fact they became such valuable players that their coach nearly wept when we went away one weekend and they had to miss a game. A week-long summer soccer camp that the three girls participated in really helped to cement their skills, and compensated for the fact that we *still* don't get out and play ball with them as often as we'd like to.

There is no question that the benefits girls derive from sports go well beyond the physical. Participating in sports is a great way to build confidence, gain social skills, and combat stereotypes about female inferiority. Once girls hit adolescence, sports participation correlates with lower rates of drug abuse, teenage pregnancy, and depression, as well as higher self-esteem and better grades. Playing with a team teaches girls of any age to pull together, to work with a coach, to share the limelight with others—and it also gives them a solid and enduring network of friendships. Since your grade school daughter is likely to be bigger than her male classmates, sports may prove to be the most effective way of conveying the clear message that anything boys can do, girls can do better—or at least just as well. "I think being good at sports is a real source of strength and independence to my daughter," said one mother. "It also helps that her friends are the same way." "Being very physical and athletic is one of the most important parts of my daughter's identity," said a New York City father of his eight-year-old. "The whole family attends her Saturday morning soccer league. She wanted to be the goalie—she is tough. Her team was 0 for 3 at the start of the season. When they finally won a game I was crying like a baby." Diana Everett, executive director of the National Association for Girls and Women in Sport, points out that the younger a girl starts playing sports, the more likely she is to stay with it over the long run. A recent national study shows that if a girl does not participate in sports by the time she is ten, there is only a 10 percent chance that she will be playing at age 25. Girls are also more likely to be active in sports and fitness if one or both of their parents participate in sports. The father-son after-dinner catch is a hallowed summertime ritual in our society—but we need to amend the ritual to include fathers (and mothers!) and daughters. One way or another your little girl is going to be exposed to sports in school, after school, in the neighborhood, through her pals. So don't wait. As soon as she's up and around, get out there and kick, throw, run, swim, and tumble around with your daughter. It will do you both a world of good.

Expressing approval, attending games, arranging for after-school transportation, and helping your daughter get the right equipment, whether ice skates, baseball gloves, or soccer balls, all make sense. Remember that your daughter will have just as many athletic opportunities in school as your son. Many parents still unconsciously stock their sons' rooms with heaps of sports paraphernalia and let their daughters fend for themselves. Take the time to find out which sports your daughter enjoys most and help her pursue them as much as she wants to.

Your daughter may be getting different messages from her peers at school or in the neighborhood, however. "Breah has always been gifted athletically," said one mother of her second-grade daughter. "She's a natural at swimming, baseball, you name it. She picks up any equipment and she does it well. I love playing sports too, and I'm out there all summer throwing the ball around with my kids. My husband and I always tell Breah she can be a baseball player or anything else. Though I wouldn't describe her as a tomboy, she's always enjoyed playing rough with the boys on the block—at least up to a point. But in the past couple years I've seen a disturbing change. She has started to say, 'Only boys can play baseball' or 'Basketball is really for boys.' I think she gets this from school. She sees the boys playing basketball at recess and the girls playing jump rope. She sees how football is the focal point of the boys' lives. She feels she can't get in boys' soccer games. She doesn't want to go out during recess—she'd rather stay inside her classroom and color. We keep talking to her about it and encouraging her, because we know how gifted she is at sports. But it's hard to fight these traditional roles and the negative pressure that comes from the other kids, especially the boys."

Breah's parents are legitimately upset, and they are doing the right thing by encouraging her to keep playing. But other parents express concern because their daughters have never warmed up to sports. Cindy says she knows her daughter would be good at sports if she gave it a chance, but Cara prefers dolls, ballet, and crafts. "She won't go near baseball, even though her brother plays all the time," says Cindy. "She stays as far away as she can from anything masculine." Kimberly, a shy and retiring six-year-old, seems to reject sports precisely because her older sister likes them. Her parents try to keep the door open by asking her if she'd like to join the T-ball team or come watch the games, but so far she has shown no interest. For a girl of this sort, nonteam sports such as ice skating, gymnastics, or tennis might be better choices. Ballet, though not exactly a sport, does give girls plenty of exercise and helps them develop strength and coordination. One teacher we interviewed complained about how few of the children in her classes were physically fit. "Parents should be more aware of fitness, for both girls and boys," she insists. "Even if a girl shies away from team sports, she can participate in aerobics for kids. This is important." Driskin, a North

Carolina father of two daughters (ages eight and six), says he hates baseball himself and thus has done little to foster his daughters' interest in the game. But he does take them on long walks through the woods and plans to take them camping.

Another sports issue to consider is whether or not coed teams are to your daughter's advantage. As a result of Title IX, girls commonly take coed gym through elementary school. (The law does permit schools to organize separate girls' and boys' teams for athletic activities involving bodily contact or where teams are formed by competitive selection, but this won't become an issue for your daughter until middle school or high school.) On the plus side, studies have found that girls often love the chance to compete against boys and that their skills improve, especially in the later years of elementary school when both sexes are becoming more competent at sports. Diana Everett notes that girls in elementary school are on average more physically mature than boys so they have a natural advantage on the playing field. Practical considerations enter in as well. "Dads are more willing to coach when teams are coed," says Everett, "and the teams often have better uniforms because sponsors are more willing to pay when boys are involved." But on the downside, some researchers have found that girls on coed teams are often left out of "game interactions," even when their skills are superior to the boys'; that boys are chosen more often as team captains; that gym teachers call on boys more than girls to demonstrate new skills for the class; and that boys tease or jeer at the girls during team games.[10] Everett adds that she sometimes hears of girls who hold back from giving their all on the playing field so they won't make the boys look bad: girls are not "supposed" to beat boys and parents sometimes loudly remind the kids of this during games. "Kids could care less about playing on mixed-sex teams," says Everett. "It's the parents who mind. They're the ones who are shouting out during games, 'Don't let that little girl knock you down!' " On balance, Everett feels that the advantages of coed sports definitely outweigh the disadvantages for girls in the first years of elementary school, and we agree.

The fact remains, however, that in many organized after-school sports programs coed teams are simply not an option, even for very young children. Whatever the political correctness of this, the girls we know (including our own daughters) have had no problem with it—in fact, they've done fine on their all-girl soccer and basketball teams. Several parents noted that in single-sex teams girls are likely to be more evenly matched with their teammates and enjoy the games more because there are no boys around to tease them or hog the ball. On the other hand, some girls on all-girl teams feel that they've been shunted aside into the B squad; that their games don't "count" as much as the boys' games; that everyone is more excited about what the boys' team does. You can help with some of these problems by proving to your daughter that you really care about her games. Try to get her on the team she chooses, which will very often be the team her friends are on. Her feeling happy and comfortable on the team is probably more important than whether it is single-sex or mixed-sex.

The American Youth Soccer Organization (AYSO), a nationwide sponsor of soccer games for children ages five to eighteen, recommends that children play in single-sex teams as early as possible. "We find that the girls are more likely to enjoy the experience when they play with other girls," says Lolly Keys, national director of public affairs for AYSO. "When girls play on the same team as boys, there is sometimes a feeling of being intimidated by what they think is greater talent. There is still a feeling that sports are for boys, and so girls may take a backseat. On girls-only teams, the girls relax more and have a lot more fun. They aren't so concerned about being second best (which they really aren't, especially at the younger ages). And the girls like the game best when their girl friends are playing with them." AYSO currently has 350,000 children participating in thirty-eight states; girls make up 30 percent of the total membership. If you'd like information on signing your daughter up in AYSO or organizing a girls' team in your area, contact the American Youth Soccer Organization, 5403 W. 138th St., Hawthorne, Calif. 90250, (310) 643-6455.

You should also be aware that your daughter may approach competitive sports in a very different spirit than the boys her age. Girls playing team sports "want to build friendships, not kill the other side," says Jody Brylinsky, a professor of physical education at Western Michigan University. "That girl playing third base is her best friend—she doesn't want to beat her out. Coaches and parents get frustrated when they don't understand this difference in values." Even Rebecca Lobo admitted to feeling embarrassed a few seasons back when she outscored her teammates by a huge margin—something that never would have occurred to Michael Jordan. Boys care more about individual success whereas girls tend to adopt a more cooperative attitude—a "let's make everybody feel good" approach, as Diana Everett puts it. "I don't think this is bad," adds Marge Snyder, Ph.D., a sports psychologist and associate executive director of the Women's Sports Foundation. "It's a different way to play the game. It remains to be seen whether girls will be changed through sports or whether girls will change sports."

Another factor to consider is the greater potential for injury in mixed-sex play, especially as children get older. "At the younger ages safety is not really a problem," said Keys of the AYSO. "But the older boys are stronger and faster than the girls, and safety then becomes a factor to consider." "Boys and girls are built differently," said one mother, "and they play differently. Would you really want your daughter playing with the boys when they get big and rough around age seven or eight?" She has a point. Sports injuries to children is a matter of growing concern, and our girls may be particularly vulnerable if they're teamed up with really aggressive boys. This is not an issue for five-year-olds, but it does gradually become an issue in middle childhood and is something to keep in mind for the future.

In any case, make sure your daughter is properly and safely outfitted for the sport.

Though for the most part girls approach sports in the spirit of pure fun, when they get older more complicated issues may enter in. A recent study revealed that by age 14, girls drop out of sports at a six times higher rate than boys. Even girls who love sports and play them well face intense social pressure to give up contact sports for more traditionally feminine activities: looking pretty, shopping, getting noticed by boys. As Everett points out, while younger girls often pride themselves on being called "tomboys," teenage girls cease to see this as a desirable category. Team sports such as basketball, soccer, and baseball are no longer "cool" among early adolescent girls (teenage girls are less likely to drop out of more "feminine" sports such as gymnastics, tennis, or ice-skating). Some teenage boys refuse to date girls who play team sports, insisting that their *own* teams should have top billing. If a girl's friends drop out, chances are she will drop out too. What fun is it being the only girl on the soccer or basketball team? The whole thing feeds on itself.

Keeping girls active in sports requires more than lip service on the part of parents and coaches, says Marge Snyder. "You have to ask yourself, What do I do to actively support my daughter? Do I buy her a baseball glove? books about sports? play catch in the yard?" She advises parents to provide their daughters with a full range of sports opportunities, and equipment. Everett adds that parents should remain involved in their daughters' sports life—if you coached her team at age seven, make the time to keep coaching when she's thirteen; go to her games; show her your pride and your support.

Girls who have unusually strong athletic skills may face different issues in their adolescent years. We've heard of several cases of girls fearing success in sports for the same reason they sometimes fear academic success: because their success makes boys look bad, because if they win it means someone else must lose, because it appears "unladylike" to be a soccer or basketball star just as it is unladylike to ace the chemistry final. One father told us of a friend of his whose college-age daughter had exceptional athletic abilities. She won a full basketball scholarship to an excellent university (unheard of for a girl just a few years ago), but she decided to chuck the whole thing because, as she put it, she just wanted to be one of the girls. Some girls in this situation don't want to enter college with the enormous pressure of competing in both sports and academics, a pressure boys run up against as well. Some worry about what serious pursuit of athletics will do to their social lives. Does athletic prowess give a college girl the same boost in status and attractiveness to the opposite sex that it gives a college boy? Frankly, we doubt it. Obviously, that isn't fair, but it's a factor that sometimes enters into a girl's decision about whether or not to pursue an athletic career in college.

Even though there are many years before you'll have to worry about the stress and sacrifice of college sports, these are issues to be aware of as you raise your daughter, especially if she shows exceptional abilities in sports.

Finally, here's a little anecdote to share with your daughter. A reporter from *Sports Illustrated* had the nerve to ask basketball superstar Rebecca Lobo about her hair-do—a neatly turned French braid. Lobo replied that the braid had a quiet message: she wanted to prove that "femininity and sport can go together." In their own wonderful ways, all of our little girls are proving the same thing every day.

For more information about getting your daughter involved in sports, contact these organizations:

Melpomene Institute
1010 University Ave.
St. Paul, Minn. 55104
(612) 642-1951

A research organization that provides resources, information, and publications devoted to health and physical activity of girls and women. "Heroes: Growing Up Female and Strong" is a video Melpomene offers focusing on the link between self-esteem and physical activity for adolescent girls.

Women's Sports Foundation
Eisenhower Park
East Meadow, N.Y. 11554
(516) 542-4700 or (800) 227-3988

A national nonprofit education organization that promotes and enhances sports and fitness opportunities for all girls and women. *SportsTalk* is their newsletter for young female athletes and their families.

National Association for Girls and Women in Sport
1900 Association Dr.
Reston, Va. 22090
(703) 476-3450

A nonprofit organization devoted to promoting sports opportunities for girls and women. Membership consists primarily of physical education teachers, coaches, and college teachers; but parents can contact them to learn more about the latest research as well as what's happening in girls' sports in their area.

6

♥

The Five- to Eight-Year-Old at Home

Remember the days when your little girl was constantly underfoot? Twined around your knees when you were in the kitchen trying to cook. Grabbing and spilling and whining when you were trying to put on makeup or tie your necktie. Moping or yelling or bouncing off the walls when you were too busy or preoccupied to launch yet another art project, game of hide-and-seek, or football scrimmage.

Now that she's in school, you're lucky if you can catch a flying kiss from your daughter before she dashes off to soccer league or ice-skating lessons, visits to friends' houses, weekend museum classes or birthday parties, religious training or karate class. When did your role as a parent change so radically from care giver to social secretary and chauffeur? Even when she is at home, your daughter is seldom at your side. Instead, she's likely to be holed up in her room, reading or dreaming or playing school with her sisters, or out in the yard kicking a ball around, clambering all over the swing set, or gathering sticks and leaves for some elaborate and mysterious project. It's a great liberation for parents—and also, at times, a source of some bewilderment. How did she grow up so fast? we wonder. How can we continue to influence her when her friends, activities, and hobbies have taken on such an important role?

It's true that our school-age daughters are moving farther and farther out into the world. But it's also true that home

remains an essential anchor; a safe harbor from the whirl of
their activities; a haven where they can come to recharge
their batteries, rest, regress, and yes, at times, cling and
whine and throw fits just as they did when they were two.
Our daughters may not always let us know how important
we still are. They are usually less demonstrative, less affectionate, and less respectful than they were a few years back.
But most of them love to be reminded—occasionally—that
they are still Mommy and Daddy's little girl and always
will be.

Family Relationships

The early school years are a time of relative calm in domestic relations. Now that she is fairly clear about both her gender identity and gender role, your daughter has probably
dispensed with a lot of the exaggerated hyperfeminine behavior of the preschool years. Chances are she is also on a more
even keel with Mom and Dad. "I remember reading that at
four little girls go through a kind of preadolescent sexuality,"
said Will, a father of two daughters. "And, sure enough, Kate
was very attached to me then—it was great. Then at five, everything was Barbies and Mommy and she had nothing to do
with me. Now [at age eight] it's evening out." His only complaint is that Kate, now in third grade, won't let him kiss her
when he drops her off at school. "She's already embarrassed
by her parents," Will says, laughing.

Mary said that her oldest daughter Sarah hit her "daddy
phase" at around five. "It's 'Daddy, take me swimming.
Daddy, give me a bath.' Every Saturday they go to the
dump together. This is a big daddy activity. I know that he
doesn't think of his time with Sarah as 'baby-sitting.' At
the stage she's in now, she wants approval from me, but
she really wants her father's love."

Driskin remarked that his younger daughter Christine
had always preferred him to his wife, and when she was
younger he had a hollow in his hip from carrying her

around so much. Now that she's six, however, she has become a little more standoffish, and she seems to go back and forth between her parents more readily. Occasionally he feels left out of the feminine world of his family (there are three daughters altogether, one in college and two in elementary school), but he makes an effort to find activities he can share with the girls, such as taking long Sunday walks, going to the park, and cooking.

Donna, a Milwaukee mother of three, said that Breah, her seven-year-old, wouldn't look at her father until she turned four. "All of a sudden, her daddy became more special, and now she seems to fall in love with him all over again every few months. They love to read together or just have long talks at the end of the day." Breah also enjoys playing sports and roughhousing with her dad, though her younger brother often takes center stage when it comes to physical activities.

A Massachusetts mother said that she likes being a role model for her three daughters, ages eight, six, and three, and that she particularly enjoys how many more things she can do with the older girls now. "They don't look to me to provide entertainment the way they used to," she remarked. "Now it's more a question of calling on me to help them get set up, to explain a game. They spend a fair amount of time in the kitchen, and I like teaching them traditional women's jobs." Conflicts do arise on occasion, however, both between the girls and between mother and daughters, and they can be really nasty because, as this mother put it, "we all know which buttons to push for each other."

Holly, whose daughters are seven and ten, feels that she and the girls are getting closer as they share more emotionally, but that at the same time the girls are becoming less dependent on her. "We look a lot alike and people comment on this, so the closeness cuts many ways," she says. "The girls definitely model themselves on me because I'm around a lot. Ashley, who is ten, spends a good deal of time watching what I do and not liking it as much as she used to. Hilary, who is seven, thinks the way I do things is the way they should be done." Though Holly is a full-time mom and her husband Steve works long hours as an investment counselor, he too is close to the girls, especially Ashley. They have always shared an interest in watching ball games together, and this continues to be a big part of their bond.

Skip said that his daughter Jamie, now ten, has always been Daddy's little girl except when she was two and three, and then she had to have Mommy do everything. She wouldn't even let him pour her milk. But that phase passed away without a trace. When she was in kindergarten and first grade, Steve used to take Jamie on "dates"—to a movie or roller skating or ice skating. Jamie's mother occasionally treats her to a night in a hotel: the two of them go to dinner, stay over at a hotel, and then have breakfast out the next morning. It's a very special time for both of them.

A couple of fathers reported that they felt the need to be more modest around their daughters once they reached elementary school age. "I sometimes find her staring at me when I'm in the tub," said one father of his six-year-old. "She doesn't ask any questions, but she's definitely curious. Maybe it's a coincidence, but she also seems to feel a little more shy around me now, too." (For more on a girl's emerging sexuality, see pages 66–71.)

Dan, a New York City father of two, sometimes worries that his eight-year-old daughter is becoming too sexualized at too young an age. "She sometimes sits with her crotch on my knees in a way that makes me uncomfortable. I think as a result I have become a little bit less affectionate with her. It has become a mild issue. I used to walk naked around the house, but when she showed more interest than she should have, I stopped doing it. It also bothers me that she is exposed to so much in school and on the street, being a New York City kid. We try to protect her as much as we can from too much exposure to sexuality."

If we're fortunate, our elementary school daughters will

have put the worst of their sibling rivalry behind them, and may even include younger siblings in their closeted conferences. Will said his daughter Kate seems to alternate between saccharine affection and cats-and-dogs clawing with her four-year-old sister Molly. But more and more, Molly is allowed to participate in the games and fantasies of the "big girls." Like many parents, Will has high hopes that the sisters will be close all their lives.

Holly and her husband Steve have always felt it was important that their two daughters, ages ten and seven, get along with each other, and they think they may have lucked out in this area. "The girls are very close," says Holly. "Different as they are, they are still good friends." Studies of twins have found that girl twins (whether identical or fraternal) tend to remain emotionally closer through life than any other twin configuration (mixed sex or two boys). Many parents have this same expectation of lifelong affection for their singly born daughters.

Chores and Household Responsibilities

As our daughters mature and settle into the school routine, we expect them to take more responsibility around the house. Unfortunately, it doesn't always seem to work out that way. Parents' complaints were pretty much unanimous. "We have intermittent success at getting Kate to pick up her room and make her bed," said Will of his eight-year-old, "but generally she is terrible at chores." "It's a constant struggle to get her to help around the house," said Marla of her eight-year-old daughter Jeanne. "Basically, she is totally uncooperative. She resists being told what to do. The result is, I'd just as soon clean up myself." Driskin said his daughters tend to be imperious, not obedient. They dress themselves, pick up their dishes—and that's about it. Jane and her husband have found that money is a big motivator. For ten cents the girls will set the table. For a dollar they'll clean their room. They help their dad in the garden for free, however, because they enjoy this. "They learned about money about a year ago," Jane said, "but we set the limits on the spending. They can only buy one thing at a time." Rachel said her daughters do chores willingly only when they do not perceive them as chores; once they get the idea that they are *supposed to* be raking up all the leaves or doing all the dishes, they quickly stop.

In assigning chores, we should make an effort to be gender-neutral. Bob, who has two sons (ages ten and eight) and a daughter (age five), has been a full-time dad for the past three years while his wife pursues a career as the principal of an elementary school. Although his role as a male primary caretaker has made him far more sensitive to sexual stereotypes than most parents, Bob realized recently that he was placing more demands on his daughter Emily to clean up her room and take care of her things than he placed on the boys. He now tries to treat all three children equally, but he notes with a laugh that the extra pressure never paid off anyway: Emily's room has always been as much of a mess as her brothers' rooms.

If the issue of chores really starts getting out of hand, it might make sense to sit down and draw up a plan of action. First of all, take a good look at your attitudes to assess whether you're placing the same demands and expectations on sons and daughters. Try to inaugurate a new regime slowly rather than lowering the boom all at once. Focus on one discrete area at a time: picking up toys one week, picking up dirty clothes another. Divide big jobs, such as cleaning up a day's worth of kid clutter, into manageable sections: one child unclutters the sofa, one puts away all the puzzle pieces, and so on.

Donna has tried posting a list of chores that Breah is supposed to accomplish each day before school: making her bed, brushing her teeth, and getting her school backpack organized. "We try to keep the chores pretty simple—I certainly don't have high expectations," she says. "I'm laid back about tidiness and certainly no perfectionist, so if she fails to perform her chores it's no big deal. I try to explain the reason behind chores rather than just lay down commands. I'll say, 'We are all in the family, and if you do these chores we'll all have more family time to play and go outside.' She has about a 50 percent success rate." Both Breah and her four-year-old brother Matthew help out occasionally with their new baby sister, and both are expected to clear their dishes from the table. Washing windows and sweeping are activities they ask to help with: they see these as fun.

If possible, match up the chores with interests and abilities. Kristi is by nature a slob, but she loves her books and is more willing to pick them up and keep them in order. Annie, age five, is obsessed with math and enjoys setting the table when her parents turn it into a math game. Offer rewards such as lavish praise, extra privileges, special desserts, trips to the park, or cash. Sarah believes in taking a more relaxed, unregimented approach to chores. "If you set rigid rules about chores, you're teaching the children that chores are tedium. Instead of handing out assignments, I tell my daughters that when I need their help, I want them to help without hesitation. I am also reasonably finicky as a housekeeper. The house looks pretty and they appreciate it."

Clothing

Progress on the chore front may be slow, but there's a good chance that the worst of the battle over clothing may be over (or at least at a prolonged stalemate) by the start of elementary school. One preschool teacher and mother of two daughters notes that among preschool girls there tends to be a lot of concern with having the right plastic beads to go with the pretty pink dress, but this eases off somewhat by elementary school. In our community nearly all the girls in preschool wear dresses every day, no matter how cold or wet it is. By kindergarten, however, girls' clothing is for the most part indistinguishable from boys': with a few exceptions, members of both sexes wear corduroys, blue jeans, and brightly colored shirts. As a result, Emily, who once whined for pretty dresses every morning, has adopted a totally practical, nonchalant attitude toward clothing. She also picks out her own outfits (always perfectly color-coordinated) and puts them on herself with only minimal prodding.

Another mother reported that her daughters are willing to wear pants, but they are choosy about the style: they have to have pockets and they can't be Osh-Kosh overalls. Carol, the mother of two girls in elementary school, admitted that her one extravagance is buying wonderful clothes for the girls. As a result, her daughters are fairly particular about what they wear; however, in the past few years, they have become more reasonable about wearing sensible clothes to school and now fuss only when some article of clothing is uncomfortable. Two of Denise's daughters were into fancy dresses, but she confirms that it definitely became less of an issue with time. "By the time they're in first or second grade they have a good sense of who they are," she said. "They don't have to put on a frilly dress to prove this." She did note, however, that concern with "looking ladylike" returns with adolescence.

Heidi avoids arguments over clothing by laying out her daughter's school outfit the night before—otherwise she'll try on thirteen different things. "Last year she wore only dresses, this year it's only pants," says Heidi with resignation. "But we still fight for ten minutes over her hair. And she still screams when I brush it." Dan, whose eight-year-old daughter Julia has been a tomboy practically from birth, says that he and his wife have to struggle to get her to wear anything but pants: "The battles over clothing got even worse when her brother, now four, was born. She tried to 'outboy' him. She wouldn't wear pants that were too puffy; she worried that her thighs were fat, even though they're not. Things really came to a head when she refused to wear a dress to a funeral. There was a huge struggle. Now we have fallen into a clothes routine, and the issue has simmered down."

On the opposite extreme are the diehard femmes fatales who hold out for the lace-trimmed shimmering chiffon confection no matter what their peers are wearing. Getting a daughter of this sort ready for the school bus five days a week can be a real trial. One mother said she has pretty much caved in on dresses (as long as they are washable), but she holds the line on shoes: sneakers for school, party shoes for indoor play and parties. Donna said she and her husband deliberately decided not to turn clothing into a battleground with their daughter Breah: it wasn't until she turned seven that she would stoop even occasionally to wearing pants, and they allowed her to have her own way. "In the winter I let her tuck her dress into her snowsuit," says Donna, "and in the summer she could play outside in party dresses. It really wasn't worth it to me to fight with her. Once she entered grade school, however, I noticed that she wouldn't turn cartwheels or do flips on the monkey bars because she was embarrassed when her panties showed. So we compromised and she agreed to wear shorts underneath. I'm glad to see that now she plays with her full exuberance again."

It may help alleviate the morning rush if the two of you agree on an appropriate outfit the night before. Or try dividing up her wardrobe into sections—school clothes, play clothes, party clothes—and set down exact rules for when she can wear what. You might also give her as much responsibility for her clothing as possible: put her in charge of keeping clothes picked up and sorted, make her pay for dry cleaning out of her allowance (which some parents start as early as preschool as a way of teaching children about the value of money), or enlist her help in choosing patterns and making clothes.

Poised on the Brink of Change

"They still look at me in admiration," one mother said of her third- and first-grade daughters. "They still think of me as knowing a great deal about everything. I'm enjoying it while it lasts—because I know some day it will be the opposite." At eight, our daughters may be nearly as big as we are, but they are still little girls. They are just starting to shed the illogic and total egocentricity of early childhood: they are acquiring a new ability to think forward and backward in time (a cognitive skill that Piaget dubbed reversibility); to use deductive reasoning; to classify and sort objects, words, and properties in groups and series. They are becoming more and more perceptive about the motives and mysteries of relationships. They have heaps of secrets. But when they play or when they fight with friends and siblings, they still seem to be locked in the solemnity and utter absorption of childhood. "When she's with her friends, she's into running around, climbing trees, and playing tag," said one father of his eight-year-old. "They go up to her room and close themselves in for hours, doing God-knows-what. Clubs are always being formed."

Eight-year-old girls are aware that Sex and Romance are "out there" in the distance like some enchanted castle. They know that girls fall in love with boys, kiss, and live happily ever after—but they can't quite imagine this happening to *them*. Most of them still have a few years left before they plunge into the turmoil of puberty. They are still free to fantasize, dream, or ignore the whole subject of Romance in favor of sports, geology, horses, or close friendships with other girls.

These girls on the brink of change show a funny mixture of innocence and sophistication. They can be terrible know-it-alls about everything that goes on in school. Even timid, retiring girls may go through a brash, arrogant phase. *Don't trouble me with anything so trivial as subtraction,* is the attitude. *I have more important things on my mind.* Younger siblings who don't know the ropes are dismissed as hopeless morons. "Cool" is a concept that they are starting to wield like a flashing knife. Having suffered from being uncool, they are determined to make others suffer in their turn. And yet when you ask these totally cool kids what they want to be when they grow up, they often reveal how much they still think of the future as an extension of the familiar world of childhood.

One of the wonderful things about little children is how hazy their notion of time is. Our little ones can speak unflinchingly about death, yet in their minds, the week, the month, the school year seem to stretch out to infinity. Our eight-year-old girls are enjoying the last few moments of this marvelous dream of childhood. Who would want to wake them up?

7

♥

Sexual Abuse of Girls

Sexual abuse of girls is a difficult subject for parents to talk about, or even to think about. Yet, unfortunately, it is a subject we cannot afford to ignore. In the past few years, child sexual abuse has received a good deal of coverage in the news media, some of it verging on the hysterical. We parents have learned that sexual abuse of girls (and boys) is far more widespread than was commonly believed, and we have heard a good deal about the long-term impact of sexual abuse on a victim's life.

The facts about child sexual abuse are upsetting, even shocking. But they are not cause for hysteria. The more we open our eyes, calmly and rationally, to the facts about abuse, the better we will be able to protect our daughters from it or help them if they become abuse victims.

This chapter describes the practical and emotional aspects of sexual abuse of girls—without hysteria. We consider the myths and realities, then offer calm, concrete information defining what child sexual abuse is, how to identify it, what to do if you discover that your daughter has been or is being abused, and how to prevent it from happening to her.

Myths and Realities About Sexual Abuse of Girls

The most shocking fact about the deeply shocking subject of child sexual abuse is that it is predominantly a family problem. The abusers are rarely strangers loitering in alleyways. Far more often, they are parents, siblings, grandparents, stepparents, uncles, boyfriends, family friends. According to statistics compiled by the American Humane Association (AHA) nearly 65 percent of the reported cases of sexual maltreatment in 1986 (the last year such figures were collected) involved family members.[1] In many cases, the child knows the abuser as a neighbor, family friend, baby-sitter, or even youth leader or minister. It is estimated that 80 percent of the children who are sexually abused are well acquainted with their abusers.

The second most shocking fact about child sexual abuse is how widespread it is. According to AHA statistics, there were 132,000 cases of child sexual abuse reported and substantiated in 1986. Other estimates run as high as 300,000. The comparable AHA figure for 1980 was 37,000 reported cases. (Part of the dramatic rise in reports stems from an increased awareness of child sexual abuse and an increased willingness to expose it.) The Federal Bureau of Investigation puts the figure at five unreported cases for every case that is reported.[2] "The incidence of sexual abuse of children is high," is the blunt conclusion that the National Committee for Prevention of Child Abuse asserts in a fact sheet on the subject. "Indeed, the actual rate may be so high that it tends to create a sense of disbelief on the part of many people."[3]

Parents of daughters may derive some meager relief from the knowledge that the pain of sexual abuse is not inflicted solely on girls. The National Committee for Prevention of Child Abuse reports that 20 percent to 25 percent of the victims of sexual abuse are boys, and the numbers of abused boys appear to be on the rise.[4] Other studies find that boys are at even greater risk of sexual abuse than girls. Mic Hunter, in a book about sexually abused boys, notes that the taboos against acknowledging or discussing sexual abuse suffered in childhood are more powerful for men than for women. "Our society mistakenly believes that 'girls get raped and hate it, but boys are seduced and love it,' " writes Hunter.[5] Because of our misconceptions and stereotypes, we make both sexually abused girls and boys suffer even more than they have to.

Parents should also be aware that children in middle childhood are more likely to be abused than teenagers (the average age of a sexually abused child is 9.2 years according to the AHA) and that the median age of the sex offender is thirty-one, with teenagers accounting for 20 percent of this group (a figure that many believe is rising rapidly).[6] So the image of the "dirty old man" is a myth. According to the AHA, women were the abusers in only an estimated 5 percent of the cases of sexual abuse of girls (for the sake of convenience, we refer to all sexual abusers as "he," even though there is a chance that the abuser is a woman).

Sexual abuse is seldom an isolated incident. Typically, the abuser "stalks" the child over a period of time, preying on her trust and affection. The longer the abuse continues, the more difficult it becomes for the child to stop it or to seek help. Children seldom lie about sexual abuse or invent stories about it.

Another common myth about sexual abuse is that the little girls are the real seducers—that they entice men through sexually provocative behavior. In fact, as one authority notes, "seductive behavior may be the result but is never the cause of sexual abuse. The responsibility lies with the adult offender."[7]

The belief that a little girl is unlikely to suffer psychological damage if she is abused at a very young age or if it is only a "mild" incident is also unfounded. Authorities differ on the exact factors that determine how emotionally crippling sexual abuse will be. Some believe that abuse involving violence, long duration, a very young victim, an adult offender, and/or a close relative is likely to have the most severe long-term effects. Others, however, conclude that even a single, "mild" incident can haunt a woman all her life and make it difficult for her to enter into close, satisfying sexual relationships.

Mary Allman, information director with the National Resource Center on Child Sexual Abuse, feels strongly that "the trauma suffered does not necessarily correlate to the number of times the abuse was committed or the specific type of sexual activity. It totally depends on the individual who was violated. Every clinician has a story about an individual seriously traumatized by one event. You have to be very cautious in generalizing in this area."[8]

Hunter singles out as "the most significant factor" in the long-term effects of sexual abuse the treatment the child receives after the abuse: "Those children who are fortunate enough to have supportive people available to them will have less difficulty than will those who are left to their own resources."[9] The authors of a guide for women who were sexually abused as children totally agree. "If a child's disclosure is met with compassion and effective intervention, the healing begins immediately," they write. But if the parents or caretakers ignore the child, refuse to believe her, or blame her for the abuse, then "the damage [is] compounded."[10]

What Is Sexual Abuse?

Child sexual abuse does not necessarily have to involve sexual intercourse or rape. It may take the form of inappropriate fondling or kissing, which is now recognized by researchers in the field as the most common form of child sexual abuse.[11] Exhibitionism and voyeurism also constitute sexual abuse. A girl who is photographed or filmed for pornography or who is shown pornographic pictures or movies has been sexually abused. Forcing a child into prostitution is obviously sexual abuse.

Violence, coercion, and threats need not be involved. A

child abuser may lead a girl gently, even affectionately, into an abusive situation. From the abuser's point of view, he may be doing nothing wrong. But it is not the abuser's point of view that matters. If the child feels that a relationship has become sexualized, if she senses that certain kinds of contact must be kept secret, if she feels threatened by a certain kind of touch or game or even by sexually suggestive conversations, then she is being sexually abused.

"My three-year-old daughter comes into our bed almost every morning to snuggle between me and my wife," one father told us. "We hug her or rub her back, and all of us seem to enjoy it. Is this sexual abuse?" The answer is no. This is normal physical affection. If, however, the father began to coax his daughter into his bed against her wishes and if he insisted on keeping these encounters a secret, then that would be an abusive situation. Some kinds of affectionate touch become less appropriate as a girl matures. One father said his daughter used to cuddle in bed with him and his wife a great deal, but when she reached six or seven neither he nor his daughter felt comfortable any longer, and so it stopped by mutual consent. A few years later, she asked him to stop walking around the house naked. He had always felt relaxed about doing this, but he respected his daughter's wishes for greater privacy.

Our kindergarten-age daughter reported casually that many of the children in her class peek at each other when they use the toilet and once, when she was over at the house of a little boy her age, they inspected each other's genitals. This is not sexual abuse but rather normal curiosity. If, however, this little boy's fourteen-year-old brother or his father made her get undressed or if the school's janitor was peeking at the children in the toilet, this would be sexual abuse. It is not only the kind of contact, but the context and the relationship and the age of the people involved.

What Is Incest?

Incest is a type of sexual abuse involving sexual relations between members of the same family. Father-daughter incest has received the most attention in the popular and professional literature, and there is a good reason: it is the most seriously damaging form for girls. Diana E. Russell, in *The Secret Trauma*, a ground-breaking book about incest based on interviews with 930 randomly chosen women, reports that 16 percent of the women in her sample had at least one experience of incestuous abuse before reaching age eighteen.[12]

There is increasing evidence that incest between brother and sister may be nearly as widespread, or perhaps even more widespread than father-daughter incest.[13] There is a tendency to view brother-sister incest as harmless exploration engaged in by shared agreement between siblings, but in fact, in most cases the brother coerces his sister into sexual games or exploration without her consent. He is experimenting sexually with the most available object; she is usually the victim, rarely the willing participant.[14] Far from being unharmed, victims of brother-sister incest are significantly less likely to marry than other women, and they have trouble maintaining successful long-term relationships, in or out of marriage.[15]

The home life of a girl who is being sexually abused by a relative becomes a nightmare of guilt, confusion, betrayal, and self-loathing. The combined toll of the sexual and emotional abuse is often devastating. Girls interviewed later in life speak of feeling emotionally numb or dirty, of living in constant fear, of feeling that their childhood has ended. Incest often goes unreported for years. In many cases the girls come to blame themselves for what has happened, and they may actually seek to protect an abusive parent from punishment.

Identifying Sexual Abuse and Incest

Girls at Risk

Child sexual abuse is not limited to one social class, racial or ethnic group, geographic area, or family situation. It is a crime inflicted on children in every sector of society. However, there are a number of high-risk indicators, which include the presence of a stepfather, a poor relationship with the mother, a mother who uses sexually punitive behavior, and extreme social isolation.[16] According to one expert, a girl who has a stepfather is twice as likely to be abused, even though the stepfather himself may not be the culprit. Girls whose mothers have live-in boyfriends and girls who have lived apart from their mothers are also at higher risk.

If any of these circumstances apply to your daughter, you need to be especially alert to the possibility of sexual abuse, particularly in the home.

Likely Perpetrators of Sexual Abuse

Child molesters, as we have seen, are likely to be parents, stepparents, uncles, grandfathers, brothers, or parents of friends. Often they are men in positions in which they can be alone with children or responsible for them. They might be youth ministers, day-care workers, schoolteachers, favorite neighbors. They are the men about whom everyone says, "Oh, he's great with kids. Kids love him." In many cases, they seem perfectly normal, and they are likely to be married and have children of their own.

Is there any way to pick out a child molester "on sight"? Do these men have any traits in common? There is no single profile, but a number of signs may help identify abusers: heavy alcohol and drug use; frequent or lengthy absence from home of the mother or father; a history of abuse to one or both parents; the presence of a stepfather or boyfriend who lives with the mother; the father placing the daughter in a maternal role, for example, giving her domestic chores and treating her as a "little wife"; wife battering; social isolation; overcrowding of the family; intellectual backwardness of parents or children; extreme overprotection by the father of his own children; a tendency to treat children as property and show no respect for their privacy; a tendency to make sexual comments about a child's appearance.[17]

These warning signs are not enough by themselves to break through the wall of secrecy that an abuser throws up around his actions, but they may put you on your guard. Even more helpful in identifying abuse is to observe carefully the appearance and behavior of the child and to listen carefully to what she tells you.

The Signs of Sexual Abuse

Your daughter is unlikely to come right out and tell you directly that she is being sexually abused. Chances are her abuser has coerced her into remaining silent. Or she may be too young to understand and describe what is happening to her or too ashamed to speak about it. Many children feel they somehow deserve the abuse, or they worry that their parents won't love them anymore if they find out what has been happening. But if your daughter does tell you she is being abused or drops hints in a vague way about some trouble she is having with an adult or sibling, believe what she is saying and follow up until you determine the exact nature of her complaint.

Often, children try to tell their parents in indirect ways. Be alert to veiled statements such as "He was fooling around with me" or "He does things to me" or "I don't like it when we're alone." As Ellen Bass and Laura Davis put it, "For a child, 'Don't make me go Poppa's house anymore' is a very clear message."[18]

It is very uncommon for a child to lie about sexual abuse or to invent stories about it. You may find your child's allegations incredible at first, but do not make the mistake of dismissing them. As noted, the single most important factor in a girl's recovery from the pain of sexual abuse is the treatment she receives after the situation is revealed. When parents choose not to understand what their daughters are telling them, when they ignore the accusations their daughters make or accuse them of lying, they are in a sense acting in collusion with the abuser.

If your daughter says nothing about the abuse, you may be able to detect it from some change in her behavior or appearance. Keep an eye out for these warning signs:

- depression, mood swings, outbursts of temper or aggression
- difficulty concentrating
- unusual quietness and docility
- sleep disorders
- bed-wetting
- weight loss
- unusual fearfulness toward adults, avoidance of touch from family members or friends
- unusual fears associated with specific places, such as bathrooms or showers
- signs of distress or fear when clothes or diapers are changed; signs of shame about her body
- fear of playing alone
- unusual or sudden interest in sexual topics or curiosity about particular sexual practices; inappropriate displays of sexual behavior at home or sexual play with friends
- any unusual appearance in or discharge from the child's vagina or anus, including itching, bleeding, swelling, rawness, complaints of pain
- noticeable straining when the child sits down or walks

If your daughter shows some or many of these warning signs over a period of time, it is essential that you take action. Try to determine who could be abusing her; take a hard look at your daughter's day, hour by hour, to see if there are any blocks of time when she is vulnerable; think about the behavior and disposition of family members who might be abusing her; sit down and talk with your daughter about your suspicions.

Parents who discover that their daughter is being sexually abused face one of the most difficult crises of parenthood. It is a crisis that must be handled swiftly but delicately, and above all in a way that spares your daughter from any more suffering. How do you discuss the situation with her without deepening her trauma? How do you put a stop to the abuse? What legal action should you take?

In the pages that follow, we attempt to answer these questions. At the end of the chapter, you will find a discussion of how you can protect your daughter from the threat of sexual abuse. In the Appendix there is a list of resources you can turn to for further help.

Taking Action

A sexually abused child requires a thorough medical examination. In the unlikely event that your daughter informs you of sexual abuse on the same day that it occurs, do not wash her or her clothing until after the exam. Carefully preserve whatever evidence you can. A prompt medical examination is a must even if you learn of the abuse long after it has happened. If you feel that your family doctor is not qualified to examine a child for sexual abuse, contact the local department of human services or the local chapter of the American Academy of Pediatrics for help in finding a doctor who is specifically trained to diagnose child sexual abuse.

Child sexual abuse is a crime, and if you know or suspect it you should report it to the police and to your state's department of social services. In many states both a police detective and a social worker will be assigned to investigate the case. Reporting an incident to a state department of social services is especially important because a social worker can provide counseling to you and your child, or assist you in finding an experienced counselor.

For advice on prosecuting a child abuse case and a discussion of the issues that prosecution raises for you and your child, see *Parents™ Book of Child Safety* by David Laskin (New York: Ballantine, 1991).

Taking Action Against Incest

Taking action in incest cases is a much more difficult issue since it profoundly threatens the family. Some experts advocate prompt reunification of the family; others insist that the incestuous parent be separated from the family. Mary Allman opts strongly for the latter. "It's too difficult to change family patterns when everyone continues as was," notes Allman, "and it leaves the victim exposed to continued abuse. If a child was raped by a stranger, would we expect her to live with the rapist? So why should she continue to live with an incestuous father?"[19]

Bass and Davis agree that leaving the family intact is rarely in the best interest of the child. An incestuous parent, they insist, cannot be trusted around his children after only a few hours of treatment or group therapy.[20]

On the other hand, the breakup of the family often condemns the nonabusive parent (usually the mother) and the children to a life of poverty. A woman whose husband is sexually abusing their daughters must frequently pit her own self-interest against that of the children. As Judith Herman puts it in her book on father-daughter incest, "Small wonder that many a mother, faced with the revelation of the incest secret, desperately tries to deny her daughter's accusations. If she believes her daughter, she has nothing to gain and everything to lose."[21] "They're in shock," one social worker described mothers in this situation. "They need instruction, they need guidelines." Above all, they need support from someone outside the family so that they don't give in to their husbands and turn against their daughters.[22]

In addition, there is very often considerable social and family pressure to hush up the case. "What are you going to accomplish by forcing him out?" relatives and friends may demand. "Is it really worth it? Was it really so bad for her? Maybe she exaggerated." This is the cycle of secrecy whereby incest is handed down from one generation to the next, with each succeeding generation too frightened or too cowed to do anything about it.

In the case of sibling incest, your first responsibility as a parent is to believe your daughter if she tells you (or hints) that her brother is abusing her. All too often, parents deny the whole thing, side with the abuser, minimize the abuse ("Oh come on, he was just playing around"), or attribute responsibility to the victim.[23] Your second responsibility is to see that the abuse ends—in many cases this means going outside the family for counseling. Mary Allman reports that, based on her experience as a social worker, sibling incest created some of her most difficult cases. "Parents have a very difficult time acknowledging that it occurred," says Allman, "and they do not handle it well or successfully. It really requires an outside authority to intervene."

How to stop incest and whether to prosecute the case are issues that should be discussed with social workers, the staff at child protective agencies, or trained counselors. For help in dealing with the crisis of incest (or abuse of any kind, inside or outside the family), call: 800-4-A-CHILD. See pages 266–69 for additional resources on sexual abuse.

Talking About the Abuse

Whether your daughter informs you that she has been sexually abused or you discover it through some other means, the first thing is to reassure her that *you* still love her. Sexually abused children are living with so much fear and shame that a display of hysteria or anger may add to their burden. No matter how shocked and furious you are, try to calm yourself before discussing the subject with your daughter. "It is a good idea to keep your feelings and reactions separate from those of your child," advise Caren Adams and Jennifer Fay, authors of a book about protecting children from sexual abuse. "The child's feelings may be completely different from your own."[24] No matter how traumatized and violated you feel, your daughter feels that much more violated—even if she can't express it or show it. You can tell your daughter that you're angry, but make sure she knows you're not angry at her.

Your role is to comfort and reassure your child, to find out what you can about the situation, and to make your child believe that you are behind her all the way. Let her know how sorry you are for what happened and how brave she is for talking about it with you. Let her know that she has done no wrong.

If possible, let your daughter take the lead and describe what happened and how she feels about it. If you barrage her with questions, you may confuse her or make her hide some crucial information. Be sensitive to the fact that the abuser may be someone your daughter loves and trusts, someone who probably still has a strong emotional hold over her. It may be very upsetting for her to hear you storm, "He deserves to go to prison for what he did to you!" She may also have complicated and contradictory feelings about the abuse itself. She may have enjoyed some of the physical sensations even though the experience was painful or confusing emotionally. Or she may have liked the attention or special favors she got from the abuser. Women do sometimes become sexually aroused by rape and even experience orgasm. To brand the sexual abuse as "disgusting" or "horrible" may only make your daughter feel guiltier. Again, try to find a way of discussing the abuse that takes your daughter's feelings into account.

Counseling Is Essential

You should be the first to discuss the sexual abuse with your daughter, and you should be willing and open to discuss the situation as often as she needs to. But no matter how consoling and understanding you are, and even if the abuse consisted of an isolated incident and involved only fondling or exhibitionism, your daughter may have been seriously traumatized. "Counseling is absolutely crucial even if the child is not displaying any symptoms," according to Jan Kirby-Gell, sexual abuse specialist at the National Center on Child Abuse and Neglect. "Without some sort of counseling the children really don't get over it." Keep in mind, however, that outside counseling does not mean that you should never discuss the situation with your daughter again. Your continuing support, affection, and openness can only benefit her.

Even with outside counseling and support from loving parents, a child may show the signs of trauma for a long time after being sexually abused. Nightmares, new fears, including a fear of going outside, and reversion to infantile behavior are common aftereffects. These symptoms may get worse after the abuse has been exposed and then, once the child is able to regain her trust in adults and in the world around her, gradually fade.

Kirby-Gell advises parents to seek out counseling aggressively and to look for counselors who have experience with abused children. Experienced counselors can be found through rape crisis centers, mental health facilities, social service agencies, local chapters of Parents United and Parents Anonymous, your child's pediatrician, or the National Organization for Victim's Assistance in Washington, D.C. (See Sexual Abuse Resources at the end of the book.)

Counseling also can be of use to you in dealing with the distress and rage you feel. Just as you don't want your child to blame herself for the abuse, so you should try not to blame yourself for what you might have or should have done. A counselor or social worker who has experience with abused children may also help you find the best way to discuss the situation with your child.

When sexual abuse occurs within the family, as it does in about two-thirds of the reported cases, Kirby-Gell advises that the entire family enter some sort of therapy. For more help on dealing with sexual abuse within the family, see *The Mother's Book: How to Survive the Incest of Your*

Child by Carolyn M. Byerly (Dubuque, Iowa: Kendall/Hunt Publishing, 1985).

For other books and organizations dealing with child sexual abuse, see the Appendix.

Keeping Your Daughter Safe from Sexual Abuse

"Parents of girls are so often hysterical about sexual abuse," said a social worker at a large suburban public school. "It's gotten to the point where they won't let their daughters play alone outside for a second. I try to calm them down and let them know that there's such a thing as being overprotective."

Prudent, wise protection means first keeping our daughters out of situations in which abuse is likely to occur, and second, teaching them how to protect themselves and how to put a stop to the abuse rapidly if it does occur.

The rules we were taught as children—never take candy from a stranger, stay out of dark alleys, never accept a ride from anyone you don't know—were really aimed at protecting us from abuse by strangers, and, as we have seen, this is relatively uncommon. "Telling kids only about strangers leaves them much more vulnerable than they need to be," note Adams and Fay.[25] It is first and foremost *your* responsibility to be alert to the possibility of sexual abuse inside the family and to act quickly to end it. If your daughter tries to inform you even in an indirect way, or if she shows any of the signs of abuse listed on page 204, get her away from the abuser at once. Do not leave her alone with her abuser. Be alert for opportunities that he may use to resume the abuse. Your daughter will not be safe until you confront the abuser and put a stop to the situation. Someone who abused you as a child is also likely to repeat the abuse on your daughter. Don't give him the opportunity.

Common sense and a healthy wariness are good guides.

Take the trouble to acquaint yourself with the family situations of her friends before letting her visit. Similarly, check the references of anyone she will be left alone with after school, such as a music teacher, computer teacher, or even religious instructor. Baby-sitters should also be screened carefully. Remember that it is less likely that some stranger is going to jump over the fence and molest her in the backyard than that she will be abused in secrecy by a friend's stepfather or older brother while she is playing at their house. Use your instincts and trust your hunches. If you have any reason for suspicion, pull her out of the situation, even if it creates some social awkwardness. And certainly, if she complains, even in indirect or subtle ways, believe her.

Unloved, neglected, and extremely timid girls are more vulnerable to sexual abuse because they lack the confidence and the self-respect to say no. A close, loving relationship with both parents is one of the best protections against abuse that you can give your daughter. You can also help her by reassuring her that she can come and talk to you about anything, no matter how awful she thinks it is, no matter who has told her to keep it a secret.

You should bring up the topic with your daughter in a low-key, nonthreatening way starting at a very young age. Bring the subject up frequently, but briefly and without much fanfare. With preschoolers, you can start with the concept of personal privacy. Teach her the correct names for all her body parts, and let her know that her body belongs to her and her alone. If she doesn't want someone to touch her in a certain way—even if it's a kiss from Grandma, or a hug from a favorite uncle—that is her right, and you should support her. Let your daughter know that you support her when she says no to an unwanted touch.

A preschooler is old enough to understand the difference between good and bad touch (bad touch makes you feel bad inside) and also that her private parts are only for her to touch. Be specific in your discussions of personal privacy: saying something like "No one except your doctor should ever touch your vagina" will make a clearer impression on a child than saying "The parts *down there* are private." You may feel embarrassed about saying *vagina* or *anus* to your children, but your children will not be embarrassed about hearing or repeating these words. If you talk about personal privacy in an offhand, matter-of-fact way, whatever embarrassment you feel will soon vanish. Introduce the subject when it comes up naturally—in the bath, for example. Again, don't make a big deal about it or turn it into a serious lecture.

All children should be taught the three cardinal rules of what to do if anyone tries to touch them in a way they don't like:

1. Say NO!
2. Run away.
3. Tell parents what has happened.

In teaching these rules, you can invent games, skits, rhymes, or any other kind of creative activity your daughter seems to enjoy. Playacting can be a good way of getting the message across. Our three-year-old twins have a great time shouting, "Those are *my* privates and *you* can't touch them. Hands off, bud!" It's silly, but it gets them in the habit of knowing about privacy and saying no. If you sense your daughter would have trouble standing up for herself, you might teach her to invoke family rules: "My mother told me not to do that . . ." or "That's against the rules of my family . . ."[26] With older girls, "What if . . ." word games can be an effective way of reinforcing the message and determining how much your daughter understands. After you've discussed the three cardinal rules, you might ask something like, "What if someone at your school told you to come in the bathroom with him and pull your pants down?" The correct response would be the three rules, or some variation on them. If your daughter comes out with a totally inappropriate answer, go back to basics with her. When playing "What if . . . ," mix in questions about other safety issues or even funny questions to keep the tone low-key. Have your daughter pose some "What if . . ." questions to you. Teach your daughter that she has a right to say no to baby-sitters in potentially abusive situations or if the sitter tries to get her to do something that she doesn't understand.[27] If the sitter offers a reward for keeping a secret, your daughter should say no and tell you about it afterward.

As your daughter gets older and spends more of her time away from home, focus your discussions on the specific dangers that she might encounter. Don't start too young or you'll just confuse her. On the other hand, don't dump the whole subject on her the day before she starts kindergarten. In a calm, nondramatic fashion, when she's around five you might explain that although most people are good-natured and kind to children, there are some sick individuals who take advantage of children. Kate, who attends third grade at a New York City public school, told her parents that a classmate had accused her aunt of sexually abusing her. They used this as an opportunity to talk about why some people do such nasty things and what she should do if anyone ever tried to abuse her. Kate's parents also talked over the idea that an abuser could be a relative or person she knows well.

It's useful to give a school-age girl details about what a child abuser might attempt: touching her in a way she doesn't like, making her take off her clothes, exposing himself, making her touch him or sit on his lap. If you merely say, "There are sick people who molest children," your daughter will either have no idea what you're talking about or will use her imagination to fill in the picture in a very frightening way. Stress that these people are the exceptions, and stress that she can keep herself safe by saying no, getting away, and telling you. Be especially gentle if your daughter is the easily frightened type. You certainly don't want to give her nightmares or make her too scared to leave your side. If the discussions of abuse are causing her undue alarm, back off for a while and tone them down. One mother who was sexually abused herself as a child is careful not to communicate her nervousness about the topic to her daughter: "We talk about it when something comes up on TV or with books. I want her to be cautious, but I don't want to overdo." A father mentioned how uncomfortable he felt when his nine-year-old daughter flirted with adult men at a party, and they flirted back in an inappropriate way. She was clearly enjoying the attention, with no sense of the potential danger. This was another good opportunity for a gentle discussion of abuse.

Another mother emphasizes to her children that they should trust their feelings. "I tell them, if someone does something that doesn't feel right to you, then it's wrong. Your feelings are always right." Jan Kirby-Gell of the National Center on Child Abuse and Neglect points out that most children have a strong intuitive sense of right and wrong: they know when something makes them feel "funny" or "creepy."

Telling a story with a pointed moral can also get the message across. A college professor in Maryland recounted this story about his twelve-year-old daughter: "She was in school when an older boy grabbed her breast in the hall, claiming that he couldn't resist. She stuck her finger in his face and said, 'If you try anything like that again I'll kick you in the crotch.' " Elementary school girls would probably find this story funny, but they'll also get the message that a girl *can* stand up for herself, that she *can* say no, and she can make it work.

Child abusers always coerce and threaten their victims into keeping the abuse a secret. If you can explain to your daughter the difference between good secrets that are okay to keep (for example, a surprise party or a birthday present) and bad secrets that she should never keep (any secret that someone older tells her to keep from you), you've made a big step toward protecting her from prolonged abuse. Younger girls probably won't get this distinction, and you can just tell them never to keep any secrets from you, and that nothing bad will happen to them if they tell secrets. You can explain to older girls in some detail how abusers may try to bribe them, offering privileges, candy, and gifts in exchange for sex and secrecy. Again, your basic message should be the following: If anyone—*no matter who*—tries this, come and tell me right away.

Another very good approach is to read a book on the subject together, or to obtain a video. (See the Appendix for a list of books, videos, and organizations.)

8

♥

Girls Who Live with
Single Parents

The number of single-parent families doubled between 1970 and 1985, and today fully one-quarter of American children under the age of eighteen live with one parent. Half of these children are under the age of twelve, and 24 percent are younger than six. Since 88 percent of America's single-family households are headed by women, we'll be primarily discussing little girls who live with single mothers.[1]

All children in single-parent families must contend with certain disadvantages: the likelihood of living in poverty or, for children of divorce, living with considerably reduced means (total family income drops by one-third immediately after a divorce);[2] the stress of living with a parent who must shoulder the physical, emotional, and spiritual work of child rearing without assistance; the problems of a missing role model, playmate, and provider of affection and information and encouragement; the social awkwardness of having only one parent in situations in which three-quarters of the other children have two parents. These are problems for boys and girls alike. But there are a number of special issues and questions that rise only for girls living with one parent, and these will be our focus here.

The Effects of Divorce on Daughters

The spiraling divorce rate of the past thirty years has loosed a flood of articles, most of which identify a curious gender gap: the experience is less devastating for girls than it is for boys. In a frequently cited study of seventy-two white middle-class young children, E. Mavis Hetherington, a psychologist at the University of Virginia, notes that boys are more vulnerable to the effects of marital discord and divorce and that the impact of such stress is "more pervasive and enduring for boys than for girls."[3] Both sexes react strongly to the crisis at first: two months after divorce, both boys and girls show an increase in fantasy aggression, negative behavior, and a greater need for attention, help, and proximity to the caretaker. Both boys and girls tend to change their play style, participating less with other children in imaginative play and spending more time as onlookers and loners. This play disruption is even more pronounced for boys, as is the severity of their antisocial behavior, aggression, and defiance both at school and at home. As one mother of a seven-year-old daughter and a five-year-old son put it, "My daughter learned to become responsible, and the experience forced her to grow up quickly, but the adjustment has been much more difficult for my son. He really resented the fact that my husband was no longer there for him."

A New Jersey preschool teacher whose marriage ended in divorce four years ago, Kathy has two daughters, Jennifer (who was six at the time) and Ashley (who was two): "Life was actually harder for Jennifer in the last days of the marriage, when things were bad; the divorce itself was more of a relief. Ashley was too young to understand much of what was going on, but Jennifer was very angry and lashed out at her peers. She wouldn't share. She got into arguments. The anger was not directed at me or at my ex-husband, but really at her friends. Her teacher called me and told me about it. Things were really tough for her for about a year, but eventually she worked through it. By third grade she was healing. Now she's fine."

Jennifer's experience accords with the findings reported in the Hetherington study. The first year after the divorce is usually the roughest for children, and even at the end of this year the girls in the study, like Jennifer, remained more anxious and unhappy than children from intact families. But by two years, these differences had largely disappeared for girls. The researchers found no major differences in behavior, adjustment, or play style between girls in divorced families and girls in intact families. Many boys had also readjusted to life two years after the divorce, but more boys than girls had failed to make the adjustment: they remained hostile, anxious, aggressive, and unhappy.[4]

Some researchers have found that children between six and eight, whether boys or girls, have the toughest time dealing with the divorce: they are old enough to grasp what is happening to their family, but their comprehension only makes the divorce that much more devastating. Many children this age retreat into a kind of mourning or even despair, blaming themselves for what has happened and consoling themselves with fantasies that everything will go "back to normal."[5] Others, like Jennifer, turn the anger outward at their peers.

Although both sexes score lower on achievement tests immediately after the divorce, five years later, boys are still doing poorly in both achievement tests and grades, while girls no longer show any adverse effects.[6] As boys' behavior deteriorates and remains impaired, mothers lose control on the home front. Sons are likely to become adversaries of their divorced mothers (some researchers speak of these mothers as the "victims" of their sons), while daughters resume "normal" relationships with their mothers—some good, some less good, but all more or less on a par with mothers and daughters in intact families.[7] In one study, researchers found that mothers showed a marked preference for their daughters after the divorce, responding more readily to the needs, problems, and questions of their girls than their boys.[8] Boys also yearn for their absent fathers more than girls do, and they are more likely than girls to become the targets of harsh and erratic punishment from their mothers. "Boys seem to experience more pain" following a divorce, sum up Galinsky and David in their book about preschool children, "to express it in less acceptable ways, to be perceived more negatively, and ultimately to receive less support from their parents, friends, and teachers than girls do."[9]

Unfortunately, these findings tell only part of the story. A major new study of the long-term impact of divorce has found that in many cases its full effect on girls is not revealed until the childhood years are over. Judith Wallerstein's study was the first to chart the lives of divorced couples and their children continuously for ten to fifteen years after the divorce took place. When the girls in her study reached their twenties, Wallerstein found that the anger and depression buried in childhood and adolescence suddenly emerged as these girls embarked on their first love affairs. "Many girls may seem relatively well adjusted even through high school and then—wham! Just as they undertake the passage to adulthood and their own first serious relationships, they encounter the sleeper effect."[10] In her study of 131 children from sixty families, Wallerstein found that 60 percent of the young women were "seriously derailed" by this "sleeper effect": they had severe anxiety and crippling fears over their budding relationships, worrying obsessively that the man they loved would reject or betray them; in some cases they too ended up in disastrous marriages, or they became involved with older men; they became entangled with many lovers simultaneously; they failed to realize career ambitions.

Behind this syndrome is the young woman's desire to shield herself from the abandonment and betrayal that she witnessed as a girl. One recently divorced mother told us, "My greatest fear is that my daughter will wind up in a marriage that ends in divorce. This is what pushed me out of my marriage—I didn't want her to continue seeing how unhappy married life was. So far [at age eleven] she seems to like boys and she talks positively about getting married herself one day. Maybe I saved her—maybe she got out in time. But I worry. You hope and pray."

Wallerstein found that young men from divorced families do not experience these anxieties over relationships or pervasive fears to the same extent as young women.[11] Other researchers have found that adolescent girls in single-parent households are more likely than girls from intact families to become single mothers themselves and to have out-of-wedlock babies while they are still teenagers.[12] "We can no longer say—as most experts have held in recent years—that girls are generally less troubled by divorce than boys," Wallerstein and coauthor Sandra Blakeslee conclude. "Our study strongly indicates, for the first time, that girls experience serious effects of divorce at the time they are entering young adulthood."[13]

A number of other difficult issues may arise. Wallerstein and Blakeslee found that the girls' relationships with their mothers often became strained over the issue of separation. Divorced mothers don't want to let their daughters go; daughters feel paralyzed by the conflict between their desire to live their own lives and their sense of obligation to their mothers.[14] A different kind of tension arises between girls and their fathers. In interviews for *Daughters of Divorce*, Deirdre S. Laiken heard over and over again about the loss and longing that these girls felt for their fathers. Even when the father became the custodial parent or shared custody, the girls felt that the relationship with their father was irreparably damaged, and that the fantasy of being "Daddy's little girl" turned creepy and frightening when Daddy was no longer married to Mommy. Laiken notes that little girls who dreamed of having Daddy all to themselves sometimes worry that the divorce is somehow their fault, and as they reach adolescence they associate their own emerging sexuality with the divorce. Intense guilt feelings around sex and painful and humiliating romantic relationships are often the result.[15]

Wallerstein and Blakeslee also identified what they called the "overburdened child syndrome," whereby the child takes on the task of keeping the parent emotionally whole— providing the stability, security, and domestic reliability that the divorced parent is no longer willing or able to provide. Martha praised her eight-year-old daughter Carrie for helping out so much with the baby after her divorce and for being such a strong emotional support for her. "She really sympathized with me when I was depressed, and she's been great with her baby sister," Martha comments. "When I was exhausted at night and the baby was crying, Carrie would come and wake me up. I don't think I could have made it without her." The more responsibility Carrie assumes, the more Martha depends on her, so mother and daughter have in a sense exchanged roles. Although Martha feels grateful to her daughter now, problems may well emerge later.

Debbi, who became a single parent four years ago when her husband died in a hit-and-run car accident, gave us another illustration of the overburdened child syndrome. Debbi's daughter Allison, now ten years old, was always a mature and nurturing child, but after her father died, she became the family's emotional anchor. "Allison is ten-going-on-being-my-mother," Debbi admits frankly. "After my husband died, she really had to take care of me, especially during the first year when I was totally crushed. She saw me cry all the time. She is *very* responsible, maybe too responsible. This is definitely a concern of mine."

"In truth, few children can really rescue a troubled parent," write Wallerstein and Blakeslee. "Many become angry at being trapped by the parent's demands, at being robbed of their separate identity and denied their childhood."[16] As with Carrie and Allison, this can be an especially acute problem for girls, who are more often expected to shoulder household responsibilities and emotional support. Boys become their mother's adversaries, but girls become their caretakers: both stand to lose a vital component of childhood.

Helping Your Daughter Recover After a Divorce

Probably the most important way to minimize the stress of divorce on children is for divorced parents to maintain some positive contact with each other and for both to remain involved with the children.[17] "What counts most is that children perceive that their parents are committed and give them priority."[18]

"Jennifer did not take sides during the divorce," her mother Kathy told us, "and she maintained a good relationship with her father. In fact, she adored him. I never said a negative thing about him to Jennifer, and he never said anything critical about me. I think this was the single most important thing for Jennifer in getting her life back to normal. It's hard when you're going through a divorce to keep your feelings to yourself and not try to get the children on your side, *but it's the worst thing you can do*. You have to remember that it's their parent you're talking about." Kathy also never stood in the way of her daughters seeing their father after the divorce. In fact, she encourages them to "keep the link" by seeing and calling him frequently. The fact that both Kathy and her ex-husband remained involved with the girls, have kept in close and friendly touch with each other, and were scrupulous about avoiding recriminations in front of the children (a major cause of trauma) have all helped the recovery and healing process enormously. As one psychologist notes, "When both parents remain involved in their child's social and school activities by meeting the child's friends and showing interest in their progress, children make a better adjustment to divorce."[19]

When the divorced father curtails his involvement, for example, by moving or by remarrying and starting another family, girls feel extremely hurt. They both long for their fathers' return and resent them for abandoning the family. Nonetheless, mothers who are able to sustain stable, loving relationships with their daughters after the divorce may be largely able to compensate for the fathers' absence.[20] Researchers have found little sign that girls living without fathers have more trouble adopting traditional female sex roles than girls from intact families.[21]

If you, as a divorced mother, have a close, loving relationship with your daughter and if you encourage her to maintain a loving relationship with her father, you're doing the best things you can to alleviate the stress of divorce. Other ways to help your daughter recover include the following:

- Don't carry out your battles in front of the children. If necessary, schedule time for discussion of loaded issues when the children are not around.
- Try to make your daughter's home life as stable and "normal" as possible. As soon as possible after the up-heaval, try to establish new routines that provide your daughter with an orderly, secure home environment.
- Accept or enlist support from grandparents, relatives, friends, or support groups. Such social support can play an important role in helping both parents and children weather the crisis of divorce and recover together.

The Father Never Known

Girls who grow up never knowing their fathers face different issues. The yearning for a father is so powerful that children raised solely by their mothers will make up fantasy images of the fathers they never had.[22] Sally, a single mother in New York City, had only a casual relationship with her daughter's father and rarely sees him. Her daughter Gaylin, who is now five, has seen pictures of her father and knows that he lives in upstate New York, but she has never had a really clear idea of who he is. "The other day I heard Gaylin talking to a friend," Sally told us, "and she was explaining that her father is very old and can't take care of her. In fact, he isn't old, but I think this fantasy is her way of explaining to herself why her father isn't around."

Leonore, a single mother of three daughters in Connecticut (seven-year-old twins and a one-year-old fathered by a different man), said that the twins really want a father figure and ask her frequently about their father and why he doesn't want to see them. "Whenever I'm involved with a man, even if he's just a friend or someone I date casually, the girls really respond to him," says Leonore. "If he's generous and caring, they'll say to me, 'We want *him* as our daddy' or 'Why can't *he* be our daddy?' They have to have someone in their heads as a daddy figure. They need the loving."

Sometimes the fantasy father compensates for everything the real mother cannot or will not do: if the mother is strict and withholding, the fantasy father is relaxed and generous; if the mother is emotionally distraught and forgetful, the fantasy father is calm, reassuring, and reliable. It's interesting to note that girls long for fathers even in environments from which male influence has been rigorously excluded, for example, in cases in which a lesbian couple adopts a daughter or conceives a daughter through artificial insemination. Just as daughters of divorce benefit from regular, affectionate contact with their fathers, so fatherless daughters need a reliable male figure in their lives. If possible, try to encourage your daughter to establish a close relationship with a grandfather, uncle, or other male relative or friend who you think might be able to fill the role of father substitute. Leonore's father lives in her building, and she feels lucky that her three daughters see their grandfather every day and have come to rely on his affection. A male preschool teacher commented that daughters of single mothers often seek him out as a kind of surrogate father. He feels it benefits these girls a great deal to see a supportive, involved adult male every day. Gaylin established just that kind of relationship with a male care giver at her day care center, and her mother feels that it has helped her tremendously. "Gaylin was lucky. Steve was there and kind of adopted her. I don't think she ever would have sought him out—she might have been overwhelmed by her need for this kind of relationship. But he fell in love with her, and she owned him. It's been great for her."

Debbi, a widowed mother, said her brother has taken a very active role with her daughter and son, and that the children adore him. He made it clear from the start that he wanted the children to look at him not as a substitute father who would lecture and discipline them, but as the "fun uncle" who takes them places and gives them a good time.

Advantages of Single-Mother Families

There is considerably less professional literature about families headed by women who were never married than about divorce. The few studies available indicate that more and more women are choosing this role for positive reasons of their own, and that despite the considerable stresses of raising children alone, single mothers enjoy being mothers and feel both satisfied and competent as parents.[23] Sandra Scarr, a professor of psychology at the University of Virginia and a single mother, notes that "one can imagine that a mature, intelligent single mother might actually give more attention to her child, without the distractions of a husband in the house. . . . My own experience suggests that [such] children get more undivided attention."[24] Debbi, who was married for six years and has spent the last four years as a single mother, totally agrees: "A husband and wife need time together and away from the children. As a single mother, I'm always very conscious of my children's needs. We do a lot more together and they have me more to themselves."

Leonore admits that the financial pressures and lack of time alone sometimes "drive me crazy," but she also feels proud of herself for managing as well as she does. "I'm doing a good job of raising my children," she comments. "They are all smart, they are good kids, and the twins are doing well in school. I think I'm a good mother—I see it in the girls. They're happy and healthy and I can take full responsibility for that. This is a good feeling." Another single mother feels that one advantage of single-parenting is that "you don't have to negotiate with anyone else the basic household decisions. You know what you can and cannot do. But this can also be a downside for the children—they don't get to see their parents working things out." One single mother spoke glowingly of her relationship with her preschool daughter: "I see my daughter growing up with an incredible trust in me since I'm the only parent she has. Since she's never known her father, she does not consider it a loss." This mother also said that the experience of motherhood has helped her grow emotionally: "Having a relationship so intense with my daughter has opened me up to other relationships and introduced me to the complexities of emotion." Debbi feels that single motherhood has forced her to become very independent and self-sufficient. The sense that she has mastered the situation, that she makes all the decisions herself, and that she's raising her two children on her own has given her a real boost in confidence—a boost that may benefit her daughter in particular in giving her a strong, competent female role model.

Just as girls seem to bounce back from divorce more quickly than boys, so girls who never had fathers have fewer social, behavioral, and academic problems than boys during middle childhood. But the "sleeper effect" of divorce that catches up with girls during adolescence and young adulthood comes into play with fatherless girls as well. "I don't know what kind of relationships she'll have with men," said Sally of her daughter Gaylin, "or how these relationships will be colored by how she interprets not having a father there with her. I guess I worry about it." "When they start going out with boys, I know I'm going to be a lot more scared," said Leonore of her seven-year-old twins. "I worry that they'll go in search of anyone who is loving to them and that they might fall prey to terrible relationships. If a girl doesn't have a lot of love from a male when she's a child, she's going to try to find it earlier than girls who have daddies at home to love and kiss them."

Statistics back up these concerns. Girls who grow up

in single-parent households are much more likely to become single parents themselves, they tend to marry at a younger age and have children early, and they are more at risk of becoming pregnant as teenagers and out of wedlock. In addition, their marriages end in divorce at a significantly higher rate than the marriages of girls who grew up in intact families.[25] Leonore has already tried to push her daughters in the direction of stable, long-term relationships. "I say to them, 'When you grow up, don't do what Mommy did. Get married first and then have the kids.' They say, 'I know, Mom.' We don't talk about it at great length, but I really think they understand." "I think I would always fight for the nuclear, intact family," said another single mother. "But if that were not an option for my daughters, it would be fine with me to be a grandmother any way I could."

As single parents of all types—divorced, widowed, and never married—become more common, social stigmas will undoubtedly decrease. Raising a daughter alone is unquestionably a challenge, but it need not be a crisis. As we are seeing all around us, more and more mothers are doing it successfully all the time.

9

Working Mothers and Their Daughters

The rise of day-care centers and all-day preschools, the growing involvement of fathers, the shift in the domestic division of labor, the eroding of sexual stereotypes: all of these social changes stem, at least in part, from the fact that in the past few years mothers have entered the workforce in unprecedented numbers. Consider the statistics: In 1960, 27.6 percent of mothers with children under eighteen were part of the U.S. labor force. By 1970, that figure was up to 39.7 percent, and it has risen steadily since then, reaching 54.1 percent in 1980, and 65 percent in 1988. Nearly as many mothers with children under three are in the workforce (54.5 percent in 1988), and that trend shows no sign of slackening off.[1] Nowadays, the norm for the American baby and toddler is a working mother.

This surge has ignited a fierce debate that remains unresolved. Is it possible for a mother to bond with her children and love them deeply and nourishingly if she returns to full-time work immediately after their birth? Is "quality time" really an adequate compensation for "quantity time"? Can a child develop normally if her mother and father split the job of raising her equally between them—or if her father is even more involved? Are dual-career couples and their surrogate care givers at day-care centers and family homes raising a generation of insecurely attached, emotionally deprived, cognitively stunted children? Common sense,

the opinions of such esteemed authorities on infant development as Drs. Burton L. White and T. Berry Brazelton, and
a considerable body of research all strongly suggest that,
everything else being equal, loving parents are the best care
givers for a child in the first few years of her life. However,
when parents cannot or choose not to provide such care, a
young child can thrive and can develop full, healthy relationships with her parents provided that the supplementary
care givers are "skilled, sensitive, and motivated," in the
words of one report, and that the child-care arrangements
are stable over time.[2] We'll let the matter rest there.

How a Girl Benefits When
Her Mother Works

Our concern is the narrower question of how an employed
mother affects a daughter. The most encouraging finding is
that maternal employment can actually benefit little girls,
particularly once they reach elementary school. Lois Wladis
Hoffman of the University of Michigan, the most prominent
researcher in this area, concludes that girls "generally appear to be more independent, outgoing, higher achievers, to
admire their mothers more, to have more respect for wom-
en's competence" when their mothers are employed.[3] Other
researchers link maternal employment and parental beliefs
in sexual equality to higher intelligence scores in preschool
girls and superior mastery of cognitive skills in middle
childhood.[4] In addition, daughters of employed mothers are
less bound by sex stereotypes: they play more with toys
and games conventionally associated with boys,[5] and when
asked what they want to be when they grow up, they are
more likely to look beyond traditional female roles such as
mom or nurse or schoolteacher.

"My daughter knows that when she grows up she can be
many different things at the same time," said Mary, who
hosts a radio talk show out of Milwaukee, of her five-year-
old daughter. Sarah's current future plans include being a

mommy, playing basketball, and holding down a job in which she can meet interesting people (she got to meet Captain Kangaroo when her mom interviewed him).

Vicki, another Milwaukee area mother, works sixteen hours a week as a home aide for elderly people. "I went back to work when Angela was ten months old, and she has been basically fine about my working. I really think she is proud that I work and wants to be like me when she grows up. She has always been very independent and self-sufficient, and maybe it has something to do with my working."

Donna, a mother of three, interrupted her career as a speech pathologist to become a full-time mom when her children were born. "I could never have left my children in the full-time care of anyone else," she says, "and we're lucky because we could make it on one income. I really wanted to give them a good start." She has no regrets about her seven years at home. "I'm happy, they're happy, I have the support of my husband—and I know I have the rest of my life to work. I've treasured my time at home with the children." Donna admits, however, that her seven-year-old can be overly dependent. "She had a very hard time when she entered first grade," notes Donna. "Since I was home full time, she felt she was missing out on something."

Nan and her husband Wayne both have demanding full-time careers as accountants in San Francisco. They have made every effort to tailor their working lives to accommodate their two daughters. Nan works fours days a week instead of five; Wayne was the first man in his office to take a paternity leave when his second daughter was born, and he has considerably curtailed his hours to spend more time with the family. There is no question that the lives of this dual-career couple are stressful, but their girls both seem to be thriving (the three-year-old with a live-in nanny and nine hours a week of play group; the six-year-old in first grade). In group situations, both of the girls know how to hold their own, how to get along with other children, how to share and stand up for themselves. It's a huge treat when their mother picks them up from school or play group on her one weekday home, but they don't fret on the other four days. For these girls, the balance of mother care and "other care" seems to be working out well.

"For daughters the benefits of maternal employment clearly outweigh the disadvantages," one psychologist concluded.[6] The same, however, cannot be said of boys. Current research indicates that middle-class sons of employed mothers perform less well academically than boys whose mothers are not employed; for working-class sons of employed mothers, the reverse is true, but they have other problems. These working-class boys often show the effects of domestic stress, and their relationships with their fathers are more difficult than those of working-class boys whose mothers are not employed. A working-class father is more likely than a middle-class father to feel like a failure if his wife works, and the sons pick up on these negative feelings. Psychologists speculate that in middle-class families, the sons may suffer academically because neither parent has the time to give sons the extra attention they might receive from a mother at home. In addition, employed mothers may have less tolerance for the boisterous, aggressive behavior of their sons, tending, like divorced mothers, to view their sons much more negatively. The push to independence that benefits middle-class girls may prove to be overwhelming for boys.[7]

Vicki, for example, feels that her employment has always been more of a problem for her two sons. "Angela never minded me going to work as much as the boys have," she says. "They are more clingy and they cry more when I have to leave. It could be birth order—being the second and third, the boys never got as much mothering." But it's also possible that her boys are troubled by shifts in the domestic balance of power. Vicki's own mother sometimes grumbles that Vicki could stay home with the kids instead of working if her husband made more money. The boys may sense that this reflects badly on their dad. Angela, on the other hand, may be benefiting from the positive role model of a strong, competent mother.

Whether her mother works as a research scientist, a secretary, an attorney, a home aide, an accountant, a musician, a bus driver, or a corporation president makes little difference to a little girl. What matters is observing that her mother can hold down a job and bring home a paycheck just as her father does (the fact that her mother's paycheck is likely to be considerably smaller than her father's, even for the same work, probably won't dawn on her until she starts working herself). She grows up with the assumption that she'll go off to work too.

Preschool and elementary school–age daughters spend a lot of time playacting their mothers' careers. A first-grade teacher and mother of three said, "I laugh to myself when I hear my four-year-old daughter say in a huffy voice, 'I have to go off and teach those kids now!'" A mother of two daughters who teaches part time recalls that she brought her younger daughter to class when she was a baby. "She learned that Mom taught and she came along. My working was never a problem. Both of the girls playact teaching all the time. Hilary wants to be a science or music teacher. Christina can't decide between being a teacher and a ballerina." A nurse's eight-year-old spends a lot of time playing nursing games. "When she's not playing nurse, she talks about owning her own restaurant or working in a grocery store." The five-year-old daughter of a publishing executive devised an elaborate fantasy in which she ran a publishing company that published the kinds of books *she* likes to read. A mother of two who owns her own advertising business with her husband said that her daughter's fantasies revolve around operating her own businesses—one week she has her own store, one week she owns a farm, another week she sells art projects (her mom is the agency's creative director).

Judy, an Ohio free-lance editor who works at home, has a different perspective: "As far as my four-year-old daughter knows, I've always worked, so she never had any expectation that life would be any other way. I do feel that I'm a good role model because I work at home and am also a devoted mother, but I see other things as good models as well. The fact that her father is very involved in her care is a good role model too. I feel an integrated life is a better model than just working. Putting in a garden is meaningful even if you don't get paid for it." Judy notes that Hanna has recently started to complain a lot about how much her mother works. "She would rather be with us than go to pre-school or be with a baby-sitter, and I totally agree. I'll try to cut back my work to half time or work in the evenings so I can be free to have time with her."

The Working Mother as Role Model

Since an employed mother is likely to be heavily involved in running the household on top of doing her job, her daughter sees her as possessing competence and mastery in two spheres. "My children know that being a mommy is my most important job," said Mary, the radio host, "but that I also work at the radio station. They're excited when they hear my voice on radio and proud of what I do. But when I'm at home, they just want to play games, tickle, and read." Mary is pleased that her children see her in both roles and that they don't feel there is any conflict or division between their mommy and the radio personality.

Studies have found that many children whose mothers work outside the home feel their mothers are even more powerful figures than their fathers.[8] For a little girl, such a perception can be a formative experience. In addition, as Anita Shreve points out in *Remaking Motherhood*, employed mothers who had to struggle to enter the workplace may make a deliberate effort to pass on strength and independence.[9] They hope their daughters can enter the working world running and jump right over the hurdles of guilt, anxiety, and self-doubt that slowed them down.

Many employed mothers want their daughters to take it

for granted that they can make it by relying on their own talents, energy, and determination. "I feel I'm being a good role model for my daughter in being responsible and in asserting my own individuality," says Marcella, who has worked full time in word processing since her daughter was two months old. "This was never instilled in me as a child. I want my daughter to feel that it's nice to have a man, but it's also important to have that pillow—whether it's education or career—to fall back on. If the man says no, she should know she can handle it by herself."

Perhaps the best way to help your daughter appreciate the importance of your job is to take her to work with you now and then and let her see what you do. The Ms. Foundation for Women recognized this essential link between work and self-esteem when it inaugurated the first annual "Take Our Daughters to Work Day" on April 28, 1993. Nearly a million girls between the ages of nine and fifteen accompanied parents and relatives to work that day, observing the myriad tasks that we do for pay each day, going to meetings and lunch dates, assisting whenever they could, and at some companies participating in special programs or lectures celebrating the contributions that they too would make in due time. The girls we observed and talked to that day were especially proud of how hard their moms worked and surprised at how many different roles they played in the course of a few hours. As Kristen Golden, the project manager of "Take Our Daughters to Work Day," wrote afterwards, "Girls were thrilled, women energized, fathers proud, employers welcoming, teachers appreciative, and the media fascinated." Being welcomed into offices, factories, hospitals, and labs, if only for one day a year, made the workplace less scary and mysterious to the girls. The girls who went to work understood what their parents did all day and they had a clearer image of what they themselves might be doing as adults. They also enjoyed the special attention that was focused on their needs and their future goals.

The first "Take Our Daughters to Work Day" was so successful that it has become a regular event, held each year on the fourth Thursday in April. By 1995, the third year of the program, participation had soared to an estimated 9 million girls, not only in the United States but in fifteen other countries as well. For more information about taking *your* daughter to work, contact the Ms. Foundation for Women, 120 Wall Street, New York, N.Y. 10005.

The Myth of Quality Time

Some researchers even make a virtue of one of the unfortunate necessities of the employed mother's life: limited time with her children. Girls tend to achieve more academically when their mothers are distant, both physically and emotionally. (The opposite is true for boys.) Thus employed mothers who cannot be as involved in the day-to-day care of their daughters may be inadvertently fostering their daughters' success in school. An employed mother would be less likely to tolerate "learned helplessness," clinginess, and whiny dependent behavior. Her message is clear: You *can* do it by yourself, and you *have to* do it by yourself because *I* won't be there to do it for you. In addition, employed mothers tend to use their limited time more efficiently for direct, stimulating interaction. Studies have found that educated, middle-class employed mothers spend as much time as their unemployed peers in such activities as reading and playing with their children.[10]

Although the notion of "quality time" has come in for a certain amount of well-deserved ridicule in recent years, we can't disregard it altogether. Whether out of guilt, devotion, or a simple desire to be with their children, many employed mothers do compensate for their long hours away from home. They lose the unstructured, informal "hanging out" time of flipping through the newspaper while the children fiddle with puzzles, or paying bills while the little ones color; but they make an effort to set aside time for reading favorite stories, playing special games, doing complicated art projects, and talking about what matters to them both.

Our own opinion is that quality time doesn't usually amount to much unless employed parents can slow down enough to take the children's needs into account. When parents are ready to provide quality time, their children are not always in quality moods. You may be all geared up to work on her scrapbook from 7 to 8 P.M., and your daughter may be falling apart with fatigue. Or you may have prepared for forty minutes of six different educational activities when she would have been far happier chatting about her day at school or having you sit next to her while she splashed in the tub. Employed parents sometimes have difficulty in reading their children's moods and emotions.[11] The parent who spends all day with the kids usually has a pretty good sense of how to pace activities, snacks, one-on-one interaction, and quiet time. A parent who has just rushed home from a high-pressure job may try to impose a let's-get-results-fast approach on the children. All too often it backfires.

Stressed Out: The Downside for Employed Mothers and Their Daughters

Carla, who teaches part time at the university level while she completes her Ph.D. in English literature, says that her eight-year-old daughter Danielle both respects and resents her work. "Danielle loves to read—in fact she reads incessantly, especially novels—and I feel that this shows respect for what I do. But whenever I have to travel to a conference or something, she gets sad and angry. On the other hand, she doesn't expect me to be around all the time. She does not have the sense that I am pulled away more than other parents. It's the rare parent these days who is totally available all the time."

Vicki notes that much as her daughter Angela respects her for working, she also resents the time she has to spend away from home, especially on weekends. "She is much more accepting of her father's job than of mine. It's a cold, hard fact of life that he goes to work every morning. There are more complaints when I have to go."

Kathy gave up a very demanding public relations job for a far less time-consuming job teaching at a preschool. She speaks for many employed mothers when she says, "My daughters did fine when I was at the car company, though they weren't thrilled about the long hours. Jennifer was in nursery school, and I had a woman come to the house to look after Ashley. It was much harder on *me*. Even though the money was good, I didn't enjoy living that way. When things got tough in my marriage [Kathy and her husband divorced four years ago], I wanted to be more available to the girls. Now I have a lot more free time, and I know the girls love it when they can walk in the door from school and I'm home. All children want their mothers when they return from school."

In her widely praised book *The Second Shift*, Arlie Hochschild gives a detailed portrait of the stressed-out life of the employed mother who puts in a full day at the office, factory, school, restaurant, or whatever, then rushes home to work the "second shift" of chores, cooking, picking up dry cleaning, feeding children, monitoring homework, and so on. This woman's daughter may grow up with lots of confidence, high self-esteem, and a positive image of women in society, but meanwhile, the woman is working herself to a frazzle. Hochschild notes that most fathers "have not adjusted themselves to this new reality" of working wives. "Most working mothers are already doing all they can" at home and with their children. "It is men who can do more." Hochschild acknowledges that some men *are* doing more— and when they do, both wives and children profit.[12]

Less Mommy But More Daddy

Though there are few hard statistics, a recent article in *Redbook* magazine on the "daddy track" reveals that fathers are increasingly turning to job sharing, paternity leaves, part-time schedules, or reduced work loads so that they can spend more time with their children and/or fill in for employed wives.[13] Another emerging trend is for couples to work split shifts—one parent working days, the other working nights—so as to share child care. Vicki and her husband Charles do this: he works 9 to 5 weekdays at a meat-packing plant, and she works sixteen hours a week as a home aide, mostly in the evenings or on weekends. The split-shift schedule has allowed them to raise their three children without relying on day care. But of course it also drastically reduces their time together.

Whatever the nature of her father's increased involvement, the daughter stands to benefit significantly. As we have seen, when fathers are actively involved, children thrive socially and emotionally.[14] When a father chooses to cut back on work so he can be with his daughter, he is sending a strong, clear message about how much he values her. A girl who sees her parents trying to split up the housework and juggle work schedules is learning a powerful lesson about equality between the sexes. In addition, she is forming an entirely different image of what men are "supposed" to be like than she would with a remote, uninvolved father. "It's good for Angela to see her daddy doing so much," comments Vicki. "He's strong and self-disciplined, and he does a lot more than most of the other fathers I see. I think this will have a positive influence on her when she gets married."

Bob, a full-time father of three in Minnesota whose wife works as an elementary school principal, believes that his involvement has helped to foster five-year-old Emily's self-assurance and an aggressive play style. Bob feels that both Emily and her older brothers have been much happier and more relaxed since he left his job as a heavy equipment operator three years ago. He's happier too. "I cherish the intimacy you only get from being home with the kids all the time," he comments.

Will, who shares a job as a newspaper reporter in Baltimore with his wife Kathy, says that his eight-year-old daughter thinks that job sharing is great and has remarked to him how lucky she is to have a parent around when she gets home from school in the afternoon. There is no question in his or his wife's mind that the arrangement has been a boon to both their daughters. (Of course, the drawback is a single salary.)

Time will tell if these children benefit from the optimal circumstances of their upbringing, and turn out as brilliantly as might be expected. Certainly they all seem to be off to an excellent start.

Social, Emotional, and Economic Factors

The encouraging package of psychological and cognitive benefits to be gained from having an employed mother only applies, however, if all elements of the system work smoothly. The employed mother must like her job and love her children, and she must value being a parent more than being a worker.[15] She must work because she wants to, not because she has to. "It would be nice if my husband earned more money," said one mother who works part time for a utilities company, "but that still wouldn't stop me from working. I happen to like my job, and I enjoy getting away from my house and children occasionally." In addition, both the employed mother and her children must be healthy enough so that they can all go off to their jobs, day-care centers, schools, or baby-sitters regularly. And it helps tremendously if the mother is educated, happily married, psychologically stable, and comfortably middle class.

That's asking a lot. And if any one of these conditions fails, the palace of advantages shatters. If, at the end of the day, the working mother walks through the door exhausted, depressed, guilty, or angry—and who hasn't?—her daughters are likely to draw negative conclusions about working. If the mother has no emotional time or energy left over for her family, her daughters are likely to grow up insecure, withdrawn, emotionally stunted. Illness hurls a paralyzing monkey wrench into the system unless the family is blessed with available grandparents, friends, or backup baby-sitters. If not, when the children get the flu, chicken pox, or sore throats, the employed mother (or father) misses work or sacrifices vacation time.

Social, cultural, racial, and ethnic factors also figure in. Maternal employment creates considerable friction between working-class husband and wife as discussed above. Girls who see their fathers attacking their mothers for going to work are clearly getting a different message from those whose fathers appreciate their employed wives. The model of the happy, self-confident, competent, independent, high-achieving daughter of an employed mother only applies within a golden circle, the bounds of which can be summed up in two words: more money.

Also debatable is whether independence and assertiveness are necessarily superior (in girls or boys) to dependence, caution, and timidity. Is the little girl who bustles uncomplainingly from kindergarten to day care to her grandmother's house really better adjusted than the little girl who panics at the idea of going to a friend's house? Why do we praise our little girls for playing by themselves but stigmatize young women who live alone? Is the little girl who doesn't seem to need her mother at all (and rarely sees her on weekdays) really stronger than the little girl who sobs when her mother goes out to a movie? Time and further research will tell. Already, preschool teachers are finding that some daughters of working mothers are showing behavior problems that once were confined almost exclusively to boys, such as hitting and acting out aggressively. Other girls seem to be suffering from neglect. "The traditional role models have been removed," notes one preschool administrator, "but they haven't been replaced with anything. The girls flounder. Daughters who don't get to spend much time with their mothers are really stressed today."

Time will also tell whether daughters of employed mothers will maintain an emotional and social edge into adulthood. The same "sleeper effect" may show up in girls later in life or in more subtle ways.

But whatever researchers eventually conclude, we in the real world have a strong intuitive sense that the employed mother phenomenon is here to stay. When they become mothers themselves, our little girls are at least as likely to be employed as we are—probably more likely. And maybe, just maybe, all those countless hours they now spend in play packing briefcases and stirring soup, taking subways to work and feeding mush to babies, teaching school and going to supermarkets, healing patients and scolding children will give them a flying start in the difficult, complicated world that will soon be theirs.

10

Looking to the Future

When we moved eight years ago, one of the first people we met in our new neighborhood was Ronni, the six-year-old girl who lived across the street. Ronni was an adorable child, with long fluffy blond hair, a piercing gaze, an extremely bold manner, and an insatiable curiosity about us, the new folks on the block. Ronni barraged us with questions about where we'd moved from, why we had moved, what we did, how we were going to fix up the house, whether we had children, why not, whether we were intending to, when. And she promptly apprised us of all the important neighborhood matters: who the other kids were and where they lived, the various schools they went to, the yappy dog who lived behind us and sometimes bit, the obnoxious three-year-old girl who lived around the corner and already wore *makeup*—could we *believe* it! (Ronni herself already sported mascara and eye shadow.)

After that first encounter, Ronni eventually calmed down, but over the next eight years we were able to monitor her progress through childhood pretty closely. (Amazing how other people's children always seem to grow up so much faster than one's own!) We saw Ronni's clothing change from frilly dresses to jazzy imported sports clothes four sizes too big to drab sweat suits and blue jeans, the uniform of middle school. We saw Ronni becoming more and more adept at tossing a baseball or football around with her older brother and sister and later at whacking a tennis ball back and forth with them in the street. We saw her fighting and laughing with her siblings (especially her sister) and hanging around in that gluelike little-sister way when her sister started coming home with boys. One summer, Ronni seemed to double in size and her features underwent a kind of sea change—her eyebrows darkened, her eyes grew wider apart, her mouth became fuller. Losing her little girl boldness, at least with us, Ronni became more polite, deferential, and self-conscious. Ronni's long nails were always done perfectly in a soft salmon pink (how she kept them from breaking during basketball games remained a mystery), and one day, we saw her chatting on her front terrace with a gawky-looking boy. Instead of rushing over to pat our dogs, Ronni waved and smiled, utterly self-possessed, then turned back to her boyfriend.

At some point after becoming parents of first one and then three daughters, we realized Ronni was providing sneak preview clips from the movie that one day would be playing in our lives. When our girls were babies, it seemed inconceivable that they would ever zoom around the block on two-wheelers, take the bus to school, or hoot with laughter with their girl friends—as Ronni did every day. But in recent years our daughters, especially five-year-old Emily, seem to be gaining fast. A few months ago, Ronni spent an entire afternoon hanging out with our girls: teaching them how to play freeze tag, doing their nails, running races, scolding them for picking their noses ("Do you want boys to like you?" she demanded. "Then you better stop doing that!"), comparing notes with Emily about the elementary school teachers ("You have Mr. MacKenzie for gym? Oh, he's cute!").

Ronni, now fourteen, is responsible enough to baby-sit our three girls; but underneath the salmon-colored nail polish, the suave teenage manner, and the rapidly maturing body, we still see the bossy, nosy, brash little girl who peppered us with questions the day we moved in. How much more vivid and startling will the continuity between infant, baby, child, and eventually teenager and adult seem with our own children? We suspect that the continuity works both ways: to our daughters, we'll always be Mom and Dad, just as they'll always be our little girls, no matter how sophisticated and independent they become.

In the preceding chapters of *The Little Girl Book*, we've followed the amazing journey a girl makes from birth to age eight. In this concluding chapter, we offer a sneak preview of some of the issues that will arise as your daughter rushes through childhood to adolescence—and beyond.

Adolescence: The Great Divide?

For those of us with little girls, adolescence looms ahead like a dark abyss into which our cherished relationships must inevitably plunge. "Things are tough enough now," said a father of life with his eight-year-old. "And it's only going to get more complicated. Already you can see puberty creeping up on her. We worry about how complex twelve or fourteen will be." "I worry that the hormones will make her a different person," said one mother of her eleven-year-old, who's right on the verge of puberty. "I fear a breakdown of communication between us more than anything."

Adolescence *is* a time of turmoil, but recent studies suggest that only rarely does it bring on the explosive upheaval that so many parents fear. (*Puberty* and *adolescence* are not interchangeable terms: puberty is defined as the period when a person's reproductive system reaches maturity, whereas adolescence refers to the psychosocial stage of development that begins at puberty and ends when a person reaches adulthood.)[1] The first sign of puberty in girls is usually a slight enlargement of the breasts, which can begin anytime from nine to thirteen (with an average age of about eleven). For most girls, pubic hair begins to appear a short time later, but the first menstrual period does not usually come until a few years after these initial signs, and true fertility usually lags some months behind menstruation. For American girls of European descent, the average age of the first menstrual period is 12.8; for American girls of African descent, 12.5. Again, the age varies widely from girl to girl: friends who are the exact same age may get their first periods several years apart. Concurrently, a pubescent girl experiences a terrific growth spurt, which usually begins at about age nine and peaks at age twelve. During the three years of most rapid growth, a girl shoots up an average of almost eight inches. And as she gets taller, her hips get broader. This precedes boys' peak growth by a full two years, which is why you see so many girls towering over their male classmates in fifth and sixth grades. (Other signs of puberty, however, such as the appearance of pubic hair, come closer together for the two sexes.)[2]

Puberty will not make your daughter a different person. In a recent book, *Altered Loves: Mothers and Daughters During Adolescence,* Terri Apter found plenty of bickering over everything from clothing to schoolwork, but little evidence of major mother-daughter rifts. In fact, she was much more struck by the continuity of affection and even admiration. When there was tension, much of it arose from the girls' need to be recognized as separate individuals with goals, desires, and interests distinct from their mothers'. The battle cries of adolescence—"You don't understand me!" "Leave me alone!" "Stop trying to run my life!"—are "as much a bid for the recognition of autonomy as a bid for freedom from constraints."[3] Arguments between mother and daughter may be hostile, angry, and frustrating, but, in Apter's view, "the aim of the argument was never to separate; it was always characterized by the underlying demand, 'See me as I am, and love me for what I am.' "[4] "We need a new model of adolescent development," concludes Apter, "one which makes sense of the continued love between child and parent, and one which makes sense of the continued support an adolescent seeks from her parents."[5]

Many of the parents, teachers, and girls we spoke to pointed to fifth grade as the watershed year in girls' lives, the time when they *really* stop being little girls. "All of a sudden, they're looking around at the boys," as one mother put it. "My daughter and her friends have been interested in boys for a while," said another. "The big difference in fifth grade is that the boys are starting to notice the girls. It's really getting intense." Sometimes it's also very funny. Girls not only have a two-year jump physically, they're also often two or more years ahead socially. In a single class you may find extremely sophisticated, poised girls sitting beside boys who seem not to have advanced much beyond kindergarten. A girl who matures early may find herself the target of all sorts of teasing by her male classmates—and an object of interest for older boys. "Early-developing girls do not simply see themselves to be ahead of others," writes Apter, "they see themselves as abnormal."[6] A young girl's self-consciousness can be excruciating, and her distress with her appearance can extend to all aspects of her self. It can all be very confusing and upsetting.

Whether she develops early or not, an adolescent girl is likely to be concerned with her appearance, even to the point of obsession. "I don't have to tell her to bathe anymore," one mother said, laughing. "She likes to dress a certain way. She is also very conscious of what her peers are wearing." Combs and makeup begin to appear in girls' desks at school. Girls who used to willingly put on jeans and T-shirts every day suddenly have a definite, sometimes expensive sense of style. This extreme self-consciousness about appearance is often a source of misery, even to popular and attractive girls. For an adolescent girl, her looks may be the most important part of who she is. In her own mind, she never looks good enough—and she frequently looks positively horrible. The low self-image that plagues so many girls in adolescence very often begins with this unshakable dissatisfaction with their appearance.

Despite her continued involvement with her parents, especially her mother, the adolescent girl is beginning to shift her center of gravity toward the world outside. Friends and after-school activities consume more of her time, and what her friends say and think about her may become more important to her than her parents' opinions. Early adolescence is often the period when peer pressure is most intense in a person's life. One mother commented that her daughter felt obliged to march in lockstep with her friends. If you think back to your own early teenage years, you'll realize that there isn't all that much you can do about it. "Keeping communication open is what I see as the most important thing," said one mother of her relationship with her twelve-year-old daughter. "I always commend her when she opens up to me. If we can talk, I feel we can get through anything together."

Special Problems of Adolescent Girls

Although your daughter's adolescence is unlikely to be as rocky as you might fear, you should still be aware of the special problems that arise for girls at this time.

Eating Disorders

Eating disorders are the dangerous underside of the obsession with appearance that haunts most adolescent girls. *I'm nothing if I'm not beautiful,* the adolescent girl secretly (or openly) believes, and beautiful means first and foremost thin. The statistics are serious enough to make any parent take notice. It is estimated that one out of five girls between the ages of twelve and nineteen has some sort of eating disorder.[7] Most often it takes the form of an obsessive pursuit of thinness: a girl will diet compulsively, weigh herself three or four times a day, refuse to eat certain types of foods, or alternate gorging with fasting.

For about one girl in a hundred, according to some estimates, these problems with food become so severe that they develop into the life-threatening syndrome known as anorexia nervosa. The closely related disorder known as bulimia is even more common, affecting about 5 percent of adolescent girls or young women. The anorexic literally starves herself, avoiding foods she regards as fattening, eating as little as possible and often in secrecy, taking great pride in controlling every bite of food she eats. The bulimic goes through wild swings: she binges on rich, high-calorie junk foods and then purges herself by cutting back drastically on all food, by taking laxatives, or by forcing herself to vomit immediately after an episode of binge eating. Bulimia is especially prevalent in college: one widely cited statistic puts the number of female college students who have engaged in episodes of bulimia as high as 20 percent.[8] Often bulimia appears as a component of anorexia: a girl will starve herself for long periods, then have a bulimic episode of binge eating and purging. In its most severe form, anorexia leads to death. According to conservative estimates, between 6 percent and 10 percent of anorexic girls starve themselves to death.[9] Although boys can suffer from anorexia, the syndrome is far more common among girls.

Anorexia and bulimia sufferers are likely to be white and to come from a solidly middle-class or upper-middle-class family.[10] They are, for the most part, described as "model daughters," "perfect girls," "never any trouble," "always tried to please." When these model daughters reach adolescence, their "good girl" behavior becomes a trap from which they cannot escape. To stop being good would mean to lose the approval of their parents and thus the foundation of their identities, but to continue being the model daughter cuts off all avenues of self-expression. By refusing to eat, these girls take control of their lives silently, passively, without seeming to rebel yet denying their parents an opportunity to help them. In her mind, the anorexic remains the model child, while secretly, perhaps unconsciously, punishing both herself and her parents. Since our culture equates slenderness with beauty, the anorexic girl can justify her self-imposed starvation as a pursuit of ideal beauty. The more emaciated she becomes, the stronger, the more in control, and the more beautiful she feels. Starving her body perversely feeds her ego.

Once she begins, the anorexic girl pursues starvation as an end in itself. Research suggests that the body chemistry reorganizes itself so that hunger pangs subside; some girls even feel a kind of runner's high of pleasurable relaxation from self-starvation. Not eating becomes a sort of addiction.[11] The anorexic may spend hours in front of a mirror hunting down telltale traces of fat, which she always manages to find and use as an excuse for continued dieting. She may throw herself into preparing huge, rich meals for her friends and family, meals she never touches. As she dwindles away, her sexual feelings diminish and she may stop menstruating. If the condition is allowed to continue long enough, she may end up in the hospital kept alive only by intravenous feeding.

Detecting anorexia in its early stages is difficult because the symptoms—excessive concern with thinness, dieting, avoidance of certain foods—are so widespread among adolescent girls. Amy Meyers, assistant director of the American Anorexia and Bulimia Association, points to these warning signs for the onset of anorexia: depression, obsessive behavior around food; eating in secret; cutting up food into tiny pieces and measuring it; repeated claims of feeling fat; setting a weight goal for a diet and then, as soon as the goal is reached, setting an even lower goal. Warning signs of bulimia include depression, strict dieting, secret eating, frequent exercise, disappearance into the bathroom for long periods, drug and/or alcohol abuse, teeth scars on the back of the hands from inducing vomiting.[12] Some girls stop menstruating even before anorexia is fully under way, and others become overactive right before anorexia sets in, throwing themselves into sports, schoolwork, and compulsive habits without showing much sign of fatigue.

The roots often are found in difficult family situations. Many mothers of anorexic girls have similar profiles, described by one authority as a "domineering, intolerant and hypercritical woman, who prevents [her daughters] from standing on their own ground and stunts their emotional development."[13] Other studies find that a high proportion of anorexic girls felt that their fathers withdrew their affection from them when they reached puberty.[14]

Medical intervention treats the symptoms of the syndrome, but not its underlying cause. A dangerously underweight girl can be kept alive through intravenous feeding, but she will not be cured. Mara Selvini Palazzoli, a well-known authority in the field, asserts that "the most satisfactory treatment of anorexia nervosa must be based on psychotherapy,"[15] and that family psychotherapy which treats the anorexic's "family as a total system" is the most effective approach. Susie Orbach, author of the popular book *Fat Is a Feminist Issue*, advocates treatment based on self-help. The patient, she believes, should ideally enter a residential treatment program designed specifically for anorexics, in which she comes into contact with other women suffering from the syndrome and where she would be involved in preparing her own food and discussing how she felt about food as she cooked and ate it.[16]

If you have any reason to suspect that your daughter is becoming anorexic or bulimic, contact a doctor or counselor trained in the treatment of eating disorders. For additional help finding a specialist in the field and for additional information, contact these foundations:

ANAD (National Association of Anorexia Nervosa and Associated Disorders)
P.O. Box 7
Highland Park, Ill. 60035
(708) 831-3438

American Anorexia and Bulimia Association
418 E. 76th St.
New York, N.Y. 10021
(212) 734-1114

Decline in Self-Esteem and School Performance

As we saw in Chapter 4, girls for the most part thrive in the early grades of school, even when the school environment is not entirely responsive to their needs. But for many, something goes wrong during adolescence. They lose their bounce and verve, becoming confused and insecure. When faced with academic challenges, especially in math and science, they start coming out with statements like, "It's too hard," "I could never figure that stuff out," or "I don't need to know about that," and their performance suffers. Their self-esteem declines, sometimes precipitously, even when there is no external reason for their negative feelings.

One principal of a girls' school noted how lost many girls seem at the onset of adolescence: they are no longer children, as their developing bodies forcefully remind them, yet they are not mature. They have outgrown children's games but are too young to date. They express more and more doubts about their abilities. Girls who painted with gusto in third grade start saying they are terrible at art. They shy away from subjects perceived as hard. They apologize before voicing an opinion. They seem embarrassed of everything about themselves: their changing bodies, their preferences in books and music, their homes, their families. They slide from "self-confidence to self-consciousness" as Emily Hancock writes in her study of female development *The Girl Within*. They no longer can hear their "inner voice." The phrase "I don't know" keeps cropping up whenever they talk about themselves and their abilities. The "invisible" school girl about whom the Sadkers have written becomes increasingly silent as well in the middle school years.

Harvard professor of education Carol Gilligan charted this disturbing change in adolescent girls in her five-year study of a group of about 100 girls at the Emma Willard private school in Troy, New York. Essentially what Gilligan found was that girls who were outspoken, self-assured, and convinced of their beliefs and values at eleven lost their way by sixteen. She concluded that adolescence is a crisis for many girls in which they run up against the secondary role of women in our culture. "Keep quiet and notice the absence of women and say nothing," is the message.[17] So many adolescents "go underground," refusing to apply themselves in school, giving up on after-school activities, withdrawing from a mainstream in which they feel doomed to fail. Gilligan published the results of her study in 1990 in a book called *Making Connections: The Relational Worlds of Adolescent Girls at Emma Willard School.*

Like her earlier work, Gilligan's *Making Connections* was controversial. Lots of women commented on how aptly Gilligan had described their own rocky transitions from carefree girlhood to anxious adolescence. But many scholars questioned Gilligan's work because her sample was so small and her subjects were for the most part from highly privileged backgrounds. Others criticized Gilligan for leaving boys out of the study: how could one say this adolescent crisis was especially characteristic of girls without including a control group of boys for comparison?

Early in 1991, however, some of Gilligan's findings received important substantiation when the American Association of University Women (AAUW) published the results of a much larger national study. The survey revealed a sharp drop in self-esteem among girls between elementary school and high school. "Girls, aged eight and nine, are confident, assertive, and feel authoritative about themselves," the survey report notes. "They emerge from adolescence with a poor self-image, constrained views of their future and their place in society, and much less confidence about themselves and their abilities." The survey results indicated that 60 percent of elementary school girls were happy with themselves, but that number had dropped to 29 percent for high school girls, and there was a similar decline in girls' perceptions of their abilities. Girls, far more frequently than boys, said "they are 'not smart enough' or 'not good enough' for their dream careers." Self-esteem declined for boys too, but at a far more moderate rate. Interestingly, black high school girls retained their early self-confidence at a significantly higher rate than white or Hispanic girls.[18] This finding may reflect the fact that black mothers are more likely than mothers of other races to run their own households and hold down full-time jobs, thus providing strong role models for their daughters. When these girls contemplated their futures, "they saw themselves as strong, economically independent individuals," writes the author of another study, "willing to engage in emotional relationships but on their own terms, not male-dominated terms."[19]

For explanations of the survey findings, Sharon Schuster, president of the American Association of University Women, points to the shortchanging of girls in the classroom[20]—an issue explored in depth in Chapter 4. If subtle sex discrimination remains rampant in our schools, as many researchers believe, then it is no wonder that girls fall silent and "go underground" by the time they reach high school. In a sense, they are only learning the lessons of the "hidden curriculum": that girls should be quiet, neat, dependent, and deferential to boys; that their good grades, especially in math and science, are due to hard work, not innate ability; that academic brilliance will make them socially unpopular, especially with boys. Gilligan looks beyond, to the culture at large. Adolescent girls, in her view, hit "the wall of Western culture" that handicaps free-thinking, self-assured, anti-authoritarian females. The Sadkers link decline in self-esteem to the fact that many girls reach puberty at the same time that they enter middle school: "Typically, boys reach puberty after they have made the shift to middle school, so they can cope with one change at a time. The trauma experienced by girls in dealing simultaneously with the metamorphosis of puberty and the adjustment to a new, more difficult school can be seen as a major contributor to the shattering of their fragile self-esteem."

Peers, the media, and popular culture also exert tremendous pressure. From all of these sources, the adolescent girl learns that what *really* counts in life is having a perfect complexion, thin legs, gorgeous hair, the right clothes, and a good-looking boyfriend, preferably one with a car and lots of spare cash. Since her standard of adolescent perfection is the cover girl of *Seventeen* or the heroine of *Sweet Valley High*, it's no wonder she doesn't like the way she looks and frequently wishes she were someone else. The AAUW survey reveals that physical appearance "is much more important to the self-image of young women than of young men," and that adolescent girls react far more negatively to the changes accompanying puberty than adolescent boys. Many boys who do feel unhappy about their appearance have the compensation of high confidence in their talents, particularly in sports. For girls, however, feeling unattractive undermines confidence in all areas.[21]

What can we as parents do to protect our daughters from this adolescent slump? To begin with, we can examine ourselves closely to see whether we are unconsciously fostering these sex stereotypes, whether we have erected the "wall of Western culture" right from the start in our own homes. Do we give our sons more freedom and responsibility than our daughters? Do we listen more attentively to what they have to say? Do we get more excited about our sons' sports activities than our daughters'? Do we believe that academic achievement—and eventually career success—matters more for our boys than our girls? Do we discourage our daughters from wild, rambunctious self-expression because it might make them unpopular?

Changing basic attitudes and assumptions is hard. Just as scores of parents of infants and toddlers told us, "We bought a truck for Debbie and a doll for Bill—but from day one each gravitated to the sex-appropriate toys," so parents of adolescent girls and boys say that they can't fight what comes naturally to the children. Teenagers want to do what their friends are doing; they'll be miserable if we make them go against the crowd. But often, it's not a question of fighting old behaviors so much as supporting new ones. A fifteen-year-old girl shouldn't have to choose between clothes and computers—she can be stylish *and* be a computer whiz. She can be captain of the basketball team *and* have a boyfriend. She can spend Wednesday afternoon shopping at the mall and Thursday afternoon at her math club. She should know that even if the cool crowd ridicules her for swimming against the current, she has your support. It's also crucial to make your sons sensitive to these issues, starting at an early age. Tell your boys about discrimination against girls and women; encourage them to treat girls as equals and help foster their friendships with girls; make sure they see both their parents sharing housework and family work; get them involved in family work and household chores in the same way you involve your daughters; try to get them to talk about their feelings.

Many of the issues raised in elementary school continue to be relevant in middle school and high school, sometimes even more so. The AAUW survey reveals a strong correlation for girls between liking math and science and aspiring to a career as a professional. In addition, adolescent girls who like math feel more confident about their appearance and worry less about whether other people like them. Our schools need to go beyond sex-neutral and become sex-affirmative if girls are to continue making progress in math and science. Girls need more positive role models of successful and powerful women in their schools; more attention paid to women in mathematics, history, literature, and science; and more female principals. Teachers need to encourage the special abilities and talents of female students, and to act as mentors for girls with extraordinary gifts or drive. As parents we can encourage middle and high schools to experiment with cooperative learning situations, to cut back on high-pressure, competitive exercises such as pop quizzes, and to introduce activities, such as journal writing, that break through the silence that so many girls impose on themselves in school. We can also push schools to give girls' teams the same support and enthusiasm that boys' teams get. And we can take the first step by cheering as loudly for our daughter's basketball team as for our son's. As awareness of the decline in self-esteem among adolescent girls increases, parents and teachers and girls themselves are working hard to address the issue. As Kristen Golden wrote in a recent issue of *Ms.* magazine, "The best news is that an exciting new girls' movement is taking shape, based on the premise that by learning to resist limiting social messages, girls can become strong, healthy young women."

Challenges Facing Fathers of Adolescent Daughters

Fathers can play an especially important role in fostering—or undermining—a daughter's self-esteem during adolescence. Playful, cuddly, energetic dads who withdraw from their daughters at the first sign of puberty are not uncommon. It's as if a girl's sexual maturity suddenly removes her from the realm of playmate or pal and makes her taboo. Some fathers worry that they can't trust themselves around their newly mature daughters, or they feel ashamed if they find themselves admiring her. Others begin to relate to their daughters in the only way they know how to relate to women: by flirting. The daughters of such men become confused, hurt, and guilt-ridden, often blaming themselves for their father's strange behavior. As Nicky Marone writes in *How to Father a Successful Daughter*, "A father walks a fine line with a teenage daughter who has just acquired breasts and all the rest that goes with it. It is imperative that he learn to give and receive affection in new ways. If he withdraws, as my father did, he creates a lasting impression of abandonment."[22]

An adolescent girl still needs to feel that her father loves her and finds her beautiful—perhaps more than ever. A father's challenge is to continue to be the relaxed, easygoing, playful companion who delighted his daughter in childhood, while at the same time taking into account her new need for privacy, her mix of pride and embarrassment over her bodily changes, and her sometimes fragile sense of self. As Marone points out, this "new style of affection" means that tickling, wrestling, and "full body contact horseplay" are out, that lap sitting may be "risky," and that a father must always knock before entering his adolescent daughter's room (a good rule for mothers too). But kisses, hugs, and gentle physical comforting in times of distress are still fine; in fact, they're essential.[23] It *is* unsettling when a little girl stops being a little girl, but that doesn't mean that the closeness between father and daughter must come to an end, or that continued intimacy necessarily leads to a dangerously sexualized relationship. With a little bit of diplomacy, some patience, and a careful examination of his own thoughts and feelings, a father can continue giving his adolescent daughter the kind of affection and support she needs most.

Girls whose parents divorced have an especially strong need for their fathers during early adolescence. As noted in Chapter 8, daughters living with single mothers frequently invent a fantasy father to compensate for the absence of a real one, and such fantasies peak during early adolescence. "Children of divorce need real fathers to encourage them at particular points in their lives," write Wallerstein and Blakeslee in their book *Second Chances*. "This is true for girls in early adolescence, around the ages of thirteen and fourteen. Many of the girls in our study do reach out for their fathers at this time."[24] If at all possible, a divorced father should make an extra effort to spend time with his daughters during this period of their lives.

Adolescent Boys Have a Rough Time Too

Sexism, often in a very subtle form, does make the going rougher for lots of adolescent girls, but adolescence is not exactly an easy or carefree time for boys. Boys may have the privileges of life on the other side of the "wall of Western culture," but with privilege comes all sorts of pressures: to achieve and excel academically, athletically, sexually; to prove themselves in a world of competitive "macho" values; and to figure out how to make contact with the very beings they have shunned for the past few years—*girls*. At a fundamental level, all parents face the same difficult task: to stay with their children during the final years of childhood; to understand how they are changing and how they are the same; to keep communications open even when they are convinced that their kids hate them (as they sometimes, inevitably, do); above all, to treat their daughters and sons as individuals with individual needs and desires that may have nothing to do with gender. The parent who can do all that all the time will no doubt sprout a halo or qualify for a Nobel Peace Prize. But at least we can give it a try.

Onward and Upward

Depending on your perspective, you may feel that your daughters are growing up at a time of triumphant achievement or unprecedented stress in the lives of women. When it's five o'clock on Tuesday and you, the employed mother or father, are rushing to get out of work, pick up some groceries, and get home in time to get your daughter from soccer practice, you may long for the simplicity of the good old days when moms were home to meet the kids after school, when little girls helped fix dinner and set the table instead of dashing around to sports events and after-school activities, when dads had dinner served to them when they got home from work and didn't even have to help with the dishes because they'd had such a tough day on the job. On the other hand, when you are standing in the bleachers watching your daughter score her first goal in soccer, when she runs home with the news that she was just elected class president, when she bubbles with enthusiasm after a Saturday morning geology trip to the local science museum, when you overhear her telling her best friend about how important her mother's job is, when her future fantasies include being a biologist, a singer, a lawyer, or all three (on top of being a mother, of course!), when you see her day by day acquiring skills, information, confidence, and spunk that you never had as a girl, you may feel that both of you are blessed to be living in the 1990s.

There is no question that feminism and the massive entry of mothers into the paid workforce have together transformed the lives of women and girls in America. More and more women have entered the ranks of professions that were once considered the special province of men: from 1972 to 1988, the percentage of female engineers jumped from 0.8 percent to 7.3 percent; female computer specialists increased from 16.8 percent to 33.4 percent; female lawyers and judges increased from 3.8 percent to 19.5 percent; female chemists from 10.1 percent to 23.7 percent; female physicians from 10.1 percent to 20 percent; and the percentage of women awarded degrees in architecture increased from 12 percent in 1970–71 to 35.5 percent in 1984.[25]

These gains by women will surely continue across the board. When today's little girls grow up, they will be in a far better position for achieving equity in pay, power, status, and they will have their mothers largely to thank for it. "I want a good job for my daughter just as much as for my son," said one mother. "I don't believe that being a woman will hold my daughter back. It's more a matter of drive and ambition. If you work hard, you can be what you want to be."[26]

In a sense, the current generation of mothers are the shock troops. They are coming under fire from every side: at work for crashing the gates of the male world; at home for "abandoning" their children to baby-sitters or day-care centers; from their own mothers for breaking out of the mold of the full-time mother; and perhaps most of all from within as they struggle with the guilt, conflict, and pressures of their new roles. Lots of employed mothers are reaching the conclusion that they can't—and *won't*—do it all by themselves: they are putting pressure on husbands, employers, government, and relatives to help shoulder the burden. There are some encouraging signs that husbands are starting to take on more of the "second shift" (the family work of running the household, caring for the children, shopping, paying bills, and so on, that begins when paid work ends), though they still have a long way to go to catch up. Maybe by the time our daughters become employed mothers, men will participate equally as a matter of course in child rearing and what used to be called homemaking. Maybe our daughters won't be forced to juggle all the responsibilities of their lives quite so frantically as their mothers do now. Maybe their employers will finally start to take the ongoing needs of families into account—not just the first six weeks of a new baby's life, but the first sixteen years.

It certainly doesn't hurt to dream. But even if some of these dreams come true, there will surely be new, even more complex issues awaiting our daughters. As we saw in Chapter 8, the problems for daughters of divorce and daughters raised without fathers often become apparent only in young adulthood. As divorce continues to be an epidemic in American marriages, we are likely to see more and more young women come of age under the shadow of anxiety, depression, and emotional deprivation. Statistics tells us that girls raised by single mothers are likely to become single mothers themselves, and daughters of divorce are more likely to enter into marriages that fail, so these problems are self-perpetuating. Sexual abuse, especially incest, continues to poison the childhoods of tens of thousands of American girls each year; the legacy of this crime will only come fully to light when these abused girls grow up. Violence against women, "date rape," wife battering persist. Our daughters may not have to fight as hard as their mothers to balance work and motherhood, but sadly, it looks as though they will have to fight many other battles even more fiercely.

It seems certain that our daughters are going to come into possession of a fragmented, contradictory world—a world where women can rule nations but cannot walk safely down some city streets; a world in which women and men will have to barter for power at work and at home, in which the question of who will raise the children is likely to have a different answer in each family. The roles of the two genders will undoubtedly continue to change dramatically, but they are unlikely to merge. The significance of the first words our daughters heard when they entered the world—"It's a girl!"—will resonate through their lives like a clear, sweet-sounding bell. Perhaps this phrase will take on meanings that we cannot even imagine when our daughters grow up and give birth to daughters of their own. Our daughters and their partners may have radically different expectations, assumptions, and future plans for their daughters. And yet, we're willing to bet that in some fundamental, ineffable, inescapable way, *their* little girls will bear an unmistakable kinship with *our* little girls.

We see so much about our own three daughters that is precious, that we would never want to change—their grace, their social acuity, their sympathy, their verbal facility, their desire to please, the grave concentration with which they tackle new tasks, their frivolity, their mental and physical agility, their high-pitched glee. And we see much about the world awaiting them that makes us sick with worry—violence and discrimination, pressure and complexity, blundering indifference to grace, sympathy, delicacy, and kindness. It is marvelous and terrible all at once to be the parent of a daughter today. Was it always this way?

Seventy years ago, the Irish poet William Butler Yeats wrote a very beautiful poem called "A Prayer for My Daughter." In the teeth of a howling storm, in a country torn by civil war, Yeats prayed that his daughter would grow up to a life of custom, ceremony, innocence, and beauty.

> And may her bridegroom bring her to a house
> Where all's accustomed, ceremonious;
> For arrogance and hatred are the wares
> Peddled in the thoroughfares.
> How but in custom and in ceremony
> Are innocence and beauty born?

Old-fashioned, quaint, and sexist as these virtues sound today, we still see their value in the lives of our daughters; we still count them among the gifts of femininity. But in our own prayer, we would add the virtues of strength, self-reliance, quick wits, indomitable character, and freedom of mind and body.

Are we praying for too much? Will the qualities in our prayer cancel out the qualities in Yeats's prayer? Can a little girl possibly have it all? By praying for beauty and strength, innocence and freedom, power and ceremony, are we dooming our daughters to strive for an even more impossible superwoman ideal than women strive for today?

We hope not. And we can add that no matter how our own little girls combine or choose among the qualities in these prayers, they will always be wonderful and we will always love them.

Appendix

Further Reading and Resources

Books About Gender Differences

Beauvoir, Simone de. *The Second Sex*. New York: Alfred A. Knopf, 1952. The classic feminist manifesto exhaustively explores the place of woman in culture and society, the biological differences between the sexes, myths about women, women's changing roles through history, and the phases of a woman's life.

Brooks-Gunn, Jeanne, and Wendy Schempp Matthews. *He & She: How Children Develop Their Sex-Role Identity*. Englewood Cliffs, N.J.: Prentice-Hall, 1979. A somewhat dated but still highly useful book for parents about how girls (and boys) are socialized to conform to their gender roles. Covers infancy, preschool, and middle childhood.

Durden-Smith, Jo, and Diane deSimone. *Sex and the Brain*. New York: Arbor House, 1983. A popularly written summary of the research into brain differences between the sexes. Remains a good introduction for the general reader.

Fausto-Sterling, Anne. *Myths of Gender: Biological Theories About Women and Men*. New York: Basic Books, 1985. A debunking of the "scientific" claims that women are biologically inferior to men in math, science, general intelligence, assertiveness, and other areas.

Gilligan, Carol. *In a Different Voice*. Cambridge, Mass.: Harvard University Press, 1982. Examines the psychological development of women and how it relates to their development of moral standards distinct from those of men.

Maccoby, E. E., and C. N. Jacklin. *The Psychology of Sex Differences*. Stanford, Calif.: Stanford University Press, 1974. The standard jumping-off point for all contemporary studies of sex differences. Written for academics, but of interest (and accessible) to parents who want to pursue the subject in some depth.

Pitcher, Evelyn Goodenough, and Lynn Hickey Schultz. *Boys and Girls at Play: The Development of Sex Roles*. New York: Praeger, 1983. Offers a detailed look at how the play styles of boys and girls diverge from the preschool years through middle childhood.

Books About Raising Daughters

Chess, M.D., Stella, and J. Whitbread. *Daughters: From Infancy to Independence*. Garden City, N.Y.: Doubleday, 1978. Goes through the major phases of a girl's life, with advice for parents.

Galinsky, Ellen, and Judy David. *The Preschool Years*. New York: Times Books, 1988. Contains terrific, practical advice for parents of preschoolers on subjects ranging from sex role stereotypes to working mothers.

Marone, Nicky. *How to Father a Successful Daughter*. New York: McGraw-Hill, 1988. Offers advice for fathers on getting involved in the care and raising of their daughters in a loving and supportive way.

Rivers, Caryl, Rosalind Barnett, and Grace Baruch. *Beyond Sugar and Spice*. New York: Ballantine, 1979. Discusses the special needs of daughters today and how parents can meet them and encourage their daughters to fulfill themselves.

Education Resources

Books About Gender-Related Issues in Education

Best, Raphaela. *We've All Got Scars*. Bloomington: Indiana University Press, 1983. A popularly written study of how children in elementary school develop sex roles and sexual identities.

Klein, Susan S., ed. *Handbook for Achieving Sex Equity Through Education*. Baltimore: Johns Hopkins University Press, 1985. A fairly technical collection of essays about sex discrimination in America's classrooms and school gyms.

Paley, Vivian Gussin. *Boys and Girls: Superheroes in the Doll Corner*. Chicago: University of Chicago Press, 1984. A kindergarten teacher reports on her observations of how boys and girls behave in the classroom.

Sadker, Myra and David. *Failing At Fairness: How Our Schools Cheat Girls*. New York: Touchstone, 1994. The most thorough and most recent book about the extent and the impact of sexism at all levels of education, from elementary school through college. The culmination of decades of excellent work on the part of the Sadkers. Contains extensive listings of books for children featuring "wonderful women and resource-ful girls."

Shapiro, June, Sylvia Kramer, and Catherine Hunerberg. *Equal Their Chances: Children's Activities for Non-Sexist Learning.* Englewood Cliffs, N.J.: Prentice-Hall, 1981. Contains practical activities for promoting equal learning in all areas.

Wellesley College Center for Research on Women. *How Schools Short-change Girls: The AAUW Report.* Washington, D.C.: American Associ-ation of University Women Educational Foundation, 1992. The ground-breaking study revealing the persistence of gender bias in Amer-ica's schools. To order a copy, call (800) 225-9998 or write AAUW Sales Office, P.O. Box 251, Annapolis Junction, Md. 20701-0251.

Books About Involving Girls in Math, Science, and Computers

Kaye, Peggy. *Games for Math, Playful Ways to Help Your Child Learn Math from Kindergarten to Third Grade.* New York: Pantheon Books, 1987. Just what the title promises.

Sanders, Jo. *The Neuter Computer: Computers for Girls and Boys.* New York: Neal-Schumann, 1986. Describes how and why to encourage girls to use computers in and out of school. The same author has written a pamphlet for parents called "Does Your Daughter Say 'No, Thanks' to the Computer?" (New York: Women's Action Alliance, 1989) for par-ents who want to help their daughters become and remain skilled in the use of computers.

Skolnick, Joan, Carol Langbort, and Lucille Day. *How to Encourage Girls in Math and Science.* Englewood Cliffs, N.J.: Prentice-Hall, 1982. A book of practical advice for parents and teachers on getting girls in-volved in and excited by these subjects.

Sprung, Barbara, et al. *What Will Happen If . . . Young Children and the Scientific Method.* New York: Education Equity Concepts, 1985. Con-tains simple ideas for enjoyable science projects that parents can involve their daughters in.

Organizations Offering Educational Resources for Girls

Girls Incorporated
30 E. 33rd St., 7th floor
New York, N.Y. 10016
(212) 689-3700

Girls Inc., a nationwide organization dedicated to helping girls become strong, smart, and bold, runs a number of skills programs including Operation SMART, a hands-on program that encourages girls to persist in science and math. Programs are offered through local affiliates and community-based organizations.

Women's Action Alliance
370 Lexington Ave.
New York, N.Y. 10017
(212) 532-8330

This organization dedicated to equality for women publishes a variety of materials about nonsexist education, computer use, girls and math, and other related issues.

Books About Working Mothers

Hochschild, Arlie. *The Second Shift: Working Parents and the Revolution at Home*. New York: Viking, 1989. A thought-provoking look at the issues raised in marriages, especially for women, when both parents work.

Scarr, Sandra. *Mother Care/Other Care*. New York: Basic Books, 1984. Offers a careful look at issues facing children of working mothers and explores the relative merits of various forms of alternative child care.

Shreve, Anita. *Remaking Motherhood*. New York: Ballantine, 1987. Examines the impact of working mothers on children, with a chapter devoted to the effects of maternal employment on daughters.

Child Sexual Abuse Resources

Books for Children About Child Sexual Abuse

Bahr, Amy C. *It's OK to Say No*. Grosset & Dunlap, 1986.

Bass, Ellen. *I Like You to Make Jokes with Me, But I Don't Want You to Touch Me*. Lollypop Power, 1981.

Bassett, Kerry. *My Very Own Special Body Book*. Hawthorne Press, 1981.

Dayee, Frances. *Private Zone*. Charles Franklin Press, 1983.

Freeman, Lory. *It's MY Body*. Parenting Press, 1984.

Gordon, Sol, and Judith Gordon. *A Better Safe Than Sorry Book*. Ed-U Press, 1984.

Haddad, Jill, and Lloyd Martin. *What If I Say No!* M. H. Cap, 1982.

Hindman, Jan. *A Very Touching Book*. McClure-Hindman, 1983.

Johnson, Karen. *The Trouble with Secrets*. Parenting Press, 1986.

Neiburg, Susan, and Janice E. Rench. *Feeling Safe, Feeling Strong*. Lerner Publication, 1984.

Appendix 267

Pawson, Barbara, and Linda Kemp Keller. *I Belong to Me*. Whortleberry Books, 1984.

Polese, Carolyn. *Promise Not to Tell*. Human Sciences Press, 1985.

Seltz, Shirly. *I Can Say No*. Seltz Associates, 1985.

Shields, Amy. *It's OK to Say No!* Playmore, 1984.

Wachter, Oralee. *No More Secrets For Me*. Little, Brown, 1983.

Walvoord Girard, Linda. *My Body Is Private*. Albert Whitman, 1984.

Videos for Children About Sexual Abuse

"Better Safe Than Sorry II" (FilmFair Communications)

"Child Sexual Abuse: What Your Children Should Know" (Indiana University Audio-Visual Center)

"Feeling Yes, Feeling No" (Perennial Education)

"Now I Can Tell You My Secret" (Walt Disney Educational Media Co.)

"Strong Kids, Safe Kids," hosted by Henry Winkler (Paramount Video)

Books for Parents About Preventing Child Sexual Abuse

Adams, Caren, and Jennifer Fay. *No More Secrets: Protecting Your Child from Sexual Assault*. Impact Publishers, 1981.

Colao, Flora, and Tamar Hosansky. *Your Children Should Know*. Bobbs-Merrill, 1983.

Kraizer, Sherryll Kerns. *The Safe Child Book*. Delacorte, 1985.

Sanford, Linda. *The Silent Children: A Parent's Guide to the Prevention of Child Sexual Abuse*. McGraw-Hill, 1980.

Organizations Dealing with Child Sexual Abuse

National Committee for Prevention of Child Abuse
332 S. Michigan Ave., Suite 1600
Chicago, Ill. 60604-4357
(312) 663-3520

An organization dedicated to preventing child abuse through advocacy, public awareness, education, and research. Provides a variety of publications on the subject as well as listings of sixty-seven local chapters. Contact them for a free list of publications and educational materials.

Clearinghouse on Child Abuse and Neglect Information
P.O. Box 1182
Washington, D.C. 20013-1182
(703) 385-7565 or (800) 394-3366

Provides extensive bibliographies on the topic of child abuse, including sexual abuse.

800-222-2000

A hotline sponsored by the National Council on Child Abuse and Family Violence that provides assistance in finding shelter for abuse victims, in reporting cases of abuse to the proper authorities, and in locating trained counselors. If you suspect a child is being sexually abused and don't know what to do about it, a support person at this number will help you.

800-4-A-CHILD

A twenty-four-hour hotline sponsored by Childhelp USA; refers callers to counselors and support groups through local chapters of Parents Anonymous and Parents United (see below); provides assistance to callers in crisis counseling and in finding the proper channels to report incidents of child abuse. Many local chapters of Parents Anonymous offer counseling to parents who are abusing their children or to the spouses of abusive parents.

Parents United/Daughters and Sons United
232 East Gish Road
San Jose, Calif. 95112
(408) 453-7616

National organization with local groups that provide assistance to families involved in child sexual abuse, for parents who were sexually abused as children and, through Daughters and Sons United, to children who are victims of sexual abuse.

C. Henry Kempe National Center for the Prevention and Treatment of Child Abuse and Neglect
1205 Oneida St.
Denver, Colo. 80220
(303) 321-3963

A clinically based resource for research, consultation, and program development in the area of child abuse. Offers a wide range of publications for sale to the general public.

National Organization for Victim's Assistance
1757 Park Road, N.W.
Washington, D.C. 20010
(202) 232-6682

Assists in therapeutic referrals for victims of child abuse; upon request will mail information packets on the subject of child sexual abuse.

Organizations Dealing with Eating Disorders

ANAD (National Association of Anorexia Nervosa and Associated Disorders)
P.O. Box 7
Highland Park, Ill., 60035
(708) 831-3438

American Anorexia and Bulimia Association
293 Central Park West, Suite 1R
New York, N.Y. 10024
(212) 501-8351

Notes

Chapter 1: Myths and Facts About Little Girls

1. J. Z. Rubin, F. J. Provenzano, and Z. Luria, "The Eye of the Beholder: Parents' Views on Sex of Newborns," *American Journal of Orthopsychiatry* 44 (1974): 512–19.

2. G. Stanley Hall, *Adolescence*, vol. 2 (New York: Appleton, 1904), 561–69.

3. J. M. Bardwick, "Psychological Conflict and the Reproductive System," as cited in J. Kagan, *The Growth of the Child: Reflections on Human Development* (New York: Norton, 1978), 120.

4. Simone de Beauvoir, *The Second Sex* (New York: Alfred A. Knopf, 1952), 301–2.

5. J. Hyde and M. Linn, eds., *The Psychology of Gender* (Baltimore: Johns Hopkins Press, 1986), 142. Although the authors concede that adult women smile more, they find "virtually no evidence for a gender difference [in smiling] among children" ages two through twelve.

6. E. O. Wilson, *Sociobiology: The New Synthesis* (Cambridge, Mass.: Harvard University Press, 1975) is the classic statement of this point of view.

7. A. Fausto-Sterling, *Myths of Gender: Biological Theories About Women and Men* (New York: Basic Books, 1985).

8. A. Barfield, "Biological Influences on Sex Differences in Behavior," in *Sex Differences: Social and Biological Perspectives*, ed. M. S. Teitelbaum (Garden City, N.Y.: Doubleday, 1976).

9. N. Pastore, *The Nature-Nurture Controversy* (New York: Kings Crown Press, 1949), as cited in Jeanne Brooks-Gunn and Wendy Schempp Matthews, *He & She: How Children Develop Their Sex-Role Identity* (Englewood Cliffs, N.J.: Prentice-Hall, 1979), 55.

10. J. Kagan, *The Growth of the Child: Reflections on Human Development* (New York: Norton, 1978), 115.

11. R. K. Unger, *Female and Male: Psychological Perspectives* (New York: Harper & Row, 1979).

12. E. E. Maccoby and C. N. Jacklin, *The Psychology of Sex Differences* (Stanford, Calif.: Stanford University Press, 1974), 1.

13. I. K. Broverman et al., "Sex-Role Stereotypes: A Current Appraisal," *Journal of Social Issues* 28 (1972): 59–78, cited in Unger, *Female and Male*.

14. M. C. Linn and A. C. Petersen in "Gender Differences and Spatial Ability: Emergence and Characterization," *Child Development* 56 (1985) use the technique of meta-analysis to reevaluate the data on superior male aggression. Other reevaluations using meta-analysis appear in Hyde and Linn, *Psychology of Gender*. Fausto-Sterling, in *Myths of Gender*, argues provocatively against the view that aggression correlates to the male hormone testosterone and persuasively challenges Maccoby and Jacklin's suggestion that the greater aggressiveness of males is biologically determined. Unger, in *Female and Male*, speculates that the male superiority in spatial visualization may result in part from boys' exposure to toys and play situations that foster their ability in this area. Kathryn E. Hood, Patricia Draper, Lisa J. Crockett, and Anne C. Petersen in "The Ontogeny and Phylogeny of Sex Differences in Development: A Biophysical Synthesis," *Current Conceptions of Sex Roles and Sex Typing: Theory and Research*, ed. D. Bruce Carter (New York: Praeger, 1987), 63, back up Unger's speculation with more recent findings that demonstrate the "plasticity" of the brain as it develops in the early years of life; they conclude that "specific experiences can alter the course of brain development" and suggest that "sex-typed socialization sufficiently constrains the activities and experiences of girls and boys to produce sex-typed cognitive performance."

15. A. Feingold, "Cognitive Gender Differences Are Disappearing," *American Psychologist* 43, no. 2 (Feb. 1988): 95–103. This study finds, however, that girls have not closed the gap at the upper levels of performance on high school mathematics. Although girls have caught up with boys in the middle of the math class, at the very top of the class, males continue to dominate, and to dominate at the same percentages as they did thirty years ago.

16. J. H. Block, "Differential Premises Arising from Differential Socialization of the Sexes: Some Conjectures," *Child Development* 54, no. 6 (1983): 335–54.

17. Jo Durden-Smith and Diane deSimone, *Sex and the Brain* (New York: Arbor House, 1983), 16. This book, originally published as a series of articles in *Playboy*, presents a popularly written summary of the research into brain differences and the implications of such research on differences in the social, intellectual, and sexual behavior of men and women.

18. The information on brain lateralization comes from the following sources: Durden-Smith and deSimone, *Sex and the Brain*; Doreen Kimura, "Male Brain, Female Brain: The Hidden Difference," *Psychology Today*

(Nov. 1985): 50–58; Sheila Moore and Roon Frost, *The Little Boy Book* (New York: Ballantine, 1987), 8–9.

19. Hood et al., "Ontogeny and Phylogeny of Sex Differences," 52.

20. Cited in Fausto-Sterling, *Myths of Gender*, 49.

21. Cited in Durden-Smith and deSimone, *Sex and the Brain*, 100.

22. June Reinisch as quoted in Winifred Gallagher, "Sex and Hormones," *The Atlantic* (Mar. 1988): 81.

23. June Reinisch as quoted in Elizabeth Hall, "June Reinisch: New Directions for the Kinsey Institute," *Psychology Today* (June 1986): 35.

24. Moore and Frost, *The Little Boy Book*, 9.

25. Kimura, "Male Brain, Female Brain," 56.

26. J. Kagan, *The Nature of the Child* (New York: Basic Books, 1984), 10.

27. Carol Tavris, "The Gender Gap," *Vogue* (Apr. 1989): 309.

28. S. Chess, M.D., and J. Whitbread, *Daughters: From Infancy to Independence* (Garden City, N.Y.: Doubleday, 1978).

29. L. B. Andrews, "How Women Think," *Parents* (Apr. 1986): 75.

30. E. Galinsky and J. David, *The Preschool Years* (New York: Times Books, 1988), 150.

31. S. Osherson, *Wrestling with Love: How Men Struggle with Intimacy with Women, Children, Parents, and Each Other* (New York: Ballantine, 1992).

Chapter 2: The Littlest Girls

1. J. M. Tanner, *Fetus Into Man: Physical Growth from Conception to Maturity* (Cambridge, Mass.: Harvard University Press, 1978), 55.

2. J. Brooks-Gunn and W. S. Matthews, *He & She: How Children Develop Their Sex-Role Identity* (Englewood Cliffs, N.J.: Prentice-Hall, 1979), 41.

3. Tanner, *Fetus Into Man*, 56–57.

4. Winifred Gallagher, "Sex and Hormones," *The Atlantic* (Mar. 1988): 79.

5. S. Chess, M.D., and J. Whitbread, *Daughters: From Infancy to Independence* (Garden City, N.Y.: Doubleday, 1978), 130.

6. Tanner, *Fetus Into Man*, Louise Bates Ames et al., *The Gesell Institute's Child from One to Six: Evaluating the Behavior of the Preschool Child* (New York: Harper & Row, 1979), 167–68.

7. See Rosalind Rosenberg, "Leta Hollingworth: Toward a Sexless Intelligence," *In the Shadow of the Past: Psychology Portrays the Sexes*, ed. Miriam Lewin (New York: Columbia University Press, 1984) for a discussion of the work of pioneering psychologists Leta Hollingworth and Helen Thompson Woolley in discrediting the theory of greater male variability.

8. Chess and Whitbread, *Daughters*, 30–31.

9. R. C. Smart and M. S. Smart, *Children: Development and Relationships* (New York: Macmillan, 1982), 102. See also S. Phillips, S. King, and L. DuBois, "Spontaneous Activities of Female vs. Male Newborns," *Child Development* 49 (1978): 590–97.

10. J. Kagan, *The Growth of the Child: Reflections on Human Development* (New York: Norton, 1978).

11. E. E. Maccoby and C. N. Jacklin, *The Psychology of Sex Differences* (Stanford, Calif.: Stanford University Press, 1974), 182–86.

12. Brooks-Gunn and Matthews, *He & She*, 67–68.

13. Sheila Moore and Roon Frost, *The Little Boy Book* (New York: Ballantine, 1987), 16–17, offers a summary of the research that supports the view that girls hear better and boys require more visual novelty.

14. Maccoby and Jacklin, *Psychology of Sex Differences*, 35.

15. See R. Q. Bell, G. M. Weller, and M. F. Waldrop, "Newborn and Preschooler: Organization of Behavior and Relations Between Periods," *Monographs of the Society for Research in Child Development*, series no. 142 (1971): 36, 1–2.

16. J. M. Bardwick, *Psychology of Women* (New York: Harper & Row, 1971), 102.

17. Maccoby and Jacklin, *Psychology of Sex Differences*, 23.

18. E. Tronick and L. Adamson, *Babies as People* (New York: Macmillan, 1980), 85–90.

19. Alexander Thomas, M.D., Stella Chess, M.D., and Herbert G. Birch, Ph.D., *Temperament and Behavior Disorders in Children* (New York: New York University Press, 1968), and Chess and Whitbread, 11–26.

20. Moore and Frost, *The Little Boy Book*, 22.

21. Alexander Thomas and Stella Chess, *Temperament and Development* (New York: Brunner/Mazel, 1977).

22. Tronick and Adamson, *Babies as People*.

23. Kagan, *The Growth of the Child*, 123.

24. H. A. Moss, "Sex, Age and State as Determinants of Mother-Infant Interaction," *Merrill-Palmer Quarterly* 13 (1967): 19–36, as cited in Tronick and Adamson, *Babies as People*.

25. Letty Cottin Pogrebin, *Growing Up Free* (New York: McGraw-Hill, 1980), 126.

26. Brooks-Gunn and Matthews, *He & She*, 69, offer a good summary of research in this area. However, Jean H. Block, in "Differential Premises Arising from Differential Socialization of the Sexes: Some Conjectures," *Child Development* 54, no. 6 (Dec. 1983), 1341, a review of the professional literature on sex differences, finds that "both mothers and fathers have been observed to react more contingently to the vocalizations of boys than to the vocalizations of girls."

27. H. A. Moss, "Early Sex Differences and Mother-Infant Interaction" in *Sex Differences in Behavior*, ed. Richard C. Friedman, Ralph M.

Richart, and Raymond L. Vande Wiele (New York: John Wiley & Sons, 1974), 151.

28. L. W. Hoffman, "Changes in Family Roles, Socialization, and Sex Differences," *American Psychologist* 32 (1977): 644–58. See also Brooks-Gunn and Matthews, *He & She*, 72.

29. R. D. Parke and S. E. O'Leary, "Father-Mother-Newborn Interaction in the Newborn Period: Some Findings, Some Observations, and Some Unresolved Issues," in *The Developing Individual in a Changing World*, vol. 2, ed. K. Riegel and J. Meacham (The Hague, Netherlands: Mouton, 1976), and R. D. Parke and D. B. Sawin, "Infant Characteristics and Behavior as Elicitors of Maternal and Paternal Responsivity in the Newborn Period" (Paper delivered at the Annual Meeting of the Society for Research in Child Development, Denver, Apr. 1975).

30. Arlie Hochschild, *The Second Shift: Working Parents and the Revolution at Home* (New York: Viking, 1989).

31. For a useful overview of the recent literature on how fathers socialize sons and daughters differently, see Phyllis Bronstein, "Father-Child Interaction: Implications for Gender-Role Socialization" in *Fatherhood Today*, ed. Phyllis Bronstein and Carolyn Pape Cowan (New York: John Wiley & Sons, 1988), pp. 125, 170.

32. J. Z. Rubin, F. J. Provenzano, and Z. Luria, "The Eye of the Beholder: Parents' Views on Sex of Newborns," *American Journal of Orthopsychiatry* 44 (1974): 512–19.

33. D. Laskin, "Snips & Snails," *American Baby* (May 1989): 26–31.

34. Rhoda Unger, personal communication, Jan. 1990.

35. Chess and Whitbread, *Daughters*, 85.

36. Carol Gilligan as quoted in Francine Prose, "Confident at 11, Confused at 16," *New York Times Magazine*, 7 Jan. 1990, 22–25, 37–40, 45–46.

37. Jerrie Ann Will, Patricia A. Self, and Nancy Datan, "Maternal Behavior and Perceived Sex of Infant," *American Journal of Orthopsychiatry*, 46 (Jan. 1976).

38. Study conducted in 1978 at the University of Sussex as cited in Richard M. Restak, M.D., *The Infant Mind* (Garden City, N.Y.: Doubleday, 1980).

39. J. Condry and S. Condry, "Sex Differences: A Study of the Eye of the Beholder," *Child Development* 47 (1976): 812–19.

40. Brad Sachs, personal communication, Feb. 1990.

41. Brooks-Gunn and Matthews, *He & She*, 72.

42. Ibid., 93–94.

43. Pogrebin, *Growing Up Free*, 141.

44. E. Galinsky and J. David, *The Preschool Years* (New York: Times Books, 1988), 155–56.

45. Brooks-Gunn and Matthews, *He & She*, 93.

Chapter 3: The Dawn of Femininity

1. E. Maccoby, *Social Development: Psychological Growth and the Parent-Child Relationship* (New York: Harcourt Brace Jovanovich, 1980), 225.

2. S. K. Thompson, "Gender Labels and Early Sex-Role Development," *Child Development* 46 (1975): 339–47.

3. Maccoby, *Social Development*, 214.

4. Ibid., 224.

5. Ibid., 230.

6. M. S. Smart and R. C. Smart, *Children: Development and Relationships*, 4th ed. (New York: Macmillan, 1982).

7. J. Brooks-Gunn and W. S. Matthews, *He & She: How Children Develop Their Sex-Role Identity* (Englewood Cliffs, N.J.: Prentice-Hall, 1979), 99 and ff. offer a good summary of theories of gender, including Freud's, and the various critiques of them. Our discussion draws on their in-depth consideration of the subject.

8. C. Gilligan, *In a Different Voice* (Cambridge, Mass.: Harvard University Press, 1982), 6.

9. L. Kohlberg, "A Cognitive-Developmental Analysis of Childrens' Sex-Role Concepts and Attitudes," in *The Development of Sex Differences*, ed. E. Maccoby (Stanford, Calif.: Stanford University Press, 1966), as cited in Brooks-Gunn and Matthews, *He & She*.

10. Brooks-Gunn and Matthews, *He & She*, 118–19, and S. K. Thompson, "Gender Labels and Early Sex Role Development," *Child Development* 46 (1975): 339–47, as cited in Brooks-Gunn and Matthews.

11. G. Melson, personal communication, March 1990.

12. See G. Mitchell, *Human Sex Differences: A Primatologist's Perspective* (New York: Van Nostrand Reinhold, 1981), 20, for a summary of this viewpoint.

13. Ibid., 20.

14. M. E. Lamb, J. H. Pleck, and J. A. Levine, "The Role of the Father in Child Development," in *Advances in Clinical Child Psychology*, ed. B. B. Lahey and A. E. Kazdin, vol. 8 (New York: Plenum, 1985), 229–66.

15. Maccoby, *Social Development*, 242–43.

16. P. K. Smith and L. Daglish, "Sex Differences in Parent and Infant Behavior in the Home," *Child Development* 48 (1977): 1250–54.

17. Maccoby, *Social Development*, 212.

18. Ibid., 211.

19. J. DiPietro, "Rough and Tumble Play: A Function of Gender," *Developmental Psychology* (1981), as cited in Smart and Smart, *Children*.

20. Evelyn Goodenough Pitcher and Lynn Hickey Schultz, *Boys and Girls at Play: The Development of Sex Roles* (New York: Praeger, 1983), 13. For comparisons of child behaviors in various cultures, see B. B. Whiting and J. W. M. Whiting, *Children of Six Cultures* (Cambridge, Mass.: Harvard University Press, 1975) and B. B. Whiting and C. P. Edwards, "A

Cross-Cultural Analysis of Sex Differences in the Behavior of Children Aged 3 Through 11," *Journal of Social Psychology* 91 (1973): 171–88.

21. Willard W. Hartup, "Peer Interaction and the Behavioral Development of the Individual Child" in *Readings in Developmental Psychology*, ed. J. Gardner (Boston: Little, Brown, 1976), cited in Pitcher and Schultz, *Boys and Girls at Play*, 16–17.

22. Pitcher and Schultz, *Boys and Girls at Play*.

23. Ibid., 32.

24. Mitchell, *Human Sex Differences*, 110.

25. Pitcher and Schultz, *Boys and Girls at Play*, 11.

26. Ibid., 73.

27. E. E. Maccoby and C. N. Jacklin, *The Psychology of Sex Differences* (Stanford, Calif.: Stanford University Press, 1974), 242–43.

28. Jean H. Block, "Differential Premises Arising from Differential Socialization of the Sexes: Some Conjectures," *Child Development* 54, no. 6 (December 1983): 1335–54.

29. Pitcher and Schultz, *Boys and Girls at Play*, 69.

30. W. R. Charlesworth and C. Dzur, "Gender Comparisons of Preschoolers' Behavior and Resource Utilization in Group Problem-Solving," *Child Development* 58 (1987): 191–200.

31. Nancy Chodorow, *The Reproduction of Mothering: Psychoanalysis and the Sociology of Gender* (Berkeley: University of California Press, 1978), 92, 110.

32. Carol Gilligan, *In a Different Voice: Psychological Theory and Women's Development* (Cambridge, Mass.: Harvard University Press, 1982), 8.

33. Ibid., 17.

34. Kyle Pruett, *The Nurturing Father* (New York: Warner Books, 1987), 210.

35. Kyle Pruett as quoted in Laura Shapiro, "Guns and Dolls," *Newsweek*, 28 May 1990, 65.

36. Chodorow, *Reproduction of Mothering*, 137–38.

37. Jamaica Kincaid, "Cold Heart," *The New Yorker*, 25 June 1990, 29.

38. Nancy Friday, *My Mother/My Self* (New York: Delacorte Press, 1977), 45–47.

39. Ibid., 68.

40. Chodorow, *Reproduction of Mothering*, 126.

41. Maccoby, *Social Development*, 240.

42. Chodorow, *Reproduction of Mothering*, 119, citing Maccoby and Jacklin, *The Psychology of Sex Differences*.

43. Maccoby, *Social Development*, 248.

44. Kyle Pruett as quoted in Shapiro, "Guns and Dolls," 65.

45. Caryl Rivers, Rosalind Barnett, and Grace Baruch, *Beyond Sugar & Spice: How Women Grow, Learn, and Thrive* (New York: G. P. Putnam's Sons, 1979), 66.

46. Brad Sachs, personal communication, Mar. 1990.

47. Sam Osherson, personal communication, Mar. 1990.

48. Lawrence Balter with Anita Shreve, *Dr. Balter's Child Sense* (New York: Poseidon Press, 1985).

49. E. Galinsky and J. David, *The Preschool Years* (New York: Times Books, 1988), 163.

50. Herman Roiphe and Anne Roiphe, *Your Child's Mind* (New York: St. Martin's, 1985).

51. Galinsky and David, *The Preschool Years*, 166.

52. Friday, *My Mother/My Self*, 69–71.

53. Galinsky and David, *The Preschool Years*, 167.

54. Friday, *My Mother/My Self*, 72.

55. Osherson, *Wrestling with Love*.

56. Beverly I. Fagot, "The Influence of Sex of Child on Parental Reactions to Toddler Children," *Child Development* 49 (1978): 459–65.

57. Harriet L. Rheingold and Kaye V. Cook, "The Contents of Boys' and Girls' Rooms as an Index of Parents' Behavior," *Child Development* 46 (1975): 459–63.

58. Arlie Hochschild, *The Second Shift* (New York: Viking, 1989), 230.

59. Bruno Bettelheim, in *The Uses of Enchantment* (New York: Knopf, 1976), 210–13, 234–35, points to the fairy tales of Sleeping Beauty and Snow White as central myths of adolescence: at the onset of puberty, the young women fall into a deep sleep, a sleep that shields them from the turmoil of sexuality until they are ready to awake to the safety of marriage with a prince. In their obsession with these fairy tales, our preschool-age daughters may be probing some of the complicated issues that await them.

60. Galinsky and David, *The Preschool Years*, 100.

61. For a summary of this issue, and a glance at cross-cultural studies conducted on the topic, see Maccoby, *Social Development*, 219.

62. Judy Dunn, *Sisters and Brothers* (Cambridge, Mass.: Harvard University Press, 1985), 77.

63. Gail Melson, personal communication, Mar. 1990.

64. Dunn, *Sisters and Brothers*, 79.

65. Ibid., 22.

66. Judy Dunn, "Sibling Relations in Early Childhood," *Child Development* 54 (1983): 787–811.

67. Galinsky and David, *The Preschool Years*, 280.

68. Pogrebin, *Growing Up Free*, 322–23.

69. Gail Melson, personal communication, Mar. 1990.

70. Barbara Brenner, *The Preschool Handbook* (New York: Pantheon Books, 1990), 11.

71. Ibid., 12.

72. See Sheila Moore and Roon Frost, *The Little Boy Book* (New York: Ballantine, 1987), 77 for a discussion of the benefits of preschool.

73. Brenner, *The Preschool Handbook*, 28.

74. Vivian Gussin Paley, *Boys and Girls: Superheroes in the Doll Corner* (Chicago: University of Chicago Press, 1984), ix–xii.

75. Bryan E. Robinson, "Vanishing Breed: Men in Child Care Programs," *Young Children* (Sept. 1988): 54–57.

76. Dr. Nancy Close, lecturer in child development at the Yale Child Study Center, as quoted in Anita Shreve, *Remaking Motherhood* (New York: Ballantine, 1987), 96.

77. Louise Derman-Sparks and the ABC Task Force, *Anti-Bias Curriculum: Tools for Empowering Young Children* (Washington, D.C.: National Association for the Education of Young Children, 1989), 51.

78. Ibid., 78.

79. David Elkind, "Superbaby Syndrome Can Lead to Elementary School Burnout," *Young Children* (Mar. 1987): 14, as cited in Galinsky and David, *The Preschool Years*, 427.

80. National Association for the Education of Young Children, "Position Statement on Developmentally Appropriate Practice in Programs for 4- and 5-Year-Olds" (Washington, D.C.: NAEYC, 1990), 2–3.

81. Ibid., 6–9.

82. See Michael E. Lamb and Jaipaul L. Roopnarine, "Peer Influences and Sex-Role Development in Preschoolers," *Child Development* 50, no. 4 (1979): 1219–22, and Eleanor E. Maccoby, "Gender as a Social Category," *Developmental Psychology* 24, no. 6 (1988): 755–65.

Chapter 4: Girls at School

1. Frances L. Ilg and Louise Bates Ames, *Behavior Tests Used at the Gesell Institute* (New York: Harper & Row, 1965) 197.

2. Sheila Moore and Roon Frost, *The Little Boy Book* (New York: Ballantine, 1987), 88–89.

3. Ilg and Ames, *Behavior Tests*, 317–26.

4. Karen de Crow, "Look, Jane, Look!" reprinted in *Sex Differences and Discrimination in Education*, ed. Scarvia Anderson (Worthington, Ohio: Charles A. Jones Publishing, 1972), 44–49.

5. "Women on Words & Images," reprinted in *Sex Differences and Discrimination*, 40.

6. Personal communication with Jo Sanders of the Women's Action Alliance, 14 Dec. 1990.

7. Myra Sadker as quoted in Claire Safran, "Hidden Lessons," *Parade Magazine*, 9 Oct. 1983, 12.

8. Myra Sadker, David Sadker, and Susan S. Klein, "Abolishing Misperceptions About Sex Equity in Education," *Theory Into Practice* 25, no. 4 (Autumn 1986): 219–26.

9. Personal communication with Dr. Katherine Canada, Nov. 1990.

10. Marshall D. Smith, "He Only Does It to Annoy," reprinted in *Sex Differences and Discrimination in Education*, 30.

11. Selma Greenberg, "Educational Equity in Early Education Environ-

ments," in *Handbook for Achieving Sex Equity through Education*, ed. Susan S. Klein (Baltimore: Johns Hopkins University Press, 1985), 461.

12. Selma Greenberg as quoted in Sadker et al., "Abolishing Misperceptions," 219–26.

13. Lisa A. Serbin, "Teachers, Peers, and Play Preferences: An Environmental Approach to Sex Typing in the Preschool," in *Perspectives on Non-Sexist Early Childhood Education*, ed. Barbara Sprung (New York: Teachers College Press, 1978), 79–93.

14. Gail Melson, personal communication, Mar. 1990.

15. Carol Dweck as quoted in Safran, "Hidden Lessons," 12.

16. J. H. Block, "Differential Premises Arising from Differential Socialization of the Sexes: Some Conjectures," *Child Development* 54, no. 6 (1983): 1339.

17. Suzanne Daley, "Little Girls Lose Their Self-Esteem on Way to Adolescence, Study Finds," *New York Times*, 9 Jan. 1991.

18. Rhoda K. Unger, *Female and Male* (New York: Harper & Row, 1979), 102.

19. Raphaela Best, *We've All Got Scars* (Bloomington: Indiana University Press, 1983), 88–105.

20. Ibid.

21. Jacquelynne Eccles Parsons, Terry F. Adler, and Caroline M. Kaczala, "Socialization of Achievement Attitudes and Beliefs: Parental Influences," *Child Development* 53 (1982): 310–21.

22. Carol Gilligan, *In a Different Voice* (Cambridge, Mass.: Harvard University Press, 1982), 10.

23. Sheila Moore and Roon Frost, *The Little Boy Book*, 127–28. From 1971 to 1988 the Educational Testing Service surveyed the reading ability of fourth graders (among others) for the U.S. Department of Education and found that girls were consistently more proficient readers than boys. Educational Testing Services, "The Reading Report Card" (Princeton, N.J.: ETS, 1990), tables 101 and 105.

24. Moore and Frost, *The Little Boy Book*, 127.

25. Camilla Benbow and Julian Stanley, "Sex Differences in Math Ability: Fact or Artifact," *Science* 210 (1980): 1262.

26. "The Gender Factor in Math," *Time*, 15 Dec. 1980, 57; "Do Males Have a Math Gene?" *Newsweek*, 15 Dec. 1980, 73.

27. Alan Feingold, "Cognitive Gender Differences Are Disappearing," *American Psychologist* 43 (Feb. 1988): 95–103.

28. Jacquelynne Eccles Parsons, et al., "Socialization of Achievement Attitudes and Beliefs: Parental Influences."

29. In her 1973 study of entering freshmen at Berkeley, Lucy Sells discovered that while 57 percent of the males had four years of high school math, only 8 percent of the females did. The result was that 92 percent of the entering females were automatically excluded from twenty-two out of forty-four possible majors. Lucy Sells, "The Mathematics Filter," in

Women and the Mathematical Mystique, ed. Lynn M. Fox et al. (Baltimore: Johns Hopkins University Press, 1980) 69–70.

30. U.S. Dept. of Education, National Center for Educational Statistics, *Digest of Educational Statistics*, 25th ed., NCES 89-643 (Washington, D.C.: GPO, 1989), table 115. It should be noted that boys do only a little better on average, completing 3.03 years of math in high school.

31. Sheila Tobias coined this term to describe a kind of acquired incapacity that afflicts both sexes, but perhaps women to a greater degree. See Sheila Tobias, *Overcoming Math Anxiety* (New York: Norton, 1978).

32. Elizabeth K. Stage et al., "Increasing the Participation and Achievement of Girls and Women in Mathematics, Science and Engineering," in *Handbook for Achieving Sex Equity through Education*, ed. Susan S. Klein (Baltimore: Johns Hopkins University Press, 1985), 244.

33. Ibid.

34. "Test Talk," *National Education Association Today* (Jan. 1988): 52–53.

35. Stage et al., "Increasing Participation," 244.

36. Joanne R. Becker, "Math Adds Up to a More Equitable Future," *Equal Play* (Fall 1984): 15–16.

37. Personal communication with Dr. Edes Gilbert of The Spence School, New York, N.Y., Jan. 1991.

38. Ibid.

39. Personal communication with Elizabeth Fennema, 1990.

40. E. Fennema and M. R. Mayer, "Gender, Equity & Mathematics," in *Handbook for Achieving Sex Equity through Education*, 149.

41. *The Mathematics Report Card: Are We Measuring Up?* (Princeton, N.J.: Educational Testing Service, 1988), 100.

42. "Test Talk," 53.

43. *The Science Report Card* (Princeton, N.J.: Educational Testing Service, 1989).

44. J. Abruscato, *Teaching Children Science* (Englewood Cliffs, N.J.: Prentice-Hall, 1982).

45. Jo Sanders, "Closing the Computer Gap," *Education Digest* (Oct. 1986).

46. U.S. Dept. of Education, *Digest of Educational Statistics*, table 359.

47. Elizabeth Fennema, personal communication, Oct. 1990.

48. "Computer Competence: The First National Assessment" (Princeton, N.J.: Educational Testing Service, 1988).

49. Henry Jack Becker, "Report #1 from a National Survey," *Journal of Computers in Mathematics and Science Teaching* 3, no. 1 (Fall 1983): 29–33, as cited in Moore and Frost, *The Little Boy Book*, 133.

50. "Computer Competence," 70–71.

51. Jo Sanders, *The Neuter Computer* (New York: Neal-Schumann, 1986), 14–15. This book and two informative pamphlets for parents and teachers on encouraging girls' use of the computer are available from the

Women's Action Alliance, 370 Lexington Ave., New York, N.Y. 10017, (212) 532-8330.

52. Dr. Barbara T. Bowman, "Sexism and Racism in Education," in Sprung, *Perspectives on Non-Sexist Early Childhood Education*, 37.

53. "He Only Does It To Annoy," reprinted in *Sex Differences and Discrimination in Education*, 28.

54. J. Roberts and J. T. Baird, Jr., *Behavior Patterns of Children in School*, Vital and Health Statistics, data from the National Health Survey, Series 11, no. 113, DHEW Publication no. (HSM) 72-1042 (Washington, D.C.: GPO, 1972), cited in M. S. Smart and R. C. Smart, *Children: Development and Relationships*, 4th ed. (New York: Macmillan, 1982), 354.

55. Myra Sadker, David Sadker, and Susan S. Klein, "Abolishing Misperceptions About Sex Equity in Education," *Theory into Practice* 25, no. 4 (Autumn 1986): 219–26.

56. Ibid.

57. Personal communication with Doris Cottham, head of lower school, The Spence School, New York, N.Y., Jan. 1991.

58. Personal communication with Dr. Katherine Canada, Goucher College, Towson, Md., Nov. 1990.

59. Personal communication with Doris Cottham, head of lower school, The Spence School, New York, N.Y., Jan. 1991. See also Best, *We've All Got Scars*.

Chapter 5: The Social Life of the Schoolgirl

1. Eleanor E. Maccoby, "Gender as a Social Category," *Developmental Psychology* 24, no. 6 (Nov. 1988): 755–65.

2. Barrie Thorne and Zella Luria, "Sexuality and Gender in Children's Daily Worlds," *Social Problems* 33, no. 3 (Feb. 1986): 176–90.

3. Ibid.

4. Roger Hart, "Sex Differences in the Use of Outdoor Space," in *Perspectives on Non-Sexist Early Childhood Education*, ed. Barbara Sprung (New York: Teachers College Press, 1978), 101–108.

5. Maccoby, "Gender as a Social Category," 756.

6. Raphaela Best, *We've All Got Scars* (Bloomington: Indiana University Press, 1983), 3–5.

7. Ibid, 18.

8. Ibid, 109–10.

9. Thorne and Luria, "Sexuality and Gender," 186.

10. Patricia L. Geadelmann et al., "Sex Equity in Physical Education and Athletics," in *Handbook for Achieving Sex Equity Through Education*, ed. Susan S. Klein (Baltimore: Johns Hopkins University Press, 1985), 327–29.

Chapter 7: Sexual Abuse of Girls

1. The American Humane Association (AHA) reports that 42 percent of the abusers were parents, 22.8 percent were other relatives. People outside the family accounted for 35.2 percent of the reported cases. However, as AHA information specialist Katie Bond points out, the nonfamily abusers are seldom strangers. They may be the boy- or girlfriend of the child's parent.

2. We know from surveys of adolescents and adults about their childhood experience that incidence of sexual abuse is far, far higher than the reported cases. One such survey of Boston-area college undergraduates found that 20 percent of the women had suffered some sort of abuse before reaching eighteen. (D. Finkelhor, *Sexually Victimized Children* [(New York: Free Press, 1979)].) In another study based on a random sampling of 900 San Francisco households, 28 percent of the women surveyed reported that they had been abused before their fourteenth birthdays and 38 percent before their eighteenth birthdays. (D. Russell, "The Incidence and Prevalence of Intra-Familial and Extra-Familial Sexual Abuse of Female Children," *Child Abuse and Neglect: The International Journal* 7 [(1983)]: 133–46.) In a telephone survey of 2,626 randomly selected people conducted in 1985, the *Los Angeles Times* found that 27 percent of the women polled and 16 percent of the men were sexually abused as children. (L. Timnick, "22% in Survey Were Child Abuse Victims," *Los Angeles Times*, 25 Aug. 1985.)

3. National Committee for Prevention of Child Abuse, "Basic Facts About Child Sexual Abuse" (Chicago: NCPCA, 1988).

4. Ibid.

5. Mic Hunter, *Abused Boys* (Lexington, Mass.: Lexington Books, 1990), 25–26.

6. NCPCA, "Basic Facts."

7. Hunter, *Abused Boys*, 22.

8. Personal communication with Mary Allman, Dec. 1990.

9. Hunter, *Abused Boys*, 45–49.

10. Ellen Bass and Laura Davis, *The Courage to Heal* (New York: Harper & Row, 1988), 34.

11. Diana H. Russell, *The Secret Trauma: Incest in the Lives of Girls and Women* (New York: Basic Books, 1986), 98.

12. Ibid., 16.

13. Diana Russell found in her survey of 930 women that among incest victims, 14 percent were abused by their biological fathers, 15 percent by stepfathers, 48 percent by uncles, and 23 percent by brothers. Ibid., 216.

14. Lada I. Tamarack, "Fifty Myths and Facts About Incest," in *Sexual Abuse of Children in the 1980s*, ed. Benjamin Schlesinger (Toronto: University of Toronto Press, 1986), 6.

15. Russell, "Incidence and Prevalence," 289.

16. David Finkelhor, "Risk Factors in the Sexual Victimization of Children," *Child Abuse and Neglect* 52 (1980): 265–73.

17. NCPCA, "Basic Facts," 9.

18. Bass and Davis, *The Courage to Heal*, 94.

19. Personal communication with Mary Allman, Dec. 1990.

20. Bass and Davis, *The Courage to Heal*, 285.

21. Judith Lewis Herman, *Father-Daughter Incest* (Cambridge, Mass.: Harvard University Press, 1981), 132.

22. Ibid., 138.

23. Vernon R. Wiehe, *Sibling Abuse* (Lexington, Mass.: Lexington Books, 1990), 76–88.

24. Caren Adams and Jennifer Fay, *No More Secrets: Protecting Your Child from Sexual Assault* (San Luis Obispo, Calif.: Impact Publishers, 1981), 64.

25. Ibid., 26.

26. Ibid., 37.

27. Ibid., 21.

Chapter 8: Girls Who Live with Single Parents

1. "More Children Live with Only One Parent," *Wall Street Journal*, 3 Mar. 1989. Of the children under six, half never knew what it was like to have two parents: their mother (or in some rare cases father) was never married; 23 percent of the under-six children in single-parent homes live with a divorced parent, and 25 percent live with a parent who is separated from her (or his) spouse.

2. "Economic Woes Mount for Children of Divorce," *Wall Street Journal*, 17 Apr. 1989.

3. E. Mavis Hetherington, "Children and Divorce," in *Parent-Child Interaction: Theory, Research and Prospects*, ed. Ronald W. Henderson (New York: Academic Press, 1981), 40.

4. E. Mavis Hetherington, Martha Cox, and Roger Cox, "Effects of Divorce on Parents and Children," in *Nontraditional Families: Parenting and Child Development*, ed. Michael E. Lamb (Hillsdale, N.J.: Lawrence Erlbaum Associates, 1982), 233–88.

5. Judith Stern Peck, "The Impact of Divorce on Children at Various Stages of the Family Life Cycle," *Journal of Divorce* 12, no. 2/3 (1988/89): 81–106.

6. Steven H. Kay, "The Impact of Divorce on Children's Academic Performance," *Journal of Divorce* 12, no. 2/3 (1988/89): 283–98.

7. Martha T. Mednick, "Single Mothers: A Review and Critique of Current Research," in *Family in Transition*, 6th ed., ed. Arlene S. Skolnick and Jerome H. Skolnick (Glenview, Ill.: Scott, Foresman, 1989), 451.

8. Judith S. Wallerstein and Joan Berlin Kelly, *Surviving the Breakup:*

How Children and Parents Cope with Divorce (New York: Basic Books, 1980), 101.

9. E. Galinsky and J. David, *The Preschool Years* (New York: Times Books, 1988), 304.

10. Judith S. Wallerstein and Sandra Blakeslee, *Second Chances: Men, Women, and Children a Decade After Divorce* (New York: Ticknor & Fields, 1989), 63.

11. Ibid., 63–64.

12. Sara McLanahan, sociologist with the University of Wisconsin, as quoted in the *Wall Street Journal*, 3 Jan. 1989.

13. Judith S. Wallerstein and Sandra Blakeslee, "Children After Divorce: Wounds that Don't Heal," *New York Times Magazine*, 22 Jan. 1989.

14. Wallerstein and Blakeslee, *Second Chances*, 99.

15. Deirdre S. Laiken, *Daughters of Divorce* (New York: William Morrow, 1981), 126–48.

16. Wallerstein and Blakeslee, *Second Chances*, 204.

17. Hetherington et al., "Effects of Divorce," 280.

18. Wallerstein and Blakeslee, *Second Chances*, 111.

19. Kathleen A. Camara, "Family Adaptation to Divorce," in *In Support of Families*, ed. Michael W. Yogman and T. Berry Brazelton (Cambridge, Mass.: Harvard University Press, 1986), 182.

20. Phyllis A. Heath and Carol Mackinnon, "Factors Related to the Social Competence of Children in Single-Parent Families," *Journal of Divorce* 11, no. 3/4 (Spring/Summer 1988): 49–66.

21. Hetherington et al., "Effects of Divorce," 275.

22. Richard N. Atkins, "Single Mothers and Joint Custody," in Yogman and Brazelton, eds., *In Support of Families*, 76.

23. Mednick, "Single Mothers," 452.

24. Sandra Scarr, *Mother Care/Other Care* (New York: Basic Books, 1984), 134.

25. Irwin Garfinkel and Sara S. McLanahan, *Single Mothers and Their Children* (Washington, D.C.: The Urban Institute Press, 1986), 30.

Chapter 9: Working Mothers and Their Daughters

1. Statistics are for married women with spouse present working in the civilian labor force. From *Handbook of Labor Statistics* (Washington, D.C.: U.S. Dept. of Labor, 1989), 242–44.

2. National Center for Clinical Infant Programs, press release, 25 Nov. 1987, as cited in E. Galinsky and J. David, *The Preschool Years* (New York: Times Books, 1988), 369.

3. Lois Wladis Hoffman, "Maternal Employment and the Young Child," *Parent-Child Interaction and Parent-Child Relations in Child Development*, ed. M. Perlmutter (Hillsdale, N.J.: Lawrence Erlbaum Associates, 1984), 101–28.

286 Notes

4. See Anita Shreve, *Remaking Motherhood* (New York: Ballantine, 1987), 91–101 for a good summary of research on the effects of maternal employment on daughters.

5. Sirgay Sanger, M.D., and John Kelly, *The Woman Who Works, the Parent Who Cares* (Boston: Little, Brown, 1987), 17.

6. Sandra Scarr, *Mother Care/Other Care* (New York: Basic Books, 1984), 24.

7. See Shreve, *Remaking Motherhood*, 111–25, for a review of the literature on sons.

8. Ibid., 73.

9. Ibid., 92.

10. Scarr, *Mother Care*, 26–27.

11. See Sanger and Kelly, *The Woman Who Works*, Chapter 4, for advice in this area.

12. Arlie Hochschild, *The Second Shift: Working Parents and the Revolution at Home* (New York: Viking, 1989), 235.

13. David Laskin, "Make Room For Daddy!" *Redbook* (Mar. 1990): 122–23.

14. See Hochschild, *The Second Shift*, 236–37 for a review of recent literature in this area.

15. Michael E. Lamb, "Maternal Employment and Child Development: A Review," in *Nontraditional Families: Parenting and Child Development*, ed. Michael E. Lamb (Hillsdale, N.J.: Lawrence Erlbaum Associates, 1982), 45–70.

Chapter 10: Looking to the Future

1. Robert R. Sears and S. Shirley Feldman, eds., *The Seven Ages of Man* (Los Altos, Calif.: William Kaufmann, 1973), 23.

2. J. M. Tanner, *Fetus Into Man: Physical Growth from Conception to Maturity* (Cambridge, Mass.: Harvard University Press, 1978), 65–69.

3. Terri Apter, *Altered Loves: Mothers and Daughters During Adolescence* (New York: St. Martin's Press, 1990), 14.

4. Ibid., 19.

5. Ibid., 2–3.

6. Ibid., 27.

7. David Elkind, "Eating Disorders," *Parents* (Apr. 1988): 190.

8. Cited in Nicky Marone, *How to Father a Successful Daughter* (New York: McGraw-Hill, 1988), 263.

9. Elkind, "Eating Disorders," 190.

10. Ibid., 12.

11. Ibid., 39.

12. Personal communication with Amy Meyers, assistant director, American Anorexia and Bulimia Association, Feb. 1991.

13. Mara Selvini Palazzoli, *Self-Starvation* (New York: Jason Aronson, 1985), 39.

14. Margo Maine, "Engaging the Disengaged Father in the Treatment of Eating Disordered Adolescents" (paper delivered at the Annual Conference of the Center for the Study of Anorexia and Bulimia, New York, N.Y., Nov. 1985), as cited in Marone, *How to Father*, 263.

15. Palazzoli, 105.

16. Susie Orbach, *Hunger Strike* (New York: W. W. Norton, 1986), 187–88.

17. Carol Gilligan as quoted in Francine Prose, "Confident at 11, Confused at 16," *New York Times Magazine*, 7 Jan. 1990.

18. American Association of University Women (AAUW), "Shortchanging Girls, Shortchanging America" (Washington, D.C.: AAUW Jan. 1991), 4.

19. Kathryn Riley, "Black Girls Speak for Themselves," in *Just a Bunch of Girls*, ed. Gaby Weiner (Philadelphia, Pa.: Open University Press, 1985), 69.

20. Sharon Schuster as quoted in Suzanne Daley, "Little Girls Lose Their Self-Esteem on Way to Adolescence, Survey Finds," *New York Times*, 9 Jan. 1991.

21. AAUW, 7.

22. Marone, *How to Father*, 242.

23. Ibid., 245–46.

24. Wallerstein and Blakeslee, *Second Chances: Men, Women, and Children a Decade After Divorce* (New York: Ticknor & Fields, 1989), 243–44.

25. The 1972 figures are from *The Statistical Abstract of the United States 1980* (U.S. Dept. of Commerce, Bureau of the Census, Washington, D.C., 1980), 418. The 1988 figures are from *The Statistical Abstract of the United States 1990* (U.S. Dept. of Commerce, Bureau of the Census, Washington, D.C., 1990), 389. The figures for architects are from Betty M. Vetter and Eleanor L. Babco, *Professional Women and Minorities: A Manpower Data Resource Service*, 7th ed. (Washington, D.C.: Commission on Professionals in Science and Technology, 1987), 72.

26. Although women have undeniably made major advances in the working world in the past two decades, it is worth noting that major inequities remain. As of 1988, the median yearly income of women working full time and year-round in America was $17,606, while for men the figure stood at $26,656 (*Statistical Abstract of the United States 1990*, 411). The low-prestige, low-paying jobs remain largely a female ghetto, as they always have been: in 1988, 95.5 percent of cleaners and servants were female, 99.1 percent of secretaries, 97.6 percent of lab technicians, and 97.1 percent of receptionists (*Statistical Abstract of the United States 1990*, 389).

Index

THE LITTLE BOY BOOK

by Sheila Moore
and Roon Frost

A valuable resource for parents that addresses the very real differences between girls and boys.

It is the only book of its kind available today!

Read on to learn more about boys....

In *Huckleberry Finn*, Mark Twain's novel of American boyhood, Huck and his friend Jim hide away on an island in the Mississippi River. Boredom sets in after several weeks and, in Huck's words, "I said it was getting slow and dull, and I wanted to get a stirring up some way...I would slip over the river and find out what was going on." Disguising himself as a girl, he rows to shore and approaches a strange house, where a woman invites him inside.

During the visit, Huck attempts to thread a needle. Unlike a girl, who would bring the thread to the needle, Huck tries to do it by bringing the needle to the thread. Suspicious, the woman complains about the number of rats scurrying about the cabin, some so bold as to peek out at her young visitor. She suggests that Huck throw a heavy lead weight at them. Huck throws the weight with his arm out to one side—like a boy would—and the woman catches him out.

"Why, I spotted you for a boy when you was threading the needle!" she exclaims with satisfaction.

* * *

Whether the tasks be threading a needle, throwing a ball, climbing a tree, or learning to write the alphabet, we often notice that boys and girls do them differently. If you have a daughter as well as a son, you can probably list a number of ways they differ in behavior without thinking about it for very long at all.

In Twain's day, people would have been amused, but hardly surprised, by the clever woman's observations about Huck. Until this century, few questioned the premise that differences in behavior between the sexes were innate—natural, desirable, and even God's plan. Most of the world is still quite comfortable with this point of view of life.

Twentieth-century experts, however, have emphasized the importance of the parents' role in bringing up their children, stressing "nurture" as opposed to "nature." Many American parents have looked to the spoken and silent messages they have transmitted and the environment they have created for the key to their children's behavior. Some of us have even felt guilty about our own actions or attitudes that may have encouraged aggression in our boys or passivity in our girls. If we just gave our daughter trucks and showed them how to be assertive, we reasoned, the girls would be independent like boys. If our sons were only taught concern for others and given dolls to cuddle, they would be less aggressive and more nurturant like their sisters.

"But it's not so simple," declares one mother, who tried to raise her children in a nonsexist way. "The biggest things in my daughters' lives right now are Barbie dolls and nail polish," she sighs. "And Jonathan—he walks like the Incredible Hulk, shovels down his food, and wants to wrestle with every boy he sees—and he's only three-and-a-half!" Speaking of the differences between her two children, a second mother added, "When she plays with something, she wants to feed it; he wants to make it fight."

For women, who do most of the hands-on rearing of young children, boys have always presented a special challenge. Their behavior sometimes seems mysterious or incomprehensible. "Why is he acting that way?" "Is it normal?" and "What should I do about this?" are questions mothers ask endlessly about their sons. "Don't worry about it," a boy's father will counter. "I did the same thing," or,

"Lots of boys do that." Because of their common sexuality, fathers understand intuitively the feelings and motivations of their sons; after all, they were once boys themselves. While it may seem an all too obvious and even trivial observation, whether you are a mother or a father affects your responses as a parent in very profound ways.

The Sequence of Development

Every child proceeds through progressive stages of development on a timetable influenced by his sex and his own particular combination of hereditary and environmental factors. In boys, acquiring self-control, learning to handle frustration, and settling in to the demands of school usually take longer than they do in girls. The vulnerability of boys to physical and environmental risks, and their delays in some aspects of development, may well mean that your son is more difficult to take care of than your daughter.

Each phase of growth is sequential, and builds upon what has gone before. Development proceeds from the simple to the complex. The child must walk before he can run; he will run for many years before he is ready to join a track team. From the awareness of his own body, the infant grows to recognize family members and his home surroundings. His thought processes gradually enlarge to encompass the outer world. If your little boy is approaching school age, you may have noticed that he is now more interested than before in who lives down the block, or what it is his big sister does when she goes to school each day.

Development of the child is multifaceted, and occurs on a number of levels. How his body grows, how he feels about himself within his family, how he learns, and how he relates to others are all important. It is difficult for a child to achieve his full potential without proper growth in all four areas of physical, emotional, intellectual, and social development. You may know a child who has been encouraged toward academic achievement at the expense of other areas of development; he may have difficulty making and keeping friends, or feel his self-worth is only as good as the grades he brings home.

Each child comes into the world with an inborn urge to learn, to become competent, and, ultimately, to achieve independence. The desire to master his body and his environment is inherent and recognizable at every stage of development. The infant who follows you with his eyes is just as determined to grasp the world around him as the three-year-old is to dress himself, by himself.

The Gift of Time

Many prominent individuals have been slow to develop, taking their time to achieve. Winston Churchill, whose words inspired half the world, had great difficulty learning as a boy. Albert Einstein's headmaster once said the boy would never succeed at anything. Beatle John Lennon's school experiences were dismal at best, and F. Scott Fitzgerald, in spite of his intelligence and obvious ability, was a poor student. Ronald Clark, in his 1984 biography of Charles Darwin, comments that the naturalist had a childhood "unmarked by the slightest trace of genius." Darwin's father once told him, "You care for nothing but shooting, dogs, and rat-catching, and you will be a disgrace to yourself and the family." Despite such unpromising beginnings, these men made contributions of lasting value to the world. Bertrand Russell once observed that a number of multitalented men of his generation all had in common a period in early childhood when they were free to do more or less as they pleased. Left to their own devices and allowed to pursue their own interests, these individuals developed, as adults, extraordinary abilities in several fields.

Time, the very currency of childhood, can be well spent or squandered on a child's behalf. The mother who pushes a little boy to unnatural levels of achievement in the preschool years may rue her zeal. The boy who recited the proper sounds in response to flash cards at three may well decide, at thirteen, that the continuing struggle to please his parents isn't worth the price he pays in time, lack of friends, and the neglect of his own interests.

The consequences of pushing children and keeping the pressure on are every day growing more apparent. Fear of failure is cited as one reason for the rise in adolescent suicide, which in less than a decade has jumped more than 40 percent in the 15–24 age group. A Virginia physical education specialist notes that a number of high-school athletes decline to play once they enter college. Others who do enroll in college athletics often play out their scholarships and then leave the sport entirely. After thirteen or more years of pressure, these young men are fed up. And who can blame them?

For little boys, time is a priceless possession. How we help them spend it can bring uncounted dividends later on. Sometimes, though, it is hard to counter pressures for too much too soon, especially when they come from those who are supposed to be "the experts." The appeal of a particular educational method, a new technique, or a book that promises the magic formula for raising or educating children is hard to resist; most of us have given in at one time or another. After all, who doesn't want the best of everything for his child? In choosing methods or techniques we use with our offspring, however, it is important to remember the significance of time to a boy and his development.

Today's boy is growing up in a world that becomes increasingly complex every day, with technological innovation, rapid social change, and shifting moral values. More than ever before, it is essential for parents to help their sons become competent people. The ability to learn at a reasonable pace, apply his knowledge, and recognize when he needs to know more will be vital attributes for the successful man in the year 2000. Adaptational skills will enable him to alter his focus or direction. Most important of all, today's boy will need the competence to make right choices among the multiplicity of alternatives that scientific advancement will present to him and his generation.

Knowing some of the characteristics that make little boys so different from girls can be of enormous help in meeting the challenge of raising a son in today's world, and in making our own choices about how to help our boys to become happy, self-assured adults.

Published by Ballantine Books
Available in your local bookstore.